Dr. Ernst Roth was born in Prague in 1896. He received his first piano lessons at the age of five from Alfredo Pellegrini of the Prague Conservatoire and subsequently went to Prague University to study law, music and philosophy. After graduating as a Doctor of Law, he moved to Vienna where he read music at Vienna University with Guido Adler. In 1922 he entered the music publishing house Wiener Philharmonische Verlag and six years later became head of the Publications Department of its parent company, Universal Edition. There he was responsible, among other things, for the new revisions of the piano works of Mozart, Schubert, Schumann and Brahms, and of an anthology of music of one hundred volumes.

In 1938 Dr. Roth joined Boosey & Hawkes in London as assistant to the late Ralph Hawkes. In 1949 he was appointed General Manager, was elected to the board the following year and afterwards became Chairman of the firm's publishing company. At Boosey & Hawkes he started and built up the series of Hawkes Pocket Scores, writing the analyses for over a hundred scores. He was responsible for publishing the later works of Richard Strauss (in particular the complete edition of his songs in four volumes) of Bartók, Stravinsky and Kodály. He also edited and arranged the works for wind instrum⸺⸺ of Bach, Beethoven, Mozart and S and has translated into German songs and operas of Britten, Wa Martinů. Since 1959 he has bec President of the Music Section of t national Publishers' Association.

Dr. Roth has contributed man on musical and historical subjects to puon-cations throughout Europe and is the e author of four books, also published in ⸺f Europe.

⸺f
st

performance of *Rake's Progress*, o⸺ ⸺ ⸺-berg, Berg and Webern; of Prokofiev and Kodály; of the withdrawn, taciturn genius of Bartók; and of Benjamin Britten. In writing of the new music of Boulez and Stockhausen and of the lesser, though by no means inarticulate, innovators, he is forthright, outspoken and controversial. The reader is left in no doubt that, for Ernst Roth, Stravinsky is the last protagonist of the golden age of music. Yet he is no philistine and accepts new music without approving of it. As he himself says in his book, 'New music is neither the destruction nor the salvation of the art.'

This is an important book, full of wit and wisdom and of the accumulated experience of a highly civilised man.

The Business of Music

The
Business of Music

Reflections of a Music Publisher

ERNST ROTH

09186

New York
OXFORD UNIVERSITY PRESS
1969

Printed in Great Britain

TO MY WIFE

CONTENTS

Author's Note

The titles of musical works always raise certain problems in translation and the reader may forgive apparent inconsistencies. Broadly speaking, I have tried to follow conventional English usage. No one would think of translating *Rosenkavalier* or *Così fan tutte*. *Die Walküre* is more widely used than *The Valkyries*. And to refer to *The Bartered Bride* by its original Czech title would be pure musical snobbery. On the other hand we have Stravinsky's own authority for substituting *The Rite of Spring* for his original *Le Sacre du printemps*. *Zauberflöte* or *Magic Flute*? *Elisir d'amore* or *Elixir of Love*? It is a matter of taste which I can safely leave to the individual reader.

PREFACE

'Why not write your memoirs?' I have often been asked. Memoirs are the fashion nowadays. In these eventful times, almost anybody who can remember anything of interest writes his or her memoirs. However, while it is true that I have spent a lifetime in contact with the most significant music and the most prominent musicians of this century—which has been, in music as in life generally, a time of tremendous change—I am still not presumptuous enough to write memoirs in the proper sense of the word.

This, I believe, should be left to those who have changed the course of history, who have spurred this world out of its lazy trot and achieved greatness: generals like Julius Caesar, statesmen like Sir Winston Churchill. I have done nothing of the kind. I am just one of the innumerable victims of the deeds and misdeeds of others, or of those mysterious high powers or low instincts which, during my lifetime, have ridden roughshod over all reason and morality and are readily blamed for everything that has happened. Victims do not write memoirs—their lives are not, and should not be, memorable.

Moreover, memoirs necessarily make their writer a central figure and that I have never been. I have served music in my own modest way, and during the last half-century music has not been an easy mistress. Indeed, I may even have lacked the blind devotion expected of a faithful servant, for I cannot pretend that I have regarded music as the most important manifestation of the human genius. Heinrich Heine, who has—involuntarily—supplied many poems to composers but who was also a great prose writer and a shrewd observer, once wrote that good people were usually bad musicians and good musicians usually bad people, and that goodness, not music, was the more important thing in life. Without sharing Heine's cynicism I must concede that his words testify to a deep insight. In the last fifty years there certainly has been more music than goodness in the world, and that is something which should be regretted by even the most ardent admirers of the art. The best music and the most vigorous musical life can offer no compensation for the absence of goodness.

However, music has assumed an unexpected importance. Our

whole existence is, so to speak, cocooned in music, from the universal din of present-day 'pop', to the lonely isolation of the most complicated sound-structures. Academics and historians, philosophers and critics and even practical musicians are busy surrounding it with an ever-growing literature, to which only one group of those closely concerned with the destinies of the art has contributed little: my own—the music-publishers.

It may be doubted whether in fact the contribution of a publisher can be at all valuable. He speaks as an interested party, so his views may be suspect. Indeed, he finds himself in a special position, different from that of any other character on the great stage of modern music. As an intermediary between art and life, between artist and public, he has to consider both the spiritual and the material existences of the art. By viewing them without prejudice he may acquire a qualification which both the pure idealist and the pure materialist lack. This, then, is the theme of this book: music between heaven and earth; between inspiration and remuneration.

In these days the heaven of music is clouded by heavy problems, which cast their shadows into every corner of its earthly existence. It is my very profession which has taught me to meet them with calm and moderation. I cannot count myself among those who unconditionally admire or condemn the past or the present. It is by no means proved that the old times were always good, nor that the new times are necessarily better. I believe in Daniel Defoe's 'Great Law of Subordination', because it is the fundamental law of all order. I have a profound respect for everything that grows by necessity, even though a melancholy thought turns to the past and to my own irretrievable youth. But I must leave it to the more courageous—or less experienced—to predict the future.

L'amour des lettres est incompatible
avec l'esprit des affaires—*Beaumarchais*

1. THE GREAT CHANGE

'Everywhere there's music.' So runs an American hit song—as if, through music, mankind had at long last recaptured its lost paradise. Indeed, music *is* everywhere: that is both its glory and its misery in these glorious and miserable times. Music appears *en grande tenue* and is regally received; music squeezes itself into everyday life where it cannot so much as make itself heard. This makes it at once the most sublime and the commonest among the arts. We are dealing with every type of music here—with the serious or 'highbrow' as well as with the light or 'popular' variety. Being of the same parentage, they each have their place in a general discussion of music, even if occasionally they regard each other with profound disdain. Together they comprise our musical life; together they supplement and, at times, replace the anonymous noise which envelops our whole existence.

The external changes which have brought about this musical explosion are familiar to everybody from personal experience: to music's detractors, who can no longer escape from it, and to its devotees, who welcome the new, easy access to an art that once relied upon its exclusiveness. Music can now be reproduced mechanically, and thereby preserved; it can be broadcast by radio and television, and thereby transported. These two developments have broken down the doors of the sanctuary, previously opened only to the priests and the initiated, like the doors of Sarastro's Temple of Wisdom. Fifty years ago one had to devote oneself to music in order to enjoy its company: one had to go to concerts and to the opera-house and, most important of all, one had to make music oneself, which required years of practice and effort.

This is no longer so. One can have music without effort. It is a terrible thought that never again will music require any exertion, except from a few professionals, composers and performers; that this handful of men and women will be able to supply the whole world with all the music that is needed. Now it has become preservable and transportable, music, particularly since the Second World War, has embarked on a truly ambitious career. It is on tap in every home, like gas, water and electricity. There is no corner where it cannot penetrate. This once delicate art has become stupendously obtrusive. One need only press a button for music to come running with mechanical servility. Workmen in factories cannot work without a loudspeaker droning out tune after tune (the BBC programme 'Music While You Work' used to reject tunes for being 'too good', liable to distract the men and women at their benches); people in bars and restaurants cannot drink or eat unless some secret device whispers music into their ears; housewives cannot cook or iron without the radio playing; in cars, coaches and planes music mixes chaotically with the noise of engines; on beaches, in fields and woods, boys and girls carry it in their transistors, like sandwiches.

Infinitely grotesque, we would all agree; indeed, we would insist that music is an art and, like any other art, mysterious. But mystery is out of fashion. We have, perhaps without realizing the deeper significance of the change, become accustomed to the most fantastic things, and can talk glibly about flying to the moon and beyond. Such a generation as ours does not easily accept a mystery, and so has lost the precious gift of wondering. When I was at school I used to think that the generation of Verdi had seen the most astonishing changes in everyday life. When Verdi was born, the few people who travelled at all did so by mail-coach at the speed at which Julius Caesar had travelled to Gaul nearly two thousand years earlier. When Verdi died, express trains were thundering along the permanent way at forty miles an hour, steamships crossing the oceans, telephones ringing in the offices of the more enterprising businessmen and postmen delivering telegrams. I thought it must have been wonderful to live while all this was still new and exciting.

Others thought so too. When, in 1843, the railways from Paris to Rouen and Orléans were inaugurated—and the *Flying Dutchman* first performed—that same Heinrich Heine (from whom, by the way, Richard Wagner had learnt the story of the Dutchman) wrote about 'the awe that possesses the thinking mind at the sight of such monstrous happenings', of the 'strong temptation of the unknown', of the 'new delights and new horrors awaiting us' and of the change such a 'providential' event would bring about. 'Our generation,' he concludes with slightly uneasy confidence, 'can be proud to have witnessed it.'

Today all this sounds rather naïve. Not Verdi's but my own hapless generation has lived through the most fundamental changes of all. Nothing since the very beginning of human history can compare with the advances of the last fifty years: with space flights, electronic microscopes and computers, antibiotics and deep-frozen foods. It is useless to speculate whether all this progress has been as salutary for the mind as it has for the body. There are some who would insist that man would be happier if he had never learnt to read and write, because it is there that the deliberate, calculated evil begins. But, though it all had to come, and we are justified in calling it a blessing, we have barely reached the fringe of the new era, of a new satisfaction and a new spiritual security, and are still left with the secret fear that one day frivolous curiosity may press a button and blast to dust this whole planet, and with it everything that thinks.

Compared with all such fateful changes, events in music are of almost total irrelevance. Indeed, how relevant *are* the arts in a world which has been divesting itself one by one of all its mysteries? Modern man has acquired a superstitious confidence in everything material. One can feel it oneself, when one is shot into the air in a jet plane at six hundred miles per hour and forgets that any one of thousands of screws and bolts may work loose and destroy the aircraft and everybody in it. There is much less confidence in the dreaming mind, in thought and inspiration for their own sakes— in the arts. From all the fantastic achievements of recent decades, one problem has arisen which was unknown to previous genera- tions: the problem of leisure. Progress provides the working man in five days or less with everything material he needs in seven. What to do with those two or more days of leisure? Who could have thought that this might ever constitute a social and moral problem? One would think that today there is more to read, more to think, more to experience, than ever before; that the ceaseless spread of education ought to produce a multiplicity of interests which even our successfully prolonged lifespans with all their spare time could not satisfy. And yet man seems to have lost the taste for his own company. One summer's day on an Italian lake, when rain and thunderstorms kept us in the hotel lounge, I had a conversation with an American lady which was characteristic of the general mood. 'Do you play bridge?' she asked me. 'No,' I said, 'I don't seem to have time for it.' 'Do you play golf?' 'No,' I replied regret- fully, 'this, too, requires more time than I have.' 'Do you paint?' she persisted. 'Unfortunately, I have no talent for painting.' She looked at me with concern. 'You'd better be careful or you'll become an introvert.' So an introvert is apparently a sick man.

New educators, new ideals, are needed if we are to prevent waste of leisure-time and consequent boredom. Can the answer be in the arts, and especially in music, which has the power to soothe the restlessness of our times as nothing else has? This, I believe, was the subconscious attitude which paved the way for the great change which was to overcome music.

It took some considerable time to produce practical results. Edison built his first sound-reproducing apparatus as early as 1878—when Brahms was busy writing his second symphony—but nobody thought then of applying the new invention to music. I had—as many middle-class families had—an uncle who was fascinated by all the small technical novelties which grew like mushrooms during the first years of this century. He had the first telephone in the family, the first typewriter, the first fountain-pen and also the first 'phonograph'.

I well remember the first performance of that unwieldy giant lily in our family circle. It played no music, but gave us 'A Scene at the Dentist's'. 'Gargle, young man,' said a hoarse voice, and the young man responded with a similarly hoarse gargle, and we all choked with laughter. That must have been about the year 1906, and it was certainly a critical time for Edison's invention, because only a few years later I heard from the same machine the current coloratura star of the Vienna Court Opera, Elisa Elizza, singing the great aria from Carl Goldmark's opera *The Queen of Sheba*, somewhat hoarse and unsteady but quite distinct, and all the fun of the first encounter had gone. There the fatal marriage of music and mechanics was solemnized. This was a very different matter from the perforated rolls, the pianolas, the musical clocks or Count Deym's 'curiosity cabinet' with its mechanical contraptions for which Mozart had written some disproportionately good pieces. Only now did 'mechanical' music become a reality, and its preservation a possibility.

But for a World War, the development of broadcasting might have taken as long again. The first morse signal went out on 12 December 1901, from Cornwall to Newfoundland, but by 1914 there was still no broadcasting of music. It is sometimes said that wars are the best stimulant for the inventive mind. This is certainly untrue. But by devaluing both money and human life they remove the most formidable traditional obstacles to progress. It was only when the First World War was over that broadcasting suddenly established itself in the midst of life—of musical life, for the broadcasting of music was one of the most attractive uses of the new medium.

It is of little value to ponder over the chronology of events. In the early twentieth century the time was not quite ripe, the deeper roots of the change were still not established. But there was a half-understood coincidence of temptation and desire, or, more crudely, of supply and demand, which pointed to a growing void that had to be filled and could best be filled with music; a presentiment of an incalculable benefit to be derived from music, as indefinable and potent as the lullaby with which a mother sings her child to sleep.

Under the increasing pressure of demand the gramophone put aside its youthful frivolity and became respectable; as did broadcasting, which abandoned such exciting absurdities as transmitting a string quartet with the first violin playing in Vienna, the second in Berlin, the viola in Paris and the violoncello in London. Could anyone believe that the new means of preserving and transporting music were more than mere adjuncts to an art, like the discovery of oil painting or the invention of the steel pen? No inner voice warned either scientists or musicians that the change might affect the whole existence of music.

Then came the 'talkies', and almost overnight an army of musicians found itself unemployed. There was some talk of a social—not a musical—crisis. It was certainly a step forward to synchronize music and picture properly and do away with improvised noises in the cinema. But if the optimists were predicting the birth of a new art, they were to be sorely disappointed. With the millstone of popularity round its neck the sound film could not rise to higher things. There were those who asked quite seriously whether it would not be possible to 'draw' on the sound-track human voices of a perfection such as nature itself could not produce. But sound 'inventors' were already busy synthesizing sounds from another source, the only human element of which was the creative brain.

So the scene was set, and it required no more than another world war to bring it all to perfection: the long-playing record, television, sound broadcasting, magnetic tape-recorder—an illustrious assembly which gave music an entirely new role in life.

*

The other arts, for the most part, have not benefited—or suffered—from technical progress. Books are more quickly printed, paintings better reproduced, than before, but books must still be read and paintings bought and looked at. There is no easier, more comfortable substitute for the enjoyment of literature or the visual arts. Only architecture seems to have been affected by the new technical possibilities and extra-artistic requirements. The design of public and private buildings is governed by their practical purpose, which they fulfil beyond the dreams of any previous generation. But all these light, hygienic blocks of steel and glass will be demolished without a thought as soon as they no longer satisfy more sophisticated demands. It is inconceivable that they should be preserved, like the Baptistry in Florence, which painfully obstructs the traffic of a modern city, let alone that their remains could be revered like those of the temples of Paestum.

I cannot help thinking of future archaeologists digging a thousand years hence for traces of our time and finding nothing worth collecting. Perhaps a modern bathroom or lavatory may survive to be displayed in a *museo lapidario*. Then people may take off their hats and say that, though we obviously had little art, we clearly enjoyed considerable comfort. But when the new architect is confronted with a task that has no practical purpose to serve he is clearly embarrassed. New churches, particularly large new churches, are half arenas, half assembly-halls or railway stations, their spiritual function curiously obscured. Between this new, purposeful architecture and the mystery that is religion there is an incongruity which the use of expensive materials alone cannot mitigate. Is the inspiration lacking which once raised eternal monuments to the gods amidst the humble dwellings of mortals?

Where this new architecture meets music the conflict between art and practical purpose is no less painfully manifest. The builders of new opera-houses and concert-halls are obsessed with acoustics. Strange shells and half-moons are being constructed, the walls clad with wooden panelling full of unbecoming holes; ugly trapezes are suspended from equally ugly ceilings, and every corner and cranny is carefully planned so that the softest, highest and lowest sounds shall reach the listener wherever in the hall he may be. How unconcerned must have been the architects who in former times festooned concert-halls with stucco ornaments and caryatids, putti and mighty chandeliers of Venetian glass!

'How were the acoustics in the old house?' Aaron Copland asked me during the opening ceremony of the new National Theatre in Munich, which, like the Scala in Milan, had risen from the rubble in all its old splendour of white and blue and red and gold. I had to admit that I could not remember. Acoustics were never discussed in the old days. It was taken for granted that in every opera-house and concert-hall there would be certain seats where one could neither hear nor see. But a great controversy arose around the Munich reconstruction; it was said and written that this noble palace with its classical façade was out of step with the times. Like all old theatres, it aimed at transporting the audience into an unreal, fantastic world of illusion and imagination, the world where music dwelt. But the *instant* music of today has lost much of its magic and is quite at ease in surroundings which give no hint of anything mysterious or unusual and replace illusion with technical perfection. There is some virtue in this change. But in spirit it is not very different from the uneasy churches of the new architecture. Should this be called a 'style' at all, or is it rather a mood?

*

Today, technical progress no longer stops deferentially on the threshold of an art—at the modern concert-halls and opera-houses—but boldly invades the inner sanctum, mechanizing and transporting the acoustic phenomenon that is music itself. One might compare this intrusion with the effect printing has had on literature and learning. Indeed, printing has done little for music; the printed copy remains what the manuscript copy was: a guide or direction for the performance. It was the preservation and transportation of the performance itself that brought to music the blessings literature and learning have received from Gutenberg's invention: the limitless expansion, the commonness.

In this way music has become a comfortable art. One might think that art and comfort are quite incompatible, but the craving for luxury is a powerful motive force in the human brain. The whole of civilization, from the wheel to the washing-machine, could be called an accumulation of comforts. It has been a spur to invention, a stimulant to the mind. There were, however, times when men themselves were aware and afraid of the dangers involved. The anchorites of early Christian days were in revolt against comfort and the evils of its attendant luxury, and even today a man sails a little boat single-handed round the world, a senseless undertaking were it not to prove that, even in these fantastically comfortable times, a man is capable of enduring and surviving great discomfort.

At bottom, the quest for comfort is a personal struggle with the devil, of which former generations had a livelier notion than we. The traveller in Italy will often wonder at the many churches built on solitary hilltops, to the enhancement of the landscape but the considerable inconvenience of worshippers. Do men, women and children in their Sunday best still climb the steep, dusty paths? One has to go far to find that exalted spirit which keeps the sacred distinct from the profane and accepts discomfort with equanimity, even joy. Once in the heart of Sicily we were passing just such a lonely sanctuary when, in the heat of the morning, a wedding procession came up the stony track from the valley—the priest with his acolyte at the head, bride and bridegroom, families and friends following, all in solemn black, wearing their rough mountain boots and carrying their better shoes wrapped in newspaper under their arms. Before entering the church they sat down in the shade, laughing and chatting, and a bottle of wine was passed round.

But such cheerful disregard of comfort is becoming rare, and where modern amenities cannot be procured in all their profusion a new generation refuses to put up with hardships which its elders accepted as a matter of course. Thus the Scottish highlands and islands and some Alpine valleys, all inhabited from time immemorial, are being deserted. In our day the old hankering has developed into a real obsession, so that every new achievement creates new needs. Compared with our grandfathers we are living in a wonderland of refrigerators, man-made fibres, antibiotics, air travel and hundreds of things which their most eccentric fancies could not have imagined.

Right up to the First World War men still had a deep, instinctive respect for the grandeur of nature. When the railway was built through the Schöllenen Gorge on the St Gotthard Pass in Switzerland it was carefully hidden in tunnels and galleries, and the engineers prided themselves on not having disturbed the romantic natural wilderness. But the new road, built a few years ago, is no place for those who like to stand and stare. Modern man is in a hurry; he cannot pause and be alone with the thundering waters and the towering rocks. The ancient 'Devil's Bridge' now stands forlorn and useless in a bend of the new road, a melancholy monument to long-lost innocence.

Even the memory of the old, uncomfortable, romantic days was treasured. I always enjoyed passing, on the way from le Bourget to Paris, the old 'Auberge aux quatre routes' with the beautifully embellished invitation: *Ici on loge à pied et à cheval*. But a few years ago the house was modernized, and the inscription—in modern characters—now reads, somewhat irrelevantly: *Ici on logeait . . .*

But I do not intend to be merely a tiresome eulogist of the past: if what is happening all round us is sad for some, it is welcome to many and therefore inevitable. But it is certainly too much when the craving for comfort takes charge of an art. The arts, one might think, should be like religions, mysterious and powerful forces, not to be approached in the same spirit as objects of everyday experience. The solitary churches on mountain-tops may be crumbling, nature may be harnessed to serve necessity rather than old-fashioned pleasures, but something intangible still prevents religion from becoming too comfortable—in spite of televised services and loudspeakers in St Peter's Square. Although it might be technically possible, nobody would seriously contemplate the construction of a mechanical or electronic device for the administration of the sacraments. Religion can be abandoned altogether, but while and where it is observed it demands sacrifice, sacrifice of time, money, comfort. Why, then, could music not resist? Surely it, too, springs from the unfathomed depths of the creative mind, to kindle the re-creative powers of those who love and believe in it? Yet when the time was ripe the need for comfort easily overcame the respect which had previously guarded the threshold of the art. Now you can buy a machine—a record-player, a radio or television set, a tape-recorder, all of which are much cheaper than a musical instrument and the tuition necessary to play it—and all you have to do is operate your machine. 'Operate' is an ominous word in connection with music or any other art or, indeed, religion. Instruments must be 'mastered', but the new devices of mechanical reproduction or transportation have only to be 'operated'. In the hierarchy of music-making, the virtuoso of yesterday is the button-pusher of today. Nothing expresses the change more dramatically. Music which is summoned by turning a knob is as far away from the living sound as preserved fruit is from the tree upon which it grew. The operator can make the music from the machine louder or softer, but he cannot change its speed or expression; he is the passive listener to a 'canned' performance which has no regard for him or his mood. Is this still the breath of the divine?

There is another motive, too, which has helped to mechanize and transport music and so make it ubiquitous, a motive which may have a higher ethical justification than the desire for comfort: the urge for better, quicker communication. If civilization is the product of our search for comfort, the urge for communication has perhaps been the source of all culture. In this field the human race has outstripped the whole animal kingdom, for we have gone beyond the communication of essential messages, which in one way or other is given to all creatures: it is the communication of the unnecessary which distinguishes us from animals. From the first rudiments of language to the communications satellite great efforts have been made and great things achieved in order that men may understand and misunderstand each other. It is remarkable that, the more perfect the means of communication become, the more frequently do large-scale misunderstandings occur.

From Marconi's morse signal communications have developed to a stage of fantastic range and velocity, which is most beneficial for the spread of political, scientific or quite irrelevant news. Music, one would think, falls into the last category, and neither requires nor justifies such speed and range. Indeed, for thousands of years it was perfectly content with the now discredited speed of sound, which is no longer good enough even for commercial travellers. One reads with some slight confusion the names of all the physicists who have, step by step, invented all the little gadgets which are now in daily use in almost every home. Which benefactor or spoiler of mankind has connected them with music so closely that they have become indispensable? I do not know whether the name of the man is even known who first dispatched music into the ether, aimlessly and without any specific destination, to be caught by anybody who had the proper apparatus and knew how to operate it. But I cannot help thinking that there must have been in this act considerable disrespect for the art, or at any rate much less respect for the art than for the invention. Musicians, such as Richard Strauss, who had grown up with the old reverence for music could never overcome their aversion to its new, comfortable image.

*

When the great change began in the 1920s and the number of radio listeners and record-buyers grew beyond all expectations, pessimists predicted that all 'live' music would come to a standstill, that concert-halls and opera-houses had outlived their usefulness and music would henceforth be produced in studios only. This has not happened. To be sure, the army of amateur musicians has been decimated, and we shall have to consider the consequences of that later. But around music there has sprung up an industry on a scale that has never been known before. There are more live concerts and a larger public everywhere, and, if attendances in opera-houses have not increased, they have certainly not fallen away.

This is a strange contradiction. Why do people still expend

trouble and money on something they can have more cheaply and more comfortably in their homes? Is this perhaps the sign of a revolt against the encroachment of technology? There will be some who say that the whole purpose of the wide and easy availability of music was to awaken the interest of a new and larger public and to arouse the desire for closer acquaintance. But it is difficult to accept that any comfort is designed to stimulate a longing for discomfort. Once the railways were running, the mail-coach was discarded; now that aeroplanes are flying, ships and railways are the poor relations of travel. The intention of the inventors of broadcasting and record-manufacture could scarcely have been to encourage the old forms of music-making and listening.

Music, however, is a very special art. Literature and the visual arts, as objects of admiration or understanding, remain as it were outside the reader or observer, like the sun or the moon or a landscape which one knows and loves without being able to make it one's own. Music, on the other hand, not only allows but demands re-creation, appropriation. Only in its re-creation does music fulfil its mission entirely. The piece of music which I play myself is 'mine' in a fundamentally different sense from the picture which hangs on my wall or the poem which I know by heart, because I participate in the musical work which I re-create. I do not participate in either the picture or the poem. While the picture and—in a somewhat less material sense—the poem *are* the works the printed or manuscript sheet of music is no more than a guide or recipe for the re-creation of a work which has no real existence otherwise.

This re-creation need not necessarily be a full-scale performance. It takes place when I recall a work in my mind or whistle a tune. It could be argued, perhaps, that the process is not so very different from reciting a poem. But the poem is an 'original', beyond any possibility of change. In music such an unalterable original does not exist. I shall deal later with the specific problems which arise from this fact: with the question of interpretation and faithfulness to the musical 'text'; of the personality of the re-creator, which unavoidably colours his performance but is only in the rarest of cases the same as that of the original creator. The possibility, or indeed necessity, of re-creation marks the essential difference between music and the other arts. The visual arts absolutely defy any attempt at it. The copyist of a painting or a sculpture creates a work of infinitely lower value than the unique original. In literature dramatic works alone leave something to the actor which vaguely compares with the performance of music, but everybody knows from personal experience that a play can be read to much greater advantage than music and does not necessarily require performance on the stage.

It follows that the mere listener, whatever pleasure he may derive from listening, is at a disadvantage. Figuratively speaking, he remains on the threshold and never enters the inner sanctum of the work that is performed for him. True, as long as it *is* performed 'for him', in a live performance and in his presence, a spark of re-creation still flashes from performer to listener, and the physical presence of the re-creator draws the listener nearer to the work. But with the new means of transporting or preserving the acoustic phenomenon that is music the re-creator is not physically present; the work is performed not for one particular listener but for an anonymous multitude. This sets a barrier of distance between the listener and the work which must harm the most precious property of music: the personal, individual appeal. Music concerns us not collectively but in a very personal sense, as if it were created for each one of us individually. It is a strange fact that the technical advances which have so successfully shortened distances in practical matters have achieved the opposite effect with an art that does not conform to practical standards. And with this growing distance between listener and work the true meaning—or, if I may be forgiven the unfashionable word, the soul—of the work tends to become separated from the physical phenomenon of the sound.

This may even, paradoxically, be the reason why the new methods of providing music comfortably and in unlimited quantities at any time and any place have fostered what, logically, they should have destroyed: the desire for live music. Wilhelm Furt-wängler's version of Beethoven's 'Eroica' with the Vienna Phil-harmonic Orchestra, in the impeccable HMV recording, cannot be bettered today by any conductor or orchestra. But owners of the recording will still flock to performances by lesser conductors and lesser orchestras. For who wants to see the 'Eroica' become petri-fied, even in the most perfect rendering? Thus it seems that all the buyers of records, all the listeners to broadcasting, are seeking the live contact with greater zeal than in the days when music had no mechanical existence. To ascribe this to the fact that easy access and omnipresence have roused the interest of a multitude which previously had no contact with music is an oversimplifica-tion. This could explain the sales of records and the number of radio licences, but not the popularity of live concerts.

One day an even more remarkable thing will happen. The manufacturer of the Furtwängler recording will delete it from the catalogues and it will no longer be available. New interpreters will come and go, and the moment will have arrived when preservation fails.

One has to penetrate to the very centre of the art in order to capture the divine spark which technical progress may have overlaid but has not destroyed; for if the divine element had been destroyed we would have no music any more. Finality is the essence of the other arts, but living change is the miracle of music, from the commonest pop-song to the most sublime manifestation of creative genius. This is something that science cannot alter.

However, it would be vain to pretend that advances which have so greatly extended access to the periphery of music have not also seriously restricted entry to the inner sanctuary. The comfort with which an abundance of music can be procured—European broadcasting organizations alone are producing three hundred hours of music per day, or a hundred thousand hours per year—has divided the musical world more sharply than ever before, into a relatively small group of highly professional performers on the one hand and on the other a vast number of passive listeners, whose relationship with the art is quite different from that of a musician who, however imperfectly, performs or re-creates music himself. Music has always been a tonic or a palliative. Present-day mass consumption has greatly emphasized these qualities, which might be called extra-musical. It is indeed difficult to believe that the current prodigious demand springs from a purely artistic need. In a wide sector of its new existence music exercises this precise side-effect—to stimulate or to soothe. Any fear that it may be brought into irrevocable disrepute by its new masters would be exaggerated, but it may equally be over-optimistic to believe that ubiquity and quantity are necessarily signs of maturity, and that the musical art has become an element of our existence, more closely connected with our everyday life than, say, were the visual arts in Periclean Athens or Medician Florence. The ever-growing din of the modern world and the nervous tension it produces have played a large part in promoting mass-production and stimulating demand. We shall have to trace the malaise which has spread from these sources throughout the whole field of music.

Although many doubts surround the vast industry which has grown up around music, one development—mechanical reproduction

—is a truly providential one. For the first time in its long history music has achieved lasting, objective existence.

Music may be the oldest of the arts. Compared with the others it requires little knowledge, little craftsmanship, little experience. Born out of an instinctive interjection, it never strayed as far from that primitive, instinctive cry of joy or despair which gave it birth as the other arts did from their origins—communication and observation. Music shaped more easily, spread more easily —and was more easily lost.

For music has indeed been lost. While an enormous treasury of works of art has accumulated over thousands of years in every corner of the civilized world, music has never survived, although it has occupied the best minds of every age. We know much about the theory and philosophy of old music, but the works themselves have vanished. We possess King David's Psalms; their poetry, their devotion and wisdom speak to us with undiminished force. But David was a musician too. At the beginning of many psalms there are the instructions: *To the chief musician on Neginoth*; *To the chief musician upon Nehiloth*. A whole arsenal of instruments is mentioned, which may be those we can see on Egyptian reliefs. But the music itself, which must have been an essential part of the psalms, is lost for ever.

Nothing can show the fundamental difference between poetry and music more clearly and convincingly. Even if it is faintly recollected in the cantillation or 'trop' as still practised in orthodox synagogues, King David's music was also instrumental music, which is banned from the orthodox service and ritual. Byzantine plainsong may represent the oldest music we know, preserved not for its artistic merit but by the orthodoxy of the liturgy, just as the Chinese, until fairly recently, could preserve the Ying Shên, the hymn to the approaching spirit of age. It is certainly true that, in the arts, later generations never accept the experience or recommendations of their forefathers, but there are certain unmistakable and imperishable artistic values which are handed down through the ages, however unfashionable their appearance may become. It is an article of faith that mankind never loses what it does not want to lose. There can be no misfortune or negligence that could deprive it of an achievement that is important for all time. Yet music has not been preserved. Generation after generation have dealt harshly with the music of their predecessors and have discarded it. We have no 'old' music.

This is a fact which has so far attracted but little attention, and few attempts have been made to explain it. Historians may even deny it altogether, arguing that the loss, so far as it has occurred, is due to the undiminished difficulties of material tradition, of the graphic expression of sounds. But the greatest works of literature have survived in languages long disused and through ages of widespread illiteracy. Similarly, great works of architecture and sculpture have been saved in spite of periods of savage destruction. There is no conceivable reason why old music in old graphs should not have been transcribed in new graphs if it had been considered worth while. Somebody, somewhere, would have rescued the old music from oblivion, just as the Arabs rescued Greek science and philosophy when the new Europeans were unmindful of their heritage.

Historians may insist, too, that we do have a sizeable knowledge of old music, while admitting that it does not go as far back as our knowledge of the other arts: we do not know what music the musicians on the walls of Sakhara are playing. It is true that, thanks to the efforts of historians, we are able to decipher most of the musical graphs of the last thousand years with some measure of accuracy. But is this really all the knowledge that is necessary for an appreciation of old music? Do we *understand* it?

Many poems of the *trouvères* and minstrels of the twelfth and thirteenth centuries are quite gay, but what we know of their music invariably sounds sad and melancholy to our ears; and this seems to indicate a basic misunderstanding. It does not mean to us what it meant to its original audience. Perotinus, the head of the School of Notre Dame in Paris in the thirteenth century, was called 'le Grand'. Do we honestly appreciate why? Even three hundred years later, when Orlando di Lasso received the title *'principe di musica'*, we cannot quite realize the margin which sets him apart from other good composers of his time. Such uncertainties apply even to J. S. Bach, the tempo of some of whose pieces, particularly among his many 'Allemandes', is doubtful.

It is not, after all, the historian who decides whether a work of art still has validity and meaning. If it were only historians who visited Rome or Athens, tourism would be in a bad way—and so would the maintenance of classical works of art, which is largely financed out of the curiosity and affection of a large public, often informed and advised by the historian but always independent in its appreciation. In music it is only the historian who cares. He can marvel at Monteverdi's anticipating the dramatic vigour of a later age, but it is Verdi who fills the opera-houses, *Rigoletto* rather than *Il Ritorno d'Ulisse*. To the unbiased mind there is always an inevitable comparison between old and new music, to the detriment of the old, while it would never occur and would seem quite unreasonable to anybody to measure Rodin beside Phidias or le Corbusier beside Brunellesco.

It is also true—and I shall deal with this aspect in its proper place—that for thousands of years music produced no truly great works, nothing comparable with the greatest manifestations of the other arts. There is no contemporary musical equivalent of Homer's *Iliad* or Kallikrates' Parthenon, of Dante's *Commedia Divina* or Michelangelo's ceiling in the Sistine Chapel, not even, one might say, of the second part of Goethe's *Faust*. Perhaps music did not look to the future as the other arts did. '*Exegi monumentum aere perennius*,' a poet could write, confident that his voice would be heard down the ages. But music, until comparatively recently, had no such ambitious purpose and was content to express the mood of the moment.

I believe, though, that the reason for the evanescence of music lies deeper than this. As I have said before, the musical score, or whatever the graphic representation of music may be called, does not constitute the work in the same simple sense as a canvas or a printed page constitutes a visual or literary work. This is the fundamental difference between music and the other arts: its glory and, if you will, its tragedy. Re-creation is not a mechanical process, just as a good cookery book is not a guarantee of good cooking. 'The real beauty of music cannot be put down on paper,' wrote Liszt, and this is not only true of beauty. Neither can the real meaning be laid down once and for all, as in the other arts; it must be guessed at or sensed. There is a void, a space, left in every work of music, which must be filled by the re-creator. This re-creation requires a large measure of mental and temperamental identity of creator with re-creator, and it is this identity which preserves our otherwise vague understanding of music. If, by the passage of time and changes in both man and his environment, it is disturbed and eventually destroyed re-creation becomes impossible and the work loses its appeal, its validity. This identity between creator and re-creator is a familiar experience to anyone making or listening to music. If somebody says that he dislikes Chopin because he is too sentimental or that he prefers Beethoven's Opus 1 to Opus 135 he expresses that very lack of identity which would prevent him from performing properly those works which he dislikes. By the change of environment, such individual differences of taste and temperament become general and 'old' music is abandoned. It is a tantalizing thought that music, which is older than any other art and perhaps even older than articulate language, has lost its past.

Now, with mechanically reproduced and preserved music, none of this should happen again. Mechanical reproduction endows music with an objective existence which it has never had before. This may not necessarily be its true nature but it is nevertheless of immense importance for future generations. Extensive archives of recordings are being assembled which preserve the actual acoustic phenomenon of an outstanding work as well as outstanding individual performances. Leaving aside all the other consequences of mechanical reproduction, this one may represent the greatest of all changes in music. Which of us would not be eager to know how Bach's *St Matthew Passion* sounded in his time and under his direction, or to listen to Paganini's wizardry on the violin? Those who come after us will be luckier than any of their predecessors since the beginning of time. They will actually hear the best performances of all that music which we are still competent to perform. Not that they will necessarily appreciate it—they may shake their heads at Stravinsky's *Rite of Spring* or consider Beethoven's *Missa Solemnis* in Toscanini's unforgettable interpretation a monstrosity. Indeed, mere preservation of the sound may not preserve the all-important identity between the creator and later generations of listeners, and therefore may not prevent the mortality of old music or keep alive the respect and affection which we feel for 'our' masterpieces. But some knowledge will be handed down, and for that our successors should be grateful.

2. INTELLECTUAL PROPERTY

....

The most diverse things—technical progress, the spread of education, mass communication and certainly some real enthusiasm—had to combine to create a monstrosity: music has become the mass-produced product of a vast industry. It has developed into a gigantic international enterprise employing hundreds of thousands of people—artists, technicians, lawyers, tradesmen, obsessed enthusiasts and cool speculators, a highly colourful world wherein the most sublime ideals rub shoulders with the most down-to-earth objectives, the *amour des lettres* with the *esprit des affaires*.

This world, like any other, needs discipline and order. At its periphery the traffic in music is subject to the ordinary rules of traffic. Debts must be paid, cheques must be honoured, offers must be binding. But the merchandise is of such a special and unusual nature that only exceptional laws can govern it: the laws of copyright, the right of intellectual property.

And here, immediately, the divine and the human, the high and the low, collide. Copyright is a cold-blooded attempt at reconciling mind with money. A cynic might even suggest that the whole idea of copyright was to care for the proprietor rather than for the property.

Copyright as we know it today is a venerable institution. But it must not be forgotten that for thousands of years mankind wrote poetry, painted pictures, built temples and composed music without any protection whatsoever, and that its absence obviously did not hamper the creative powers of artists; nor has its presence apparently enhanced them. The arts are very old, but copyright is very young.

Unlike jurisprudence generally, the law of copyright has not grown with and out of particular conditions. The Ancient Greeks, who were exceptionally capable artistically but rather simple-minded in legal matters, never thought of it. Even the Romans, less gifted creators but eminent lawyers and administrators, never tried to find a formula for the protection of the artist. There must have been no need for it. After all, Roman art prospered to no small extent on the imitation and reproduction of great examples, and this may not have allowed the idea of the exclusiveness and inviolability of intellectual creation to be developed. It was, on the contrary, the natural function of a good sculpture to be copied, of a good thought to be re-thought. Nor, apparently, did the living-conditions of creative artists justify any intervention by the legislators. Sculptors, painters, architects and cutters of gems and medallions were certainly paid in accordance with their capabilities and with the importance of their task. From a legal point of view this was no different from any other contract of service, purchase or sale, unaffected by any consideration of the intangible or the divine. How most poets and philosophers made their living we do not know, though some, like Aristotle, had wealthy and munificent pupils and others, like Horace, had liberal patrons. Nothing suits the arts better than liberal patronage, which rewards generosity of the mind with generosity of money. It ensures the dignity of both, and the Roman system must have produced an enviable balance between the artist and society: the artists 'gave' their works to the world and the world proved grateful without any sense of obligation. We still speak of a work of art's being 'given' to the world, although the phrase is no longer accurate. Great works have been created and given to mankind under this rule of generosity, and no complaint about the conflicting needs of mind or money reaches our ears from those distant, happy days.

It was more than a thousand years after Virgil that the first murmurs of discontent were heard—characteristically, from poets. Whereas sculptors, architects and painters still enjoyed the advantage of supplying material objects at a price which fully covered both their intangible and their tangible work, poets, such as the most famous of German minstrels, Walther von der Vogelweide, could and did complain of the discrepancy between the richness of their art and the poverty of their reward.

It was the advent of printing which decisively disturbed the peace and brought to the surface the problems which had been gathering in the subsoil of artistic creation. Printing allowed a degree of exploitation far beyond the former business of scribes and copyists. The printer was now also the distributor of the printed work, the publisher, a businessman who invested money in presses, founts and paper—and who demanded protection from his competitors. This was the real issue. Emperors, kings and sovereign princes sold privileges to printers. *Con licenza dei superiori; Cum gratia et privilegio Christianissimi Francorum Regis; By privilege of His*

Roman Imperial Majesty not to be reprinted within ten years—such are the notices printed on the title-pages of early books, warning against infringement of the monopoly given to the printer-publisher (though not, it must be emphasized, to the *author*).

Anglo-Saxon thinking has still not really advanced beyond this point. The technical term for the author's right, the *droit d'auteur*, the *Urheberrecht*, is still 'copyright', the right in the copy and not in its intangible contents which resist legal definition. Copyright today is no more than a misnomer, although with one ominous exception: neither the British nor the American Copyright Act acknowledges the *droit moral*, the inalienable, non-transferable right of the author or composer to prevent and to prosecute anything which he considers to be a disfigurement of his work, such as cuts, changes in instrumentation or even an objectively bad performance.

Privileges are not rights but exemptions from rights. They were not granted as a matter of course but had to be applied for and paid for. By granting them the sovereign secured for himself a share in the revenue from the intellectual creations of his subjects, to which he was as legitimately entitled as to treasure trove. The creators themselves acquired no title and were fully exposed to the predatory practices of the printers—and Martin Luther was not the only author who complained ineffectively about the way they exploited the works of others. Also, the privilege had no validity outside the country where it was granted, which was particularly serious for musicians. (Peter Paul Rubens was probably the first 'author' to enjoy international protection of his works when, in 1619 and 1620, the Dutch States General and the Kings of England, France and Spain granted him the exclusive right to execute and distribute etchings of his own paintings. This, no doubt, required an artist-diplomat with good connections, and for a long time it remained a rare exception.)

However, the growing discontent of authors led in the end to a kind of conspiracy. In 1776 Beaumarchais (whose sarcastic comment stands at the beginning of this section) founded, together with some like-minded friends, the *Société des auteurs et compositeurs dramatiques*, a society of dramatists and opera-composers who were determined thenceforth to make the most of their talents. Only those theatre-directors or impresarios who paid a royalty to them and to nobody else should be entitled to have access to their works. This was intended to protect them from the greed of the entrepreneurs as much as from the weakness of their own characters, for corruption and intrigue were rife, while goodwill and co-operation had to be bought with substantial bribes payable to everyone from the managers down to the porters at the stage doors. What a pity that Beaumarchais himself was such a scoundrel! It would be more pleasant to think of Apollo coming down from Parnassus to take arts and artists under his protection. But the prize must go to the inventor of the clever, eloquent and rapacious Figaro, and it is his name which shines in resplendent golden letters outside the premises of the still flourishing society in the rue Ballu in Paris.

Since then Frenchmen have never ceased to speculate about the peculiar position of art and artists in a world which felt the coming upheaval in its bones. The revived determination to recognize beauty and do good led to the conviction that an orderly world would have to do justice both to the god in man and to the man in god. Jurists had their qualms. Neither Gaius's *Institutions* nor Justinian's *Pandektae*, which between them still formed the basis of legal thought in France, gave a clue as to how the abstract product of the mind could be made into a protectable object—its concrete representation, paper and ink, canvas and colour, marble and mortar, being irrelevant. Then the American Congress, and subsequently the French Revolution, proclaimed the doctrine of 'Human Rights', equally unknown to the classical authors and equally abstract. This pointed the way, and on 19 July 1793 the *propriété intellectuelle* was formally enthroned. This may be called the birth of copyright.

The basic doctrine was new: the author is by *nature* rather than by law or grace the exclusive owner of his work. In one respect only did the jurists not give way: to this day mere ideas, improvisations, cannot be protected. There must be an incontestable record, a 'work', a manuscript, a picture, a building. Beyond this, however, no formalities need be complied with, no applications made, no fees paid to secure protection. Both entrepreneurs and public are alike forbidden to take possession of the work. Only with the author's consent can they make use of it.

This must have created some serious problems, especially in music. The exclusive right of the composer operates not only against the exploiters and the public but also against his fellow musicians. And it was in music that respect for other people's property was most lax. Borrowings were frequent, forgeries not rare. More works were published under the name of Pergolesi than he could have written in a long life—and he died at twenty-six. Haydn's name figures on several dozen works of which he knew nothing. When Mozart became fashionable at the beginning of the nineteenth century his name was not spared either. Such a casual attitude is difficult to understand today. J. S. Bach did not bother to indicate the source of any of his transcriptions of works by Vivaldi, Marcello, Telemann and others, although in his case there was no intention to mislead anyone. It was simply a matter of no importance. Opera-composers showed a similar attitude to the authors of their libretti. 'A certain individual called Mozart in Vienna has had the effrontery to misuse my play *Belmont and Constanza* for an opera libretto,' exclaimed the outraged author in a Leipzig newspaper after a performance of *Die Entführung aus dem Serail*. It was quite true. He had not been asked for permission, he had not been invited to co-operate, he was paid nothing, his anger was perfectly justified—but he had no redress.

Under the rule of copyright such things should not happen again. The State places all its judicial and punitive resources at the artist's disposal, and every infringement becomes a punishable offence. The new conception establishes both the material interests and the respect for the creation of the intellect, in the same way as material property is protected by the law. The borrowings of yesterday become thefts; forgery becomes scandalous. Nothing in art is more contemptible than plagiarism.

Let us remark here that plagiarism is more difficult to prove in music than in literature. 'Style' in music is no more than an accumulation of phrases and turns which are common to most composers of the time—in the case of Mozart, Hermann Abert has shown this in great detail and with remarkable diligence. Thus only the most blatant examples can be prosecuted successfully. In my career I remember only one such case, when a song was reissued with a different text and title. The original was long forgotten and the new, unauthorized version became a great popular success. So all concerned, the defenders and the offenders, agreed to let the desecrated original (whose composer was dead) be forgotten and to share as honestly as the peculiar circumstances permitted the considerable revenue from the more successful version.

*

The newly discovered and formulated 'author's right' did not by any means capture the imagination of the world at one stroke. Although its revolutionary character soon lost its menace and the idea became more acceptable outside France it was more than fifty years before a codified copyright spread to the greater part of the civilized world. Once it had reached that stage, however, there was no holding it. The arts, unlike the men and women who produce and enjoy them, cannot be confined to one particular country. The new means of travel and communication brought once distant countries closer together, and with the growth of international trade in all types of goods it was felt necessary to supplement national copyright laws with international agreements. In 1886 the Berne Convention for the Protection of Literary and Artistic Works was signed, and most civilized countries adhered to it, with the notable exceptions of the United States of America and Russia. The Berne Convention is certainly one of the few effective instruments of international law. Others exist more in theory than in practice, and one would like to think that artistic matters have brought about a union of peoples and governments which purely material considerations and interests have never achieved.

In broad outline, the Berne Convention stipulates certain minimum requirements of protection to be included in the national legislation of each convention country, and demands that foreign works should enjoy the same protection as 'national' works, the nationality of a work being decided by the place of publication and not by the nationality of the author. Thus a Russian author obtains protection in all convention countries if his work is first published in one of these, irrespective of the fact that Russia has never ratified the convention. This has been of particular importance for music, and Russian publishers such as Belaieff, Jurgenson, Gutheil and Bessel opened their own publishing houses in Paris, Berlin and Leipzig in order to secure protection for the enormously successful new Russian music of Tchaikovsky, Borodin and Rimsky-Korsakov.

The United States, on the other hand, concluded bilateral treaties with the most important countries—though not with Russia—by which reciprocal protection was granted, though the formality and fee of registration with the Library of Congress in Washington had still to be complied with. The fee has only fairly recently been waived. Protection depends on the nationality of the author and a Russian, for example, not domiciled in the United States cannot obtain it even if his work is published in a country which has a treaty with the States.

So, at the end of the nineteenth century, everything seemed well provided for. Artists could not ask for more. Jurisprudence had mastered the difficult problem.

✳

As early as 1793 certain doubts had arisen. Material property is basically everlasting. A reward of land and title bestowed centuries ago by a king on a loyal follower can be perpetuated as long as the lineage flourishes, however unworthy the descendants may be. Only the owner's free will, insolvency or bankruptcy, or actual physical destruction, can change the ownership of material goods. Copyright, in appointing the artist the sole owner of his work, applied essentially the same rules. But, while it was accepted by all legislative bodies of the time that property in general should benefit its owner alone, there remained the awkward contradiction that works of art were destined for mankind and that mankind, too, was entitled to a benefit. Here was an obvious conflict. Many an established legal principle had been violated to produce the concept of intellectual property, but now the jurists had to go one step further. No sooner had the artist's rights been established than the legislators had to consider how dispossessed mankind could recover its cultural heritage. This has remained a dilemma ever since copyright was introduced. Nothing that has happened since 19 July 1793 has reconciled the opposing interests of artist and public. As recently as 1959 the first paragraph of the decree by which a Ministry of Culture was created in France (where the idea of the intellectual property originated) says solemnly: 'It is the task of the Ministry of Culture to make the major works of mankind in general and of France in particular accessible to the largest possible number of Frenchmen.' This almost sounds as if the new ministry had the power to override the exclusive rights of the artist if they restricted access to his work. To the layman—and, especially, to many people in the musical profession—this may seem reasonable enough, but no lawyer could accept such blatant disregard of rights which are nowhere defended with more determination than in the French courts. In fact, the Ministry of Culture has no such power.

It was clear from the outset that some means had to be devised to circumvent the difficulty, and that intellectual property could not simply be equated with material property by the award to the artist and all his successors of an everlasting, exclusive proprietary right. The theory is that it is neither the Government nor the people of any particular country which bestows copyright, but mankind itself—and that mankind therefore reserves for itself a reversionary right. The works are, ideally, everlasting; the rights in the works are not. The day must come when the creation of the intellect can be returned to the public. The original French terminology, still in use today, calls it characteristically '*la chute dans le domaine public*', the 'lapse' into public property or the public domain. When this day arrives all the barred and bolted doors are flung open and mankind invades the sanctuary to take possession of its patrimony, to which it is entitled by virtue of its kinship with the original creative mind. All the limitations previously imposed by law become null and void, including the 'moral right'.

A work 'in the public domain' can be freely altered, arranged and rearranged, used or abused at will, for it is nobody's and everybody's property. Mozart's piano sonata in C (K. 545) becomes 'In an Eighteenth-Century Drawing-Room'; Mendelssohn's overture to *A Midsummer Night's Dream* has three trombones added to the orchestration, although Mendelssohn himself deliberately avoided them; *Carmen* becomes *Carmen Jones*; *Romeo and Juliet* becomes *West Side Story*. Unscrupulous arrangers and publishers must not be held responsible for such outrages. It is for the public to discourage them. Such misdeeds are committed simply for the sake of money, which only the public can provide. So it is for the public and public conscience to prevent them, for there is no authority to safeguard unprotected property against the vandalism of its owners. True, there are a few countries which have introduced a so-called '*domaine public payant*'; Italy for *all* artistic works, France for literary works only. For such works a royalty must be paid for the reprinting or performing of unprotected works, but this represents only a form of taxation and not protection.

The 'period of copyright' is one serious anomaly in the artificial edifice of copyright legislation dealing with goods which lead a peculiar material and spiritual double life. Every period of copyright is arbitrary. The only natural moment for protection to cease would be on the death of the author, but mankind and the legislators could hardly be so callous. No other time-limit could be anything but arbitrary. In France, a period of fifty years *post mortem auctoris* was stipulated from the beginning. Most other European countries would not go beyond thirty years, which, in French eyes, prematurely surrendered the works of Wagner, Brahms, Johann Strauss and Dvořák, together with French works still protected in France such as those of Bizet, Gounod and Delibes. Germany did not introduce the fifty-year period until 1934, but in 1965 she extended it to seventy years. There was and is little uniformity: Spain has eighty years, Brazil sixty,

Portugal an everlasting copyright. There is no reasonable justification for any of these limits, as there is, for example, in the close
season for hunting or fishing. The period of copyright is a compromise between artist and public, hesitantly sanctioned by
legislation.

Even the motives behind this 'period of copyright' are not clear.
Since 1871 France has extended it by the war years 1870–1,
1914–18 and 1939–45, so that it stands at present at sixty-one
years plus several months and days, the reason being that during
those years the works could not be properly exploited. The principle, therefore, is unashamedly materialistic. Since the Second
World War Italy and the Scandinavian countries have followed the
French example.

On the other hand the United States has introduced an altogether different system, and it is anybody's guess whether this was
prompted by spiritual or commercial considerations. The American
law allows the artist a total of fifty-six years (two periods of twenty-
eight years each) from the date of publication, which date is
ascertainable by the entry in the Copyright Register at the Library
of Congress in Washington. It therefore happens not infrequently
that a work falls into the public domain not just soon after the
artist's death but actually during his lifetime, which seems rather
inconsiderate on the part of the legislators. Certainly it is a galling
experience for the artist, more particularly for the European artist,
who is used to more respectful treatment. True, up to the beginning
of this century America owed more to the rest of the world than
she had to offer, and the case for better copyright protection was
not very strong. However, since America has become an important contributor to science, literature and serious music, as well as
the greatest power in the realm of popular music, the copyright
law is in the process of being revised and the fifty-year period
after the death of the composer is to be introduced.

As the purpose of copyright is the protection of the artist from
society it is of a certain piquancy to see how communist countries
are dealing with it, the overriding communist doctrine demanding
that the interests of the individual be subordinated to the interests
of the community.

Those communist countries which were members of the Berne
Convention before the war, such as Czechoslovakia, Hungary and
Poland, have remained members and are fulfilling their international obligations as best they can. They have not materially
altered their national legislation under communism except that

they have accelerated the 'lapse into the public domain' by reducing the period of protection to twenty-five years from the death of the author, this applying equally to their own works and to foreign works in their territory.

Communist Russia, like Tsarist Russia before it, scorns all international conventions and still finds it more profitable to abandon all rights in Russian works abroad and gain free access to the artistic and scientific production of the rest of the world in exchange. Russia has, however, a national copyright law, first promulgated in 1928 and thoroughly revised in 1961. In the special circumstances of communism this law gives a more vivid picture of the conflict between art, artist and society than the laws of capitalist countries, which tend to obscure the deeper issues. Contrary to basic communist principle, which allows private ownership of minor assets only, the Russian copyright law stipulates the exclusive proprietary right of the author in his work, which is a capital asset—provided, however, that the work is in line with official ideology. Napoleon, in more primitive times, hated all ideology and ideologists; communism loves both and makes the arts its ideological vehicle. Arts and artists are privileged and, if necessary, punished, and the obedient exponents of official ideology enjoy concessions nobody else could expect from such a doctrinaire way of life.

Ideology is easily identifiable in literature and also to some extent in science. When it comes to music it becomes more hypothetical. There is no explicable reason why Tchaikovsky's music should conform better to communist ideology than Boulez's, unless it is simply that one has a wider appeal and is more accessible than the other. But the alleged modernity of communist society admits of no modernity in the arts. The experiments and efforts of 'decadent' and 'bourgeois' Western composers to create a new music are forbidden to their Russian counterparts. It is noteworthy that the abolition of such restrictive and ill-defined ideological rules in music have led to a true explosion of new talent in Poland.

If a work does not conform to the official, authoritatively imposed ideology it remains unprotected. The law simply states the fact, without disclosing who makes the decision or indicating any procedure or right of appeal. In a capitalist country this withholding of protection would mean only that the work would be free for all. In Russia it means suppression and prohibition, the State being the only authorized publisher and distributor. If the State Publishing House rejects a work there remain only illegal ways of bringing it to the notice of the public. A work like *Dr Zhivago* has to be smuggled out of the country and published abroad, and the smugglers and their helpers risk their freedom.

If, however, the work is in line with ideological requirements it is given protection, and the exclusive ownership thus conferred at once collides with the existing order. The author can destroy his work or bury it in his desk. There is nothing in the law which can compel him to part with it. (Communist legislation is not generally deterred by unenforceable laws, since if need be they can be supplemented by violence.) But if an artist wants his work to be exhibited, printed, performed or distributed, he has no alternative but to assign his rights to the State authority. He cannot cast around for the highest bidder or the most suitable publisher. The State decides the conditions on which the rights must be assigned and the law itself provides a guide as to the percentage of royalties due to the artist on the sale of books and music, a rule which contradicts all the experience and usage of a 'free economy': the greater the print, the smaller the royalty. Thus, while the period of protection may still be of material importance for the author, for the public it is irrelevant. In capitalist countries a work 'in the public domain' is normally cheaper than a protected work; in Russia there is no discernible difference between them, both being in the hands of the State as the sole owner and virtual infringer of copyright. Indeed, the law promulgated by the Central Government treats the period of protection with complete indifference. The Copyright Act of 1928 stipulated fifteen years after the death of the author; the new act indicates no definite period but leaves it to the member countries of the Soviet Union to decide within their own jurisdiction, which so far they do not seem to have done. It is open to debate whether this in effect means that every work or no work is 'free'.

It will largely depend on his good personal relations with the executives of the State Publishing House what influence a composer, say, has on the typographical appearance, distribution and publicity of his work. The law itself gives him no remedy for any failure on the part of the publisher. It regularly happens that even the most important works are restricted to a single edition, the demand being declared to have been satisfied when libraries, schools, orchestras and opera-houses, theatres and broadcasting organizations have been supplied with copies. Shostakovitch's 'Forty-eight Preludes and Fugues' for piano were sold out in this manner within two months and have never been reprinted.

The State takes good care of its tame artists, and does so in prominent cases very generously, far exceeding the minimum conditions laid down by the law. But copyright in its true sense remains an empty gesture.

In spite of the apparent weakness of this system of simultaneous award and expropriation of rights, some Western artists—mostly dissatisfied and disillusioned ones—believe that the magic formula has been found to rescue them from their brutal struggle for artistic and material existence. But there must be unsuccessful, dissatisfied and disillusioned authors in Russia, too, who do not share in the bounty available to the successful on either side of the Iron Curtain.

*

In the deliberations which led to the institution of copyright music played but a minor part. The text of the Berne Convention still names literature specifically, but lumps music along with 'the other arts'. Despite this, all further development at both national and international levels was dictated by music and by the technical progress to which it was increasingly subjected. Since the beginning of this century music has been a matter of concern for the legal profession. Before the First World War the legal nature of mechanical reproduction (mainly of music) had to be defined; and this was not as easy as it may appear. A judgement of 1911 described the phonographic cylinder as an interchangeable part of a machine, which had no independent existence within the meaning of copyright and which therefore could neither be said to constitute an infringement nor receive protection. Those cylinders, discs and perforated rolls could not be called 'graphic reproductions' either, since, having no graphic quality, they could not be read. There was no precedent to indicate the proper place for this novelty, and in the end special provisions had to be made in order to accommodate mechanical reproduction in the growing edifice of copyright. It was primarily for this purpose that most of the existing copyright acts were revised between 1900 and 1911. They declared the author the sole owner of the new right of mechanical reproduction. Reproduction without his consent would constitute an infringement in the same way as an unauthorized reprint would. 'Consent' always means money. A new source of revenue had been tapped, which was primarily to benefit composers.

This had hardly been achieved when broadcasting arrived on the scene. This provided jurists with more new problems, as it would fit into none of the laboriously devised categories of foreseeable and protectable uses of a work of art. Broadcasting was not a public performance. In its early years performances regularly took place in studios, to which the public was not admitted. Reception in the home was strictly private. There was no mechanical reproduction of the sound, only transmission. A new category had to be established which added this to the rights reserved exclusively to the author. A new rampart was built to keep the public at arm's length and add yet another source of income to those already existing. Film, sound film and magnetic tape rounded off the picture of the ever-growing means of making use of works of art in general and of music in particular.

The Berne Convention therefore found itself out of date and had to be revised in order to keep pace with developments, first in Rome in 1928, then in Brussels in 1948 and finally in Stockholm in 1967. While the revision of 1928 emphatically reasserted the moral and material protection of the artist in the face of technical innovation, the revision of 1948 produced some hesitation and doubts on the part of the legislators, who felt that they might have gone too far in their concern to protect the artist. Certain exemptions were introduced for broadcasting, public libraries and other institutions not dedicated to direct material gain—restrictions on the exercise of proprietary rights such as could not be applied to other, material types of property. The Stockholm revision has confirmed and tightened these restrictions, so, if it was music which had led to the refinement and extension of the notion of intellectual property, it is also music which has now caused a certain contraction.

Eventually, in 1952, the Berne Convention was supplemented by a Universal Copyright Convention designed to extend reciprocal protection, without cumbersome formalities, to those countries which were not signatories to the Berne Convention, especially the United States and the Latin-American republics. Only Russia again refused to participate. ('We have no political motives,' a high official of the Russian Trade Delegation in London said to me, 'but we cannot accept a convention of which Spain is a member.')

Among all the achievements in the field of copyright one rule deserves particular mention because it has done more than anything else to change the economic status of composers: the protection of public performance.

It was never too difficult to control performances of dramatic works, as the Société des Auteurs et Compositeurs Dramatiques had proved. Long before there was any legal protection of dramatic performances opera-composers kept their orchestral scores and sold copies to the theatres at an inclusive price in lieu of royalties. It sometimes happened—Mozart, for instance, experienced it—that dishonest copyists made copies for themselves and sold them for their own profit in a foreign country, where no law or privilege protected the work. The first French Copyright Act introduced protection of the dramatic performance, and since the middle of the nineteenth century other European legislative bodies have followed this example—Verdi and Wagner made considerable capital out of it. But symphonic, instrumental and vocal music remained outside any such jurisdiction. It seemed that it would be impossible to control the innumerable performances that took place in a multitude of concert-halls and other places of entertainment, even if the principle had been recognized. Once such a work was printed and distributed it had to be left to its fate, and the composer had to be content with his sheet royalties.

The story is told of a long-forgotten French composer of light music who once dined at a Paris Café-Concert while the orchestra was playing some of his work. When he was presented with the bill for his dinner he refused to accept it: if his music was played without any payment being made to him, he said, he would not pay for his dinner. The matter came before a court and the composer won his case. This was in 1849. A dramatic and ominous precedent had been established. Even the most benevolent observer must have felt it outrageous that, at least in France, orchestras, singers, violinists and pianists should be unable to carry on their professions without the composer's consent—for that was the real issue, at a time when old or unprotected music was unwanted and new, protected music was all the rage. No concert artist could have made a living by playing or singing only the old masters and not the works of Chopin or Liszt, Rossini or Auber. But a few months later, in May 1850, the Agence Centrale pour la Perception des Droits des Auteurs et Compositeurs de Musique opened its offices and collected performing fees from concert-halls, cafés, restaurants and cabarets in the same way as the Société dramatique did in theatres. In the first seven months of its existence it collected the sum of 7,500 francs, which was encouraging enough for it to continue with increased vigour. There was a great deal of noise and argument about it, but under the protection of tribunals and the police and of a legal monopoly conferred upon it the new Society became a considerable power.

Outside France, legal men had serious objections. It seemed to them unjustifiable that a man who acquired a copy of printed music, often for the express purpose of public performance, should not by the act of purchase also acquire the right to use it. Even composers and publishers hesitated to support the claims of their French colleagues, fearing a reduction in sales and performances. In Germany Richard Strauss worked on the authorities, members of parliament and public opinion until, in 1903, a society similar to the French one was founded; most other countries then followed suit. The revised Copyright Acts eventually recognized the exclusive right of the composer to authorize all public performances of his works, dramatic and non-dramatic. Thereafter the former were called 'grand' rights, the latter 'small'—though there was nothing small about the financial benefits.

In the comparatively virgin soil of music there were thus discovered new mines of phenomenal yield, whose riches cannot be exhausted as long as music is publicly performed, transmitted by sound broadcasting and television or used in films. So far as fees are concerned it is immaterial how the performance is effected, whether by live musicians, sound-tracks, discs or tapes. Legislation could not have been more generous to composers and their lyric-writers, who are in a much happier position than poets, writers, sculptors, painters or architects. Public recitals of poems or novels are comparatively rare—they are intended to be read individually, and reading a book is the quintessence of privacy. Sculptures and buildings in public places may not be photographed for material gain without the sculptor's or architect's consent, but they are there to be looked at free of charge. Entrance fees may be payable at exhibitions of works of art, but they rarely go to the artist whose works are exhibited. Music, however, is not meant just to be read or looked at. Its very nature requires performance, and this deeper significance of the musical work, which will repeatedly engage our attention, finds expression in legal terms as well as in financial demands.

I could not therefore agree that the general protection of performing rights introduced a purely material element into the theory and practice of the rights of intellectual property. It has often been said that Richard Strauss, by his championship of the new laws, was taking revenge for the misery inflicted on former generations of composers. However, his was an act of extraordinary foresight. In 1898, when he started his campaign in earnest, he could not have known that, in the course of the changes music was to undergo, the traditional revenue of the composer would almost dry up. Without their income from performances and mechanical reproductions composers today would be much poorer than their hungriest predecessors. Sales of sheet music and the consequent royalties are lower than they were a century ago, but the revenue from performances and mechanical reproductions has reached fantastic proportions.

*

Everything which has happened in the field of copyright during the first decades of this century has conspired to entangle the fairest child of the muses in a web of claims and counterclaims. The more complete the protection of music becomes, the more painful the friction between the rights of the artist and the rights of mankind. As long as education and taste were largely the prerogatives of a well-to-do upper class, music and the other arts were counted among the more luxurious furnishings of life. The idea that an artist might rob mankind was inconceivable. Now, under a meticulous system of copyright, and with the coming oɪ mass education, the public—that is to say, the 'users' of the art— feel oppressed by the manifold demands of artists, and of composers in particular. This represents a fundamental change in the respective positions of the two parties and has led to the introduction of exemptions from the otherwise stringent laws which are just as illogical and arbitrary as the period of subsistence of copyright.

In a number of countries cultural, religious, charitable and educational performances do not require the composer's consent. A compulsory or legal licence replaces that normally issued on behalf of the composer, to whom, therefore, no payment is due. The performers, who sometimes—but not always—supply their services free of charge, are publicly praised for their generosity; in extreme cases they are awarded medals and titles. But the generosity of the composer, being enforced by the law, calls for no recognition. The English Copyright Act of 1956 has even introduced a Copyright Tribunal, accessible to anybody who feels wronged by a charge for the use of copyright material, which can not only declare such charge to be excessive but can fix the price at which the author has to allow the use of his work. From such innovations one can gauge the degree of suspicion and uneasiness which has arisen between the artist and his public. There is a public lien on works of art, and especially on music, which will not allow the owner to open or shut the door to his work at will.

Other problems which could not have been foreseen when the idea of intellectual property was first propounded also presented themselves. The sharp light of jurisprudence revealed that the contours of artistic creation were not as clearly defined as the romantic notion of them had suggested. The compilation and codification of the first copyright acts coincided with the Industrial Revolution, and the creative mind was distracted by many new avenues of approach. It could be said that it burst its banks and flooded the lower fields of invention. The first version of the Berne Convention included among the protectable arts the 'applied arts', such as fashions, model dresses and model hats, which are certainly products of 'creation' but of a creation motivated more directly by material gain than by purely artistic considerations and which is therefore 'applied' creation, not intended to provide any lasting intellectual benefit. Although a system of national and international protection of patents and trade-marks, reminiscent of the old privileges, grew up alongside copyright, disputes are frequent and often unresolved: quite recently a rose-grower sued a gardener for the infringement of his copyright because the gardener had illicitly secured a cutting of a 'protected' rose.

The new copyright acts which, after the Second World War, had to cope with new conditions were not drafted with the cool detachment such delicate matters required. They came into being amidst a clamour of demands and protestations from many quarters. Music, which formerly had stood modestly in the background, became the main target. The new technical advances with all their consequences introduced whole new classes of participants in the creative process, all of whom claimed a legal share in both protection and profit: the manufacturers of gramophone records, the producers of films and television programmes, even the cameramen and, last but not least, the army of professional performers. The creative contributions of all these new shareholders in the great enterprise of copyright are naturally limited, conditional upon the original works which they serve, but their material interests are overwhelming. How the composer fares largely depends on them. So the record-manufacturer is given a copyright in recordings reproducing the works of someone else; the film producer has a copyright in a film using the intellectual property of someone else; television acquires a copyright in programmes which themselves consist of someone else's copyrights; the cameraman receives a copyright in the photography of someone else's ideas; and, finally, the performers enjoy a copyright in the performance of someone else's work. The legislators of the 1950s would have been better advised to distinguish between the creators of original works and all those who render important but ancillary services, rather than to graft more and more 'secondary copyrights' on to the basic intellectual property.

While it could be argued that gramophone records, films and television programmes still complied with one fundamental requirement of copyright by being exclusive while they lasted, the same argument does not apply to performers and their performances. A work such as Benjamin Britten's 'Variations on a Theme of Purcell' has several hundred performances every year, some of them simultaneous, in different places, and all those conductors and orchestras acquire the same right in their particular rendering of the work. It may have been with this anomaly in mind that performers' rights were officially termed *droits voisins*, 'neighbouring rights'. We shall have to consider these in greater detail, because they open up a view of present-day musical life which the legislators themselves may not fully have envisaged.

Artists, and composers in particular, find themselves surrounded by a whole crowd of co-artists or 'neighbours' threatening to engulf them by their numbers and material power. If it was once preferred, in all matters concerning intellectual property, to camouflage material interests by disguising them as ideals, such modesty—or hypocrisy—has been abandoned in this latest development. It is the material interests, which would not have been secure enough under the less rigorous protection of industrial rights, that have forced themselves upon copyright itself. In a most remarkable manner the original, idealistic conception of intellectual property is thus rapidly silting up. Nothing has brought mind and money closer together than this tendency of modern legislation to procure a share in the financial proceeds for every executive in the industry which has developed around music. As essentially industrial rights and copyrights are merged into a single legal entity, protection of the artistic creation itself has almost become a secondary purpose.

All this has tended to make copyright extremely complicated—so complicated, indeed, that neither the artist nor the tens of thousands of people who daily come into contact and conflict with it are able to understand all its implications. The new rights of self-appointed co-authors and the *droits voisins* of the performers should not, in the intention of the legislators, impinge on the basic copyright of the author proper; but this is just what must inevitably happen. If a public concert is to be broadcast permission is required from both the composer and the performers, and if one of them withholds it his—involuntary—partner must suffer. Innumerable 'users', such as publicans and café- and restaurant-proprietors who entertain their clients by playing records or tapes, are often unaware that, unless they have first obtained a whole series of licences, they are committing a punishable offence: a licence from the composer to play his work in a public place; one from the same composer to play it by means of a mechanical reproduction; one from the manufacturer of the mechanical reproduction; and finally one from the performers whose rendering is mechanically reproduced. This is clearly too much for what must appear to be one single use. No wonder that the multitude of small users find themselves perpetually on the brink of prosecution and that actual offences, in spite of a fairly widespread system of control and supervision, occur daily.

When one has to deal with constant inquiries, demands and complaints, as the publisher has, one becomes aware of the atmosphere of dissatisfaction which surrounds copyright today. There can be little doubt that protection of the composer has passed its peak. The future development of musical copyright will have to revoke some of the rights granted by an over-zealous legislation under the impact of technical change. In the meantime, music will have to tread the hard road of money and commerce.

3. ORGANIZATION

It takes many brains and many hands to carry music to the masses. Music must be composed, or adapted; someone has to choose the works which are to be performed, recorded on disc and tape or synchronized with films. Somebody has to engage the performers, for the big symphony orchestras and opera-houses, from the famous stars down to the cabaret and night-club singers. Somebody has to build transmitters and turntables, pay fees and salaries, print and sell tickets, put advertisements in papers and paste posters on hoardings. Somebody even has to print music, collect royalties, performing and mechanical fees and account for them—there is no end to what has to be done if music is to be available like drinking-water in a large city, and its material usefulness ensured.

The laws plot only the boundaries of the territory upon which the great spectacle of present-day musical life is to unfold. It is for the interested parties themselves to establish the necessary organization. In this thoroughly organized world two groups are almost automatically forming which set the industry in motion and keep it going: the creators or producers on the one hand and the group of users or consumers on the other. The public, standing between them, plays no part in the organization: but it buys or rejects the goods offered, and in its hands the ultimate success or failure of the other two lies.

It cannot be said that the two groups of 'producers' and 'consumers' are living together in harmony. They probably never do in any field, but when the 'product' is an art their differences can be sharp and distasteful. Although music has become the subject of regular trade certain factors of general commercial practice are still inapplicable to it. First and foremost, it has no accepted price, as have other goods in daily demand. Differences in quality are quite conspicuous, but differences in price are difficult to assess. In the practical world of commerce a cheaper, inferior product has a legitimate place—margarine instead of butter, the bicycle instead of the motor car. True, this applies also to performers and places of performance. But who would buy or perform a piece of music which is worse than another simply because it is cheaper? Every work, rightly or wrongly, has to aim at being thought excellent of its kind—whether it is serious or popular or simply background music. This unavoidable state of affairs invalidates the normal usages of commerce. The services rendered to music, the fees payable for the performance, have no accepted material level. The users demand as much as they dare and the public resists as much as it can, and this creates the shifting ground upon which our musical life rests.

The composers, from whom all the power and influence should derive, are only loosely organized. In almost every country there are composers' guilds or associations but they recruit their members mainly from the ranks of the disappointed. More ruthlessly than any other vocation, art separates the qualified from the unqualified. If the captain of industry has some difficulty in sympathizing with the troubles of the one-man firm, genius has nothing in common with mediocrity. Neither Igor Stravinsky nor Richard Rodgers can fit into a professional organization, for their ambitions are fulfilled and the complaints of the smaller fry are not their complaints. Thus the absence of all the most prominent figures robs composers' associations of any real influence.

However, authors and composers—and publishers—do have organizations for the protection of their material interests, and these have achieved a high degree of efficiency. Starting modestly enough as a Société Dramatique or an Agence Centrale they have become great powers. There is now a society of this kind in every civilized country, its presence and purpose almost unknown to the millions of music consumers. These societies are not merely social or debating clubs dealing with the art of music: they are the organizations which had to be created if the rights conferred upon composers and their *paroliers* or song-writers were to be operated and enforced—the right to authorize public performances, broadcasts and mechanical reproductions and, more important still, to establish scales of payments for all such authorizations, to collect them and to distribute them.

This is no small undertaking—too big, at any rate, for the individual composer. Capable organizers were needed to distil the '*esprit des affaires*' from the '*amour des lettres*'. Forced by the boom in all things musical like plants in a hothouse, these societies have united into a world-wide organization which disciplines the whole of musical life. The PRS (Performing Right Society) in Britain, the ASCAP (American Society of Composers, Authors and Publishers) in the USA, the SACEM (Société des auteurs, compositeurs et éditeurs de musique) in France, and so on, are the bodies which control public performances. Other, similar organizations control mechanical reproduction, and every country has its societies and every society its acrostic. Whoever performs or reproduces music—broadcasting organizations, orchestras, dance-bands, the solitary pianist in a bar—has to submit his programme to his national society, obtain a licence and pay for it. A vast network of 'supervisors', or snoopers, sees to it that only the smallest fish escape. The national societies are united in an international confederation, and treaties of affiliation provide a world-wide exchange of programmes, controls and money, so that, for example, the British composer receives his performing and mechanical rights from the Argentine, the American composer his from Italy.

Any composer or song-writer with a number of published works to his credit is admitted to the membership of his national society; he assigns his performing and mechanical rights to it and the society then exercises them as his representative. Enormous card-indexes have been set up, listing hundreds of thousands of titles and thousands of names, and these are exchanged between all the societies. This requires a large personnel, extensive premises, directors and managers and a great deal of money, which is readily available. Regular mass consumers, such as the broadcasting and television organizations, pay yearly sums, running into millions. Record-manufacturers have to pay a percentage of the selling-price of every disc as a royalty; concert-promoters pay for every protected work according to the size of the hall. Those who do not pay are automatically delivered into the hands of justice. In this way these societies have become the heavily armed and highly mobile international police of musical life. An enormous stream of money flows through their tills, and even though administration costs are high a sizeable sum remains for composers and publishers.

In all this the art itself is but a secondary issue. For the societies music exists only as a record of names, titles and duration of performance. It is true that most performing-right—as opposed to 'mechanical'—societies make certain concessions to serious music* by granting a higher reimbursement to the playing-time of, say, a symphony than to the playing-time of a popular song, and some societies have even recognized a secondary category of serious music, namely 'distinguished entertainment' music, which is cheaper than serious music proper but more expensive than popular music, a distinction which introduces an element of 'expensive'

----

* It will be noticed here and throughout this book that I do not adopt the deplorable habit of calling all serious music "classical" as distinct from "popular".

and 'cheap'. However, this is of no concern to the promoters, being a matter of internal accounting between the societies and their members. As the adaptor or arranger of unprotected music, whose contribution is protected, has a claim to performing and mechanical fees for his protected version smaller than those of a genuine composer the societies have set up committees of musicians whose task it is to assign the works declared by members to their respective categories. (Many years ago I had an ill-tempered argument with one such committee which refused to accord the status of 'original compositions' to the folk-song arrangements of Béla Bartók.)

However, duration of performance remains the yardstick, and here the system does not do justice to the composer's labours. A symphonic work for large orchestra has the same 'point value' as a solo sonata for flute of similar duration, whereas, though the original conception of those two works may take the same time, the physical writing of a full score of, say, a hundred pages is a much more slow and laborious task. But the administration of a world repertoire is too complicated to allow for further itemization. Eschewing preference for the good and aversion to the bad, the societies register success but not its reasons. Despite this aloofness they present themselves as guardians of the art. Composers must live if they are to compose, and no other institution in our musical life supplies them with the means as bountifully and regularly as the societies.

Perhaps the greatest blessing of the whole system is that all patronage is banned. The composers receive no more than is due to them, but payment of what *is* due—and it is a good deal—can be enforced without their incurring the displeasure of a patron, as happened to Beethoven. However, nothing remains for the beginner. Some societies have a pension fund for their old members but the encouragement of the young, of the new and unproven, has no place in their statutes. It is left to the care of others—the music-publishers.

I am always trying to find the beating heart of the living music beneath the hard armour of organizational endeavours and legal and financial operations. There is something more than a shrewd business sense in this protection of the performance and mechanical reproduction of a musical work. A breath of the '*amour des lettres*', however faint, clings to all these carefully guarded material interests. Music will be actively re-created. It cannot become completely detached from its creator, like a poem or a picture; his shadow follows it as the ghost of Hamlet's father dogs the wavering son. Even without the interference of the law the purchaser of sheet music acquires only the shell of a hypothetical content. He normally overlooks the threats and warnings in small print: *Performing rights reserved* or even, *All rights reserved.* These are no product of commercial acumen but a somewhat bizarre expression of the greater mystery that unites the creator with his work.

Among the consumers broadcasting and television take first place. Even those who may never have thought about it must have some vague idea of the size of an organization which every day, from early morning till late at night, educates, informs and—especially with music—entertains hundreds of millions of listeners and viewers. This is, in fact, a heavy industry of the immaterial, having no other purpose but the hope of a better, happier, more educated society. In many countries broadcasting is nationalized, because the improvement of men's minds is an obligation upon governments rather than upon individuals. The farther west one travels, the more the grip of the state loosens, both on broadcasting and on the individual. In France the Organisation de Radiodiffusion et Télévision française (ORTF) is still a department of the Ministry of Communications, but the moment we cross the Channel we find broadcasting and television independent and the state exercising only a peripheral control. Farther west again, in the Western Hemisphere, broadcasting is left to private enterprise. In North, Central and South America there are hundreds of private broadcasting organizations, and anybody who understands the business can start and operate a transmitter or a network. Some clever people have even discovered that the freedom of the high seas has preserved some of the romance of the old days of piracy and have established commercial stations on old ships and forts outside territorial waters and official control.

One cannot repress a slight shudder when one reads the statistics of sound and television broadcasting. Reliable figures are available only for Europe—excluding Russia and a few other communist countries. The number of listeners and viewers in North and South America cannot be ascertained, as no licence-fees are payable. We must therefore confine ourselves to the figures as published by the European Broadcasting Union, for all Europe with the exceptions mentioned above.

The number of licences for sound broadcasting rose from 31,000,000 in 1950 to 60,000,000 in 1955, to 71,000,000 in 1960 and to 84,000,000 in 1965, while television licences increased during the same period from 285,000 to 4,500,000, to 18,500,000 and finally to 44,000,000. Experts deny that saturation point has been reached; in a world of insatiable need for noise that may never happen. But the figures give a good idea of the gigantic scope of the new means of communication. European broadcasting and television organizations employ some 100,000 people, from directors general down to doorkeepers. They engage thousands of performers of every type and standard every year; and music is the commonest of all the forms of entertainment they project into the ether, to be caught by those millions of receivers.

In Europe all this began rather pompously, with lofty cultural ambitions. Until quite recently an inherent respect prevented the desecration of art and culture at the profane hands of commerce. Sound and television broadcasting, it was felt, should be financed out of licence-fees collected by the agencies of the state, and these fees are not a selling-price but a tax. A comparatively small amount pays for an enormous volume of information and entertainment. But in the United States broadcasting was designed for profit from the very beginning. Education, information and pleasure are free, and this is a laudable ideal. Yet the broadcasting organizations, deriving their revenue from advertisements, are commercial, which hardly seems compatible with such idealism. The revenue is quite fabulous; so is the value of the advertisements, which can recommend all types of goods much more persuasively than printed notices in newspapers.

This American example, like others, was bound in the end to undermine stubborn European morale. For many years commercialism prowled round European broadcasting and television like a hungry wolf round the sheepfold. Only a few small countries, such as Luxembourg or Andorra, let it in, leaving the responsibility for art and culture to their more affluent neighbours. Eventually the temptation became too great for the big countries and for their state-owned or state-controlled organizations, and the wolf was ceremoniously received at the front door.

It may be some time yet before Europeans rid themselves altogether of a nagging feeling of impropriety. The method of 'sponsored programmes', so well established in the Americas, is not admitted in Europe: in the United States General Motors or Camel cigarettes can engage the New York Philharmonic, book time on sound radio or television and enliven a one-hour concert of sterling music under a sterling conductor of their own choice with their own advertisements. In Europe the advertiser is firmly excluded from any interference with the programme, and art and commerce are carefully separated. This, quite bluntly, is sheer hypocrisy. The advertiser pays a very high price for his spot, and will do so only if he can be assured that the programmes preceding and following it are so popular that millions of listeners will endure his advertisement. Hypocrisy has always been an excellent sedative for a troubled conscience.

So in Europe, too, commercial broadcasting and commercial television established themselves—causing, incidentally, a bloody massacre in the world of illustrated journals and magazines. As was to be expected, commercialism avoids art as best it can. In the undignified disguise of the 'jingle', music becomes the salesman of a multitude of goods, and clever composers—who could perhaps produce something better but certainly nothing more remunerative —are making considerable fortunes by providing the right noise for the right article.

Cosmopolitanism was not, at first, one of the visible preoccupations of broadcasting, but since the Second World War it has become its proudest achievement. Performances from the Salzburg Festival can be heard throughout the world, either by direct transmission or on tape-recordings; programmes are being exchanged; the communications satellite has even overcome the curvature of our planet. This has so increased organizational and legal problems that not only do broadcasters run their own legal departments but the European (with some non-European) organizations have formed the European Broadcasting Union to take care of such common technical problems as how they should avoid each other in the ether, and to steer them through the treacherous waters of international copyright.

The other great power in our musical life is the record industry— as it is honest enough to call itself. It has become a heavy industry. It is estimated that sales, excluding Russia and Japan, amount to 500,000,000 records annually, which is no mean achievement considering that more than one-third of the world's population has not yet arrived at the stage of buying records. But the record-manufacturers are no music-promoters in the ordinary sense. Recording sessions take place behind closed doors, and what is eventually sold to the public is often the result of much trial and error. This accounts in no small measure for its undoubted technical excellence. Also, manufacturers secure the exclusive services of prominent performers and popular stars, and often first-recording rights of important composers; all this, of course, against payment of substantial fees and with an eye more on their competitors than on the art itself. Sound broadcasting and television have clear—if rarely fulfilled—cultural obligations; record-manufacturers have none. Broadcasting is quite frequently criticized on artistic grounds by the Press or by Parliament because of its programme policy, and the public follows such activities with suspicion. But record-manufacturers, who are likewise mass distributors of cultural goods, are immune to any criticism. One regularly reads about their new issues and the technical quality of their products, but their artistic policy is not a subject of public discussion. The words 'manufacturers' and 'industry' distinguish them from all other servants or patrons of the art. The manufacture of records is 'business', pure and unashamed, and not a particularly risky business at that. In a few countries, such as the United States and Great Britain, this has even aroused the sympathies of the legislators, and a legal and compulsory licence limits the sacred prerogatives of composers by declaring that a work, once recorded, may further be recorded by any other manufacturer without the composer's prior consent, though not without payment of the usual or statutory royalties.

All this stirs up considerable resentment among composers, publishers and performers, but the power of the manufacturer and the possibilities he offers are so great that few would be brave enough to invite his wrath. One day, perhaps, some independent spirit may measure the enormous influence of the mass distribution of records on the whole existence of music and may discover that, overwhelmed as it is by public taste, it tends to vitiate the efforts of many serious promoters and distributors. The young composer, the unfulfilled promise, can expect nothing from the gramophone industry. It is for others to take risks and the industry to pick the plums; for others to encourage budding talent and the industry to exploit success. But the gramophone record has fantastically increased the commercial potential of music, and for this achievement alone has secured a place of honour in the annals of the art. Being international, and in almost constant conflict with the artists' and performers' rights, the industry has established an international federation for the world-wide protection of its interests.

This, then, is the formidable array of forces which has ringed Apollo's grove with a series of fortified camps. Great battles are fought behind the scenes between producers (the artists' societies) and consumers (broadcasters, record-manufacturers and concert-promoters), with ever-rising costs of living on the one hand and ever-increasing demands on the other to ensure that there should be no lasting peace.

Mention must also be made here of the army of performers, though more will have to be said about them in their proper place. They include all those who perform music professionally: star conductors, singers, instrumentalists, down to the humblest musicians in the humblest dance-band.

Although the individual star performer has a fairly long and distinguished pedigree, the respectable orchestra musician is a product of more recent times. While music remained an aristocratic pastime the ordinary musician was a proletarian, badly educated and badly paid. There was nothing exceptional about the Salzburg Court Orchestra as described by Mozart in 1778: 'One of the main reasons why I hate Salzburg is the rude, wretched and disorderly behaviour of the court musicians. No honest, well-behaved man can live with them. Instead of taking their part one has to be ashamed of them.' Twenty years later Carl Maria von Weber confirmed Mozart's verdict: 'There is no lack of personalities, but they all are disorderly drunkards.' Conditions were to change profoundly before the rank and file of professional musicians could rise to the commanding position they now hold in the musical hierarchy. Growing professionalism and, in its train, growing perfection have given them a sense of purpose and pride such as they never knew before. Without them our whole musical life would come to a standstill.

In the face of technological progress there grew up in some quarters the fear that the live musician might eventually become dispensable, but the very opposite has happened: there are more professional musicians than ever before, they are more urgently needed and they are more proficient. Their strength had only to be co-ordinated to make itself felt. In most countries performers are organized in trade unions, demanding fixed minimum wages and maximum working-hours; they strike to enforce their demands and generally like to emulate other workers in other industries. This attitude has a peculiar flavour when applied to an art, which, apart from talent, requires enthusiasm. Enthusiasm should be above timetables and collective bargaining. But this is just one more case of the '*amour des lettres*' and the '*esprit des affaires*' entering into an uneasy partnership. A performance is no longer aimed at a comparatively small audience: its preservability and portability make it available to millions, a development which, theoretically at least, deprives the performer of many of his opportunities.

Confronted by the powerful consumer organizations, he would be crushed if he did not have the strength to resist. The performer's new status, his powers and rights, have played an important part in the development of musical life over the last fifty years, and we shall meet him again when we come to consider the fundamental change that has occurred in the art itself.

4. THE MUSIC PUBLISHER: I

Among all those who live for and off music, the music-publisher plays the most ambiguous part. He stands at the crossroads of art and commerce, where enthusiasm for the art and business sense meet or miss each other; between artistic obsession and commercial acumen, promoting the art and translating it into good money. Composers expect from him both fame and fortune.

The musical profession knows him as the man whose curious way of life it is to give with one hand and take with the other; but the millions of music-lovers hardly hear about him, although he supposedly renders them considerable services behind the scenes. Occasionally, though less frequently than formerly, they read his name on printed copies. There are even some publishers of operas and ballets who insist that their names be printed on the programmes, alongside those of the purveyors of shoes and wigs. This may flatter their vanity, but attracts no attention.

The publisher is a trader, but his trade is as specialized as his merchandise, which is not really his in the same way that a house or a pair of trousers would be. He acquires it from its first owner with many liens and on many conditions, and he acquires it in order not to sell but to exploit it. 'Exploitation' may seem an incongruous word in connection with works of the spirit, but it describes the publisher's function quite correctly, for in this new world the methods of distributing music and making it pay have greatly changed. It is true that the publisher of educational and classical music, in its proper sense, is no different from the book publisher. Both are simply selling their publications. But the publisher of contemporary or, more generally, protected music not only has to sell it—so far as that is still possible—but must deal with all the new aspects of music which were unknown fifty years ago and are of paramount moral and material importance for the composer today. This exploitation of all the old and new opportunities gives the music-publisher a much greater responsibility for, and greater influence over, the destinies of the musical art generally than the book- or art-publisher exerts on his own field. This has hardly added to the music-publisher's reputation, but it has made his position more delicate. He is—like Abraham Mendelssohn between his famous father Moses and his even more famous son Felix—a parenthesis between the author and the public.

One might assume that the profession of a music-publisher is an eminently musical one. When music-publishing on a grand scale began, although there were some engravers among the founding fathers, such as Breitkopf or Artaria, the majority were in fact musicians, if of minor rank. Neither Anton Diabelli nor Giovanni Ricordi nor Nicolaus Simrock were composers of distinction—Muzio Clementi was probably the only notable exception—and these men were shrewd enough to recognize that they could achieve more with the genius of others than with their own modest talents. However, as businesses passed on to sons and grandsons and distant relatives, or changed hands altogether, while at the same time music became a permanent and reliable source of income with a future of growing promise, commercial problems tended to overshadow the purely musical aspects, and today one finds only a few musicians among publishers of serious music.

I have interviewed many young people who wanted to go into publishing because they were 'mad on music'. But the young man who is only mad on music sits reading proofs in a back room for the rest of his life. The musician who wants to be a publisher needs great powers of self-denial, and perhaps even a dose of frivolity to teach him that not everything he likes is necessarily good, that there is a type of music which one can publish only if one does not know it, that he must not be guided by the professional critic but that the public represents a supreme court against whose verdict there is no appeal—and other similar maxims which override the publisher's own personal leanings and convictions. His time is taken up by never-ending routine work and by legal, commercial and technical problems, and only now and then, for all-too-short periods, can he retire from the tumult of business to the quieter realm of the art he serves. And if he is just a lawyer or businessman he can well do without such respite.

On the other hand, musicians are usually in the forefront of 'popular' publishing. Managers of publishing enterprises concerned with pop-songs are often hard-boiled practitioners, former band-leaders or pop-singers or at least song-writers, people who cultivate the closest contact with the public and its fickle tastes, to which they have to conform instantly and unconditionally. Their attitude is much appreciated by the composers of popular music and their lyricists, eager to know what the public wants. But a similar attitude would quickly bring the serious publisher into disrepute. His task is to make the public like what his composers produce, to defy its preferences, to educate or even force it into accepting what at first may seem unacceptable—even to him.

There is small comfort in the fact that the expert popular publishers too, with all their eagerness to please, make mistake after mistake.

How, and why, does one become a serious music publisher without inheriting a publishing business? There can be no specific gift, no sense of vocation, which would leave no other choice. One does not become a music-publisher out of the sense of duty that might call one to be a doctor, a mathematician or a minister of the church. Moreover, the young man or woman who decides to go into music-publishing seldom has a clear idea of the career it offers. It is a rather careless decision to make.

As a warning, or encouragement, I can only tell how I became a music-publisher myself.

My parents must have considered music an important thing in life, for I began having piano lessons before I started school. (I can still feel some of the fascination of that first encounter with music, and in quiet moments the notes can look at me as they did then: like messengers of an impenetrable mystery. It is a fleeting but delightful feeling not to have been completely overwhelmed by so many years of involvement.) I must have made quick progress and spent more time at the piano than my father liked. After my teacher, a pedant with a moustache, pince-nez and smoothly parted hair, had presented me in private circles, he arrived one day, put Mozart's piano concerto in E flat, K. 271, on the piano and said peremptorily that I would play the work with orchestra in public. I then had five years of hard practising behind me, was ten years old and sure of myself as I was never to be again.

My father, when told, said nothing; my mother was not quite certain what to make of it. The concert took place in the small hall of the Rudolfinum in Prague; the success was as great as expected and the papers next morning were most flattering. But my father took me aside and spoke wisely and sternly to me: he was very happy with my dexterity on the piano, he knew that I imagined the life of a pianist to be wonderful and he knew that in this I was sadly mistaken. He disclosed to me that my music-teacher had once hoped to become a great pianist himself, which impressed me very much. As an artist, he said, one had to be among the very best, a genius, in order to be really happy. Woe unto those who had no more than a pleasing talent! They would blame the whole world for not having the taste to recognize them, and would lead an embittered existence. In every other walk of life one could be satisfied with a nice income and good friends—one would not become a doctor, a lawyer or a merchant with the sole intention of being the best in the world. But without such ambition one could not even begin to think of becoming a pianist or musician, and such ambition was itself dangerous, for it held within it the seeds of lifelong disappointment. After all, the pursuit of music should not be a profession, it should be a sanctuary, a shelter in life. But a livelihood? Never! I should continue with my piano lessons, but I should also study, play tennis in summer and skate in winter. Father would leave the choice of a profession entirely to me, provided only that I chose a regular job because regularity was the most important thing in life. If I did not understand it then, I would do so later on and be grateful to him.

This was an unexpected sequel to the great event. But I was not as disappointed as one might think. My parents disliked everything ostentatious and never encouraged us children to attract attention. Modesty, if not actual subordination, was the guiding principle of our upbringing, and it must have suited my own constitution. Like all middle-class children at the end of last century I was born for a quiet life in secure circumstances. Even today I still belong to that small and slightly comic band who never drop a piece of paper where they should not; who with perfect sincerity declare to customs officers at frontiers and airports everything they carry, thereby making those officials all the more suspicious; who never tire of establishing a cordial understanding with all those appointed to run their lives, from the park-attendant to the tax-collector. At the root of such an upbringing and education was certainly a belief in the higher wisdom of Governments, and a longing for normality.

As soon as this normality was disturbed, however—and in my time it was more violently disturbed than it had been since the collapse of the Roman Empire and the Great Migration—that hankering after reason, tranquillity and order dangerously reduced one's chances of survival. It must have been the much-maligned hand of providence which has guided me without permanent harm, and even with some inner gain, through the adversities of two world wars and emigration. I could hardly reproach my parents and teachers for having sent me into this world without any wholesome suspicion. A Bantu boy—at least at that time—had still to be taught what to do in order not to be eaten by a lion. After all, wild beasts are fanatics for order and regularity, but who can fathom human nature?

So I believed my father when he told me that integral calculus and the history of the War of the Spanish Succession were even more important for my future happiness than music. I was quite content not to have my interests confined to a single subject, and this was particularly important in the last years before and the first few years after the First World War, when so much new and astounding knowledge was demanding attention. I well remember those first terms at Prague University, still housed in its old building of AD 1346, with its dark, vaulted corridors and lecture-rooms where Philip Frank, Albert Einstein's successor in the chair of theoretical physics, said blasphemous things about the universe. I remember too the mixture of fear and amazement with which we greeted the traces of broken atoms in Wilson's cloud chamber, and how hesitatingly we allowed ourselves to be persuaded that the difference between a car and a carrot was 'structural' and not material.

For a time music, unable to compete with all these revolutionary and revolting things, withdrew to the very edge of my world, but I was in no real doubt that I wanted to spend my life in her company. Having strayed through many fields, physics and mathematics, philosophy and history, the piano master-class at Prague Conservatoire, I obtained my law degree and entered music-publishing, which seemed a sensible compromise between realistic necessity and idealistic fancy. I expected nothing more than to render some useful service to the goddess to our mutual benefit. To this end I also spent some eighteen months in a special school for the graphic arts, in printing offices and paper-mills, anticipating that, even for music-publishing, a general attitude would not be enough and that some specialized knowledge of a technical nature must be useful, if not actually necessary. The rest has followed as if it could never have been otherwise, and I have seen music in all its aspects: as an art and as a commodity; as a system of staff lines, heads and tails, dots and slurs hammered into the zinc plate by the engraver and printed by the offset machine with monumental indifference. But music, in spite of it all, has remained a true friend, graciously forgiving me my pianistic shortcomings.

How does the publisher find a composer, or the composer a publisher? This is a vital question for both.

A publisher rarely has the good fortune of a Cimabue who, on his travels, met the boy Giotto scratching a masterpiece on a rock. Every post heaps mountains of unsolicited manuscripts on his desk, and these—contrary to widespread suspicion—are examined, because there is always a possibility of an undiscovered talent. The music-publisher is better placed in this respect than the book-publisher, who has to deal with typed offerings of no immediately recognizable individuality. Music, conveniently, must be written by hand, and to do this well requires years of practice. Nothing gives away the immature dilettante more mercilessly than an inexperienced hand, and so a quick glance is often enough for a manuscript to be returned with the stereotyped friendly phrase in which the unhappy recipient reads only the word 'no'. In more than forty years I remember only one case when I found a good piece in this way and published it. It was quite successful, but the composer never wrote another. Once, too, I heard a piece on the radio which attracted my attention. The name of the composer was not announced. My inquiries led to a reprimand for the conductor, who had smuggled the work into his programme without first submitting it to the controlling panel; but the composer was found and has made quite a respectable career.

However, these are exceptions. Normally a relationship begins more prosaically. In this well-organized world nobody can hope to be discovered in anonymous seclusion: the young composer must go to school, his teachers must observe the first signs of talent and recommend their pupil. It then remains the publisher's task to separate winged genius from crawling mediocrity. Here, perhaps, is the one gift the publisher needs; the flair which is unaffected by experience.

It cannot have been easy at any time, because the great mass of published music has always been mediocre. Even in the nineteenth century, when every work seemed to be stamped with unmistakable signs either of excellence or of imperfection, only the average could really have been beyond doubt, conforming as it did to all the accepted precepts. True greatness, like true incompetence, is no respecter of rules. In times of greater artistic security composers could be divided into two types: the traditionalist and the original genius. Bach, Haydn, Mozart and Brahms fall easily into the first group; Beethoven, Chopin, Wagner and Debussy into the second. The original genius writes music such as nobody before him has written; the traditional genius writes essentially the same music as his contemporaries but does it better. It is a question of temperament rather than of artistic merit.

The publisher may not always recognize the traditional genius as a genius, but he will always find his work remarkable. If, however, he is confronted with an original genius, with music thoroughly new and unproven, he cannot be blamed if he is beset by doubts. Imagine seeing for the first time the first of Chopin's Preludes, Op. 28, in manuscript, a graphic image such as had never been put on paper before, and having to decide whether publication would be a sound investment. (One should not take umbrage at that word. It is the publisher's profession to invest money in art so that the art, the artist and the publisher himself may all three benefit. Only then does the publisher completely fulfil his mission. The possible sales potential remains a necessary, though not always acknowledged, consideration because it produces both fame and fortune.) So Chopin's first publisher—a little swindler, by the way—had his qualms, but times were secure, and the passion of the public for new music still burned fiercely.

Even so, the young Wagner could not find a publisher. Today it sounds rather comical that Franz Schott, when offered *Rienzi* six months after its successful première, could reply that he was too busy with Herr Lindpaintner's new opera *The Sicilian Vespers* to find time for Wagner. *Rienzi* may not be particularly alive today, but it is certainly not as dead as Lindpaintner's whole *œuvre*. But at that point, in 1843, Lindpaintner was *arrivé* and Wagner a beginner. Wagner did not find Schott's refusal improper, although, a few months later, he did take exception when Breitkopf and Härtel declined *The Flying Dutchman* and published Halévy's *Charles VI* instead. Wagner had no choice but to finance the publication of his first operas—*Rienzi*, *The Flying Dutchman* and *Tannhäuser*—himself, and it took him thirty years to settle the resulting difficulties.

The young Richard Strauss fared little better. Had he started by writing such voluminous and costly operas as Wagner, he too would have had to publish them at his own expense. As it was he found a small publisher who bought—for a pittance—his early songs and his best symphonic poems. Gustav Mahler, with his gigantic symphonies, was not so lucky and had to pay all the costs of having them published under the imprint of a Viennese printing firm. Among the avant-garde at the turn of the century only Debussy seems to have had no difficulty in finding a proper publisher.

All this figures in the publisher's register of sins of omission. It must not be forgotten, however, that the old and powerful publishing houses followed the changes in music with greater anxiety than Press and public. If music strayed from the well-trodden path to success to throw itself into doubtful experiments they had much to lose. Publishers north of the Alps in particular must have been irritated by events in Italy, where composers continued with irrepressible vigour to write their operas to the old recipes and carry home the laurels from an enraptured musical and unmusical world. Little had altered since the days of Rossini. While the ageing Verdi produced his amazing *Otello* and still more amazing *Falstaff*, the young Puccini, Mascagni and Leoncavallo, and lesser figures such as Ponchielli, Giordano and Cilea, were waiting on the doorstep of the hall of fame. The massive chain of mountains seemed to be having on music the effect it has always had on the weather: the stormy, unsettled conditions which beset composers and publishers in the north were unknown in the south.

Historians often call the nineteenth century the 'century of German music'. It is certainly true that German symphonic, chamber and instrumental music far outshone the comparable achievements of other nations. But in the domain of opera, which occupied a very large section of musical life, if not the largest, Italian was still the common language. Mozart's operas took a long time to become internationally accepted. Even such standard German works as Beethoven's *Fidelio* or Weber's *Freischütz* still remain comparatively provincial successes, within the German *Kulturkreis*. Wagner, in the second half of the century, heralded a general change of national emphasis in music; but in the crisis of the 1890s Italian opera stood firm, and the publishers on the banks of the Po did not share the worries and consequent frequent mistakes of their northern colleagues.

The latter's fears soon proved to be well founded. The years before the First World War, disturbed not only by Debussy and Richard Struass but also by Stravinsky and Schoenberg, were only the beginning—though these composers made Wagner sound traditional. After the war atonality seemed to outpace Debussy and Strauss. By the time I entered music-publishing in 1922 it had become almost impossible to discover unmistakable signs of merit or futility in music. The publisher could only choose between resisting the aggressive beliefs of 'new' composers and their friends and being carried away by their arguments. Defying all conventional ideas about music, this new generation demanded not only the professional services of the publisher but also his artistic conviction. Wagner had previously started what seemed to be a new relationship between composer and publisher when he wrote that he could deal only with a publisher who had faith in his mature works. No word has been handed down from Beethoven to suggest that he expected more from his publisher than a fee. Now that music had embarked upon the rejection of its past achievements and the quest for a new promised land it became an article of faith; the publisher became a crusader.

Persistent success often creates treacherous ideals. Music-publishing owed its standing and prosperity to the music of the nineteenth century. The new atonality, and the dodecaphony which followed it, were so much at loggerheads with everything that had made music great, successful and remunerative that they could scarcely fail to appear as sinful iconoclasm. Publishers could muster neither the faith nor the money to embark on adventures whose success was, to say the least, very doubtful. This new music was not for them.

So it was perhaps to be expected that, instead of one of the great and long-established publishers, it should be an outsider who threw in his lot with the New Music. Universal Edition, of Vienna, and its director Emil Hertzka owed nothing to the past but a 'classical edition', thought to be impervious to changes, the early works of Richard Strauss and some minor works of Max Reger.

Hertzka rose from obscurity to become the figurehead of everything new in music. The last shot of the Great War had hardly been fired when he clashed head-on with public opinion by assembling all new music of no fixed abode under the roof of his publishing business—first and foremost the 'star' trio of Arnold Schoenberg, Alban Berg and Anton Webern, but also many others who did not belong to that 'school', such as Béla Bartók, Zoltán Kodály, Alfredo Casella, Ernst Křenek, Kurt Weill, Gianfrancesco Malipiero, Darius Milhaud and a host of lesser names who are now forgotten.

Emil Hertzka was no doctrinaire; nor was he fastidious. He also published operas by Franz Schreker and Eugen d'Albert without blushing, and in the midst of all the noise created by 'new music' the successes of Křenek's *Jonny spielt auf*, Jaromir Weinberger's *Schwanda* and, particularly, Weill–Brecht's *Dreigroschenoper* were as welcome to him as the riots and fisticuffs which surrounded *Pierrot lunaire* and *Wozzeck*. There was no clear intention, no consistent, exclusive conviction in his policy. Anyone who had a grudge against 'old' music—or against its representatives—was welcome at Universal Edition. Hertzka almost seemed to specialize in works rejected by other publishers. But he may have had the feeling that a new art was about to arise, and that he could seize an opportunity which older and wealthier publishers were sure to misjudge and therefore miss. This hectic activity brought not only a few operatic successes but also some best-sellers, such as Bartók's 'Allegro barbaro' and Casella's 'Pièces enfantines'. But the bulk of his publications mouldered on the shelves, awaiting their day. This was unusual, for a publisher habitually has an eye on the paying (and buying) opera- and concert-going public.

Emil Hertzka was a strange man, a mixture of commercial astuteness and rash idealism. True enough, Europe was suffering from a degree of inflation which pre-war economists would have thought impossible, and money lost both its value and its appeal. But Hertzka could have spent his worthless money on something more pleasurable than the printing and publishing of music which nobody else printed and nobody wanted to perform or to hear.

His appearance seemed to contradict his actions: he looked as old-fashioned as any *fin-de-siècle* artist, with his long hair, long beard, brown velvet jacket and large black tie—a majestic figure, half Wotan and half Brahms, who contrasted strangely with revolutionary music and its vociferous composers and propagandists. Although I worked for quite a few years next door to him I never discovered whether he could even read music, nor did I ever hear him talk about it with enthusiasm or even sympathy. He was more feared than loved; his thin, sharp voice seemed not to belong to his imposing figure. He was not a kindly or genial man but displayed a biting and often cynical sarcasm (which, incidentally, was apparently his most effective weapon in dealing with Arnold Schoenberg). It was said that Hertzka, for all his costly and unremunerative patronage of new ideals, never lost sight of his own personal interests, and we, his assistants, used to sing an uncomplimentary little song about it to a tune from Tchaikovsky's 'Pathétique'. And still he did what no other music-publisher at that time dared to do, and considerable sums of money were spent not only on engraving, printing, paper, binding and publicity but also on supporting financially the struggling prophets of the new art. All this was done without charm, grace or warmheartedness, without any evident generosity—and yet it was still a unique undertaking. Finally, in the great economic crisis of the late twenties and early thirties, trouble came to Emil Hertzka and his publishing house and a timely death spared him much humiliation. The orator at his

funeral declared that no one would ever be able to speak of the new
music without mentioning Hertzka's name.

Now, since the end of the Second World War, more has been
said and written about new music than ever before, but Emil
Hertzka is forgotten. It is futile to speculate on what might have
happened to mankind without Julius Caesar and Napoleon—and
to music without Emil Hertzka. I do not believe that one man can
change the course of events, for this is pre-destined by forces more
powerful and incalculable than the whims of any individual. But
one man of genius can accelerate or slow down the otherwise
inevitable development. This alone is his glory or his damnation.
And Emil Hertzka should be remembered.

However—and it is perhaps characteristic of the general attitude
—although some kind of halo surrounds the names of less adventurous but better rewarded music-publishers of the nineteenth
century, no publisher of our own pioneering age has attained any
comparable fame. With great reverence the story is told of that
patriarch of all publishers Aldo Manucci, who risked his fortune
by printing the first Greek books. He died a wealthy man and
nobody seems to begrudge it. But today it would be said that the
music-publisher's patronage of the arts is marred by his expectation
of future profits, while his business sense is put in question by his
speculating with an unsuitable product. Hertzka did not die in
the poor house either—and posterity seems to owe him nothing.

*

The revolution of the 1920s was only a rumble of distant thunder; the storm broke in earnest after the Second World War.
Schoenberg, Berg and Webern have almost become classics, and the
publisher, while still insisting on being the promoter and protector of
art and artist, is faced by a young generation of composers to whom
experience is repulsive, tradition a burden, concession an abomina-
tion. In more secure times, both artistically and generally, even the
original genius wanted to be heard and performed—to be successful
in the normal, uncomplicated sense. If Schoenberg once wrote that
he had as little consideration for the listener as the listener had for
him he probably meant no more than Beethoven when he refused
to consider Schuppanzigh's violin. But today we are solemnly told
that, in a world of mass civilization, true art must be reserved for a
select few, for an élite whose understanding is more important than
the applause of the multitude. It is proclaimed, with a kind of
hollow pride, that artistic value and public rejection are synonymous.

This was not so in happier times: when Titian's 'Assunta' was unveiled in the Frari in Venice on 20 March 1518 there was a public holiday!

And yet even those composers who profess to care little for public recognition still seek a publisher. What can the publisher do? It is not for him to share the solitude of those who scorn the world. On the contrary, he has to promote music, he has to make it known and, if at all possible, liked. He is not in the happy position of the art-dealer who has achieved everything expected of him if he finds a single member of a wealthy élite to buy an abstruse painting or sculpture. It is a sad fact that the élite of music-lovers, the young men and women at the beginning of their careers, are mostly impecunious and can contribute little more than the encouragement of their applause to the well-being of composer and publisher. The publisher needs that general public which, as Richard Strauss once put it in his blunt Bavarian way, fills the concert-halls and pays the full price for its tickets.

But this paying public is indifferent to 'new music', and we shall have to deal specifically with this attitude, which is novel and quite unprecedented. 'New' music occupies an extremely small place in both the performers' repertoire and the publishers' catalogues. It is idle to speculate which comes first. The problems are too deep seated to be solved by the new means of mass communication, let alone by the old means of publishing, printing and promoting by letters and words of mouth. The question of how composer and publisher get together is therefore more momentous now than ever; for each is equally incapable of managing without the other.

Once composer and publisher have found each other they conclude an agreement in writing: such is now the rule. This agreement is the foundation on which rest the spiritual and material well-being of the composer.

Book- and art-publishers have, in general, a better reputation than music-publishers who are frequently represented as hard-boiled businessmen living off their unworldly victims. Who has not been touched and angered by the stories of Pergolesi, Mozart, Schubert, Chopin and Schumann and has not, secretly or openly, held their publishers responsible for their early deaths? The past hangs over the publishers like a dark stormcloud.

Among the money-making arts music is certainly the youngest. Whereas for thousands of years it seemed that music and money had nothing in common, literature was an object of commerce long before printing was invented. Famous works were copied and sold by professional scribes or by professional dealers—more than three hundred fourteenth- and fifteenth-century hand-written copies of Dante's *Commedia Divina* are still known. Yet there is no trace of a similar trade in music. Only a few copies of renowned pieces were made, not enough to create a commercial market. Even when, two generations after the first books were printed, music too could be duplicated mechanically, the trade remained small and could not provide a living for the composer.

But then music itself was a minor art. Even after the beginning of its great upsurge it lacked the standing of the visual arts or poetry, being regarded as a craft rather than an art, and the composer-musician as an artisan rather than an artist.

How easily, by comparison, did the visual arts come to terms with money! One can read this in Vasari's *Vite*, where, with frankness and pride, he tells how Domenico Ghirlandaio received 1,200 gold ducats for the Capella Tornabuoni; Filippino Lippi 2,000 ducats for the Capella Caraffa; Jacopo della Quercia 2,200 gold pieces for the Fonte Gaia; and so on. 'Much money and great honour' (in that order) is his usual expression, although he does not disclose his own fees. Later, when the fine arts had had their golden age, one no longer finds such frankness. Carlo Ridolfi, almost a century after Vasari, writes of Carpaccio only, '*Acquistò Vittore non poco grido*' ('Vittore acquired no small reputation'). But even today the papers busily report the fantastic prices paid at auctions—half a million pounds for a medium-sized Cézanne, a sum which must have made Cézanne shake his head wherever he is now. Not to mention Picasso and the fortune he can legitimately amass.

This has never happened to music. It was, no doubt, much appreciated, but it never enjoyed that respect which finds expression in large sums of money. Composers, however prominent, were employed in 'tied' jobs which they owed to their craftsmanship, to their aptitude for providing the right type of music for the right occasion. They may have expected no more. When copies of their works circulated, it enhanced their reputations but not their incomes.

Palestrina was certainly held in great esteem, but the 'Maestro di cappella' had not the standing of the architect of St Peter's. Musicians in fixed employment led a modest but secure life. Even J. S. Bach, with his extravagantly large family, was never really hard up, although, like Palestrina and other outstanding musicians before him, he had to quarrel with his employers about every increase in his salary and sometimes lost his patience with them. But he lived at the meeting-point of two ages and wavered time and again between the respectability of an appointment in the church and the much less respectable station of musical 'valet' who had then begun to replace the Cantor. In the next generation the musician was indeed a valet, condemned to seek his material security in his livery, a man without dignity who must have felt that he was born for the highest purpose and reduced to the lowest. This was the critical time, when music became aware of its own greatness, and it could not pass without social and moral difficulties.

The date 8 June 1781 is something of a red-letter day in the social history of music. On that day a forgotten nobleman, Count Arco, dispatched Mozart from the security of the retained musician into the uncertain existence of the freelance composer. His contemporaries could not appreciate the importance of this event. Leopold Mozart, who had the highest opinion of his son's genius and hated his own servile position intensely, could not believe that anyone could live by composing alone. It was, indeed, not easy, even if it was not quite as bad as Mozart's heartbreaking letters and subsequent historians make out. Anyone who takes the trouble to find out what Mozart earned, even in the dark years of 1789–91, will discover that, while it was no princely income, it was by no means desperately little. If he and Constanze had not had the fatal habit of always spending more than they had there should have been no misery. Joseph Haydn died a wealthy man; Gluck had money to spare for speculating in stocks and is said to have left a fortune of 600,000 florins, thereby rivalling any composer or publisher who ever made money with music. But that era had not yet arrived.

When it did, things changed rapidly and radically. A sentence from a letter written by Beethoven to his schoolfriend Wegeler on 20 June 1800 shows the new situation: '. . . my compositions are earning much and I can say that I have more commissions than I can carry out; also I can choose for each work from six or seven publishers, or more if I tried; no one bargains with me, I demand and they pay. . . .' Music had come of age at last; for it must be the measure of the maturity of any art that it is not only appreciated but paid for, just as the artists of the Italian Renaissance were rewarded not only with honours but with money. In Beethoven's later life commissions disappeared and the publishers' fees replaced the generosity of patrons. They provided him with all the amenities he wanted—and, at the end of his life, with the absurd idea that he was poor. Even literature had not achieved so much. In Beethoven's day writers could hardly live on the revenue from their works, however successful. They had to earn their livings as professors, librarians or preceptors, and could write only in their spare time.

But a fair system of monetary reward for the composer could not be easily or quickly found. One would like to think that no amount of money could pay for the pleasure *The Magic Flute* has given to succeeding generations of music-lovers. But we have seen, when discussing the period of subsistence of copyright, that it is only the spirit, not the money, which is eternal

When music became a regular livelihood for composers and publishers there seemed to be only one reasonable method of paying the composer: the publisher bought a work outright for a flat sum. It was almost impossible to calculate that sum; it was a guess, based on the chances of the work's success as the publisher saw them. If he sold more copies than expected he had a good bargain and the composer lost; but the reverse was more frequently the case, because failures are always more numerous than successes, although history does not register them. There was no need to sign formal documents; an exchange of correspondence was sufficient. If, like Beethoven, the composer had the public behind him the publisher could not bargain. He probably did not even try because he had to outbid the five or six other competitors. If the composer was less well established the publisher secured for himself a premium for the risk he took.

How the overall price of music had risen appears from the fact that for *each* of his late string quartets Beethoven received exactly as much as Mozart thirty years earlier had received for a complete opera. Carl Maria von Weber's cousin Aloysia Lange recounted that Weber had earned more with his *Oberon* alone than Mozart with all his operas together. This custom of the flat rate, *à fonds perdu*, as it was called with a hint of sarcasm, continued well into this century, which may be taken as a sign that both composers and publishers were satisfied. Beethoven had many successors, other composers with whom the publisher could not bargain, who demanded and obtained what seemed equitable to them. Richard Strauss still sold his publishing rights for lump sums, reserving for himself performing and mechanical rights.

As a rule this system both protected the composer against total loss and barred him from total success. In retrospect nothing seems to have done more harm to the reputation of music-publishers. Generations of publishers are said to have bought the best works for a pittance and made great fortunes without ever concerning themselves with the misguided composer. The few known cases are stains which no detergent can remove, where art and money are in head-on collision. If an ordinary tradesman knows how to buy cheaply and sell at a profit, and so legitimately accumulates a large fortune, people take off their hats and praise his efficiency. He may even be knighted. But a similarly shrewd music-publisher is suspect to everybody, contemptible to many. His wealth has an air of illegitimacy and it will be whispered that the degree of his comfort varies according to the degree of discomfort of his composers.

Those who take this line always adduce one of the same handful of cases to 'prove' their point. For example, in 1859, the year of the first performance of his *Faust*, Gounod sold his 'Ave Maria, méditation religieuse sur le premier prélude de J. S. Bach' for five hundred francs, then a very modest sum. After a performance by Pasdeloup the piece was badly received by the Press and the publisher probably thought little of it. But composer, publisher and expert critics were all mistaken, and the absurd assumption that the absent-minded Bach had omitted the melody which his 'accompaniment' required resulted in a work which became—and probably still is—a worldwide success. Millions of copies of dozens of different arrangements must have been sold. Gounod himself—described by his biographers as a dreamy, unworldly man—saw this happening but made no complaint. His successors, however, took exception to his short-sightedness. They engaged the best lawyers they could find, and almost a century after the unhappy deal the matter came before the courts, which did not hesitate to take the side of the composer and make the publisher pay a huge sum so that justice was seen to be done.

Such things happened in the nineteenth century. It is often forgotten that, in those days of defenceless composers and rapacious publishers, the most cordial relationships nevertheless existed between the best of both sides. Giulio Ricordi was a true friend of Verdi and Puccini; Fritz August Simrock a close friend of Brahms; Marie-Auguste Durand an intimate of Debussy. Generally, composers and publishers trusted each other, so much so that the 'agreements' which were concluded were often curiously informal documents. When I once tried to establish exactly what rights Boosey & Hawkes held in Offenbach's *Vie parisienne* a long search

produced a handwritten letter, dated 1868, from Offenbach himself which simply said: *Monsieur, bien reçu la somme de 1,000 frs.
pour 'la Vie parisienne'. Agréez*... This was the document covering
the rights for Great Britain and the British Empire—half the
world at that time.

All this has changed. Thanks not to charity but to their art
the beggars of other days have become a community of high standing and repute, and every rise in the social scale has invariably been
followed by a widening of worldly experience. The successful but
naïve composer no longer exists. Today he is no long-haired
dreamer but dresses like other mortals and receives sound advice
from many quarters about the debt mankind and publishers owe
him for his gifts. So an agreement is made which bears as little
resemblance to the contracts of the last century as the jet plane
does to the mail coach.

In some countries, such as France and Germany, the law has
declared the substance of copyright inalienable and ruled that only
the 'right of exploitation' can be assigned by the composer to a
third party. This is not much more than a polite compliment to
the mystery of the creative mind which is foreign to the more
prosaic Anglo-Saxon outlook. In Britain and the United States
the composer regularly assigns the copyright itself, this assignment
usually being made for the whole period of copyright and all possible future extensions, a stipulation not recognized in every
country. With serious music it is normally made for all countries
of the world, though French publishers, following scientific
developments with greater attention than others, are now demanding the rights for the entire universe.

According to his importance—and thence his bargaining-power
—the composer receives a varying share in the proceeds of his
music: a sheet royalty of 10–15% of the selling-price of all copies
sold; 25–50% of hire fees or rentals for orchestral materials;
66–75% of performing fees of dramatic works, operas, musicals,
ballets, which also covers the librettist's cut; 50–66% of all
royalties resulting from mechanical reproductions; 50% of all
fees paid for the inclusion and synchronization of single excerpts
in films, but 66% of such fees if the composer's work supplies all
or the major part of the music for the film; and finally 50% of all
fees and royalties payable by a sub-publisher, if any. This makes
an impressive catalogue of financial expectations.

But this is not all. In one critical respect the new face of music
has affected the relationship of composer and publisher: the composer

not only receives money from the publisher but also has to pay something in return. When becoming a member of a society he must undertake to assign to it the performing rights in all his present and future works. At the time of signing his agreement with the publisher, therefore, he does not dispose of these rights. The agreement with the publisher provides for the share in them which the composer allows the publisher, and the statutes of the societies establish the maximum the publisher can claim: normally 33%, exceptionally—in the United States and Great Britain—50%. The societies would not recognize and would not pay a larger share to the publisher, but he may have to be content with less than the statutory maximum. As performing fees are a substantial part of the potential earnings of a musical work, this payment by the composer is as important to the publisher as his revenue from all other sources.

All this is well established, and the publisher's scope for shrewdness in his dealings with the composer is strictly limited. However, the object of the agreement is a curious one. No composer would be happy if the publisher were to behave as one behaves in normal commerce, correctly and punctiliously fulfiling the letter of a legal document. In spite of all the commercialization there is an invisible wall between art and commerce which prevents music from becoming merely merchandise and the publisher's business from degenerating into mere commerce.

Indeed, the publisher is expected to do many things for the composer which either defy legal definition altogether or at best can only be hinted at in a written document. The most important of these is obviously publicity. Almost every agreement contains a clause to the effect that the publisher will 'use his best efforts', which can mean everything or very little, in this direction. Composers who have already achieved fame require little publicity. A new work by Stravinsky need only be advertised; any attempt at recommendation would be ludicrous. But the young composer, the new music, require an effort beyond any contractual obligation. It rarely happens that the composer is satisfied with his publisher's efforts—he, and many others, are inclined to overrate the power and influence publicity can exercise. There is a widespread notion among composers that every success is due to them and every failure due to the publisher, implying that the publisher could compel success and prevent failure.

Indeed, there are many who believe that music might have been spared the tribulations of the twelve-note doctrine if Emil Hertzka had not drummed it into so many heads with his ruthless and aggressive propaganda, spearheaded by a periodical called *Anbruch* (*Daybreak*, or *Dawn of a New Era*), which was as uncompromising as day and night themselves. When this publicity was unleashed, however, although it was sustained for quite a few years, it was largely ineffective. The general public, which never read the famous *Anbruch* or saw any of the countless leaflets, remained unaffected and could not be persuaded to like the new music. The small circle of converts which supplied the contributors and readers of *Anbruch* were certainly fortified in their belief, but the overwhelming majority of musicians—composers, conductors, singers and instrumentalists alike—were indifferent and impervious to all the frantic recommendation and abuse. During the economic and political troubles of the 1930s this propaganda became much more subdued and finally ceased. When twelve-note music rose from the ashes of the Second World War, there was no publicity at all. Its surviving supporters were themselves surprised.

This unexpected resurrection demonstrated the true task of the publisher: to put a work, even a controversial work, before the world and render discussion and appreciation possible. It is for others, both experts and laymen, to form their own opinions and for the anonymous public to deliver the verdict. After more than forty years in publishing, years which have seen the greatest upheaval in music as an art and as a commodity, I do not believe that the publisher and his publicity have any other power or function but that of starting the debate. The course it takes, the result it produces, are outside the publisher's domain. He is powerful only if his publications are successful, which means only if they are good in the sense of being a valid expression of their time. It is my unshakable belief that the sham and the bogus, however cleverly and insistently publicized, will be discovered and discarded sooner rather than later. But it is equally true that in this world, flooded with music and publicity as it is, a good work may also find it difficult to rise to the surface without the help of publicity, though he would be a sad pessimist who thought that it might remain for ever unknown.

The regular activity of the publisher starts with the production of the work assigned to him by the composer. Quite a few publishers of serious contemporary works produce only a few copies; this is an expression not so much of lack of confidence in the quality of the works concerned as of a rather heartless realism in assessing their possibilities. They are justly reproached with not properly fulfilling their task, although the alternative—rejection—is no less painful for the composer. At a time of transition like ours the boundary between professional decorum and reason is not easily defined. In principle the publisher is still expected to print the works and to offer them to the general public.

As far as printing goes, the music-publisher is at a great disadvantage compared with his colleagues in the field of literature. The book-publisher is concerned with the presentation of his publications; he chooses the fount, the size, the printing-area, the title-page, the binding—things which the public accepts without noticing them if they are well done and recognizes at a glance if they are not. In this way the book-publisher makes a creative contribution which plays no small part in the fate of a book.

Nothing similar happens to the music-publisher. Everything he does is dictated by hard necessity and inviolable convention. The format is dictated by practical experience: music is to be not only read but played, so the size must be so chosen that the player need not turn the pages too often; where he does have to turn them there must be a suitable rest or sustained note, which often disturbs the even distribution of the engraving. Moreover there is only one musical fount or typeface, the size again being chosen from the practical viewpoint of quick legibility and not on aesthetic grounds. But the most serious, indeed unsolved, problem is that of the graphic presentation of music itself, which in every respect is only a poor relation of ordinary script.

There are, of course, various means of written communication. The old Chinese symbols for words and sentences were independent of any particular spoken language. Born out of wit and intelligence, they were meant to appeal to the imagination and so could be 'read' in any language. A particularly well-conceived and well-designed symbol might be hung on the wall, like a picture. At its highest level writing was for the Chinese a spiritual and artistic exercise, and it is said that up to the communist revolution the well-educated Chinese traditionalists refused to read the standardized letters of printed books and newspapers, just as Guido da Montefeltro would not tolerate printed books in his library.

Scripts formed from an alphabet of letters, on the other hand, are to a considerable extent phonetic. They not only combine letters to form words which communicate unmistakably a special meaning but also indicate the pronunciation, the sound of the written word. This is the real problem of spelling; with different peoples this leads to different solutions which the foreigner, assuming that his own language possesses the only correct and logical spelling, will always find somewhat unnatural. The sound *sh*, for instance, is spelt in French *ch*, in Italian *sc* before *e* and *i*, in German *sch*, in Swedish *sj* and so on.

After the conversion of the Czech people to Christianity their language, like Russian, was written in Cyrillic script, which derived from the Greek alphabet but added a number of extra letters in order to better reproduce the actual sound of the spoken word. In the course of the fourteenth and fifteenth centuries, under pressure from the surrounding Germans and persecuted for religious reforms, they adopted instead the Latin alphabet, a form which in no way indicates the sound. As a consequence a multitude of accents had to be added to the letters, to mark not only long and short syllables but also the hard, medium and soft vowels characteristic of all Slav languages.

In the case of English pronunciation differs so widely from spelling that quite often only natural instinct can guess at either, though efforts are being made to simplify spelling, thus facilitating written communication at the expense of etymology. The very small inflexion that distinguishes 'wring' from 'ring', 'write' from 'right', is important not only phonetically but as an aid to the understanding of the meaning. But in spite of phonetic spelling many of the acoustic properties of a language remain unconsidered, not only open and closed vowels and accents but even essentials such as speed, melody and cadence. However, the unmistakable identity of letters, words and sentences can dispense with all this. Tongue and the temperament of the people know it and the foreigner will learn it only from years of constant use.

In music on the other hand the entire meaning comes from the acoustic phenomenon. It is not therefore sufficient merely to suggest or paraphrase it, as spelling does; musical signs or graphs should be as precise as letters, words or sentences. This has never quite been achieved, music having always demanded more than could be graphically expressed. Once letters seemed sufficient; then a kind of shorthand had to be introduced to give better information about the music; then it became necessary to indicate pitch; no sooner was this done than the duration of every note had to be fixed; and so on. The music of the last century has to all intents and purposes outgrown our means of writing it down. What would old Guido of Arezzo say if he saw the score of, say, Richard Strauss's *Elektra*? Our musical texts not only consist of notes in intricate rhythmic arrangement but are filled with all sorts of additional markings and directions without which the pure musical text would not be intelligible. J. S. Bach and Handel were still able to rely on the self-evidence of notes in their context; Mozart could do with few additional markings; but for Beethoven the mere musical graphs were no longer sufficient, and from his time onwards composers grew increasingly mistrustful. The scores of Gustav Mahler are full of exhortations, explanations, warnings and commands inserted to make the meaning of the music clear. This is a perfect analogy with the application of Latin characters to the Czech language: cumbersome and inadequate.

That letters should be clearly and immediately recognizable was one prerequisite of the calligraphic art. The scribe, and after him the type-founder, could invent characters without impairing their legibility. A special aesthetic developed, which was handed down from the earliest scribes to the printers. From Gutenberg to Eric Gill much industry and imagination has gone into the design of the letters from which the modern publisher and printer can choose. Only where the need for quick legibility is the first concern of the graphic artist is there little choice. In old musical manuscripts the words and initials are often beautiful; the heavy, black, square notes and staff lines are not.

Nor can the first music prints compare with early letterpress prints. For a short time the spirit of baroque art tried to reform the shape of music script. A *canzona* by Frescobaldi, engraved freehand on to the copperplate, with ledger lines drawn across its whole width, the stems and tails embellished with flourishes, is a true ornamental pattern. But the danger of illegibility was apparently too great. The musician has not the leisure of the reader; he must read at a glance where the reader of a book can enjoy the graphic quality. Frescobaldi's engraver had no successor, and no Bodoni arose among engravers and writers of music. There is little consolation to be found in the pompous title-pages of the seventeenth century and the daintier ones of the eighteenth. The script demanded standardization; ambiguity had to be avoided. Prints of the eighteenth and early nineteenth centuries still have that certain distinction which so often transfigures everything antique, but it needed only Senefelder's discovery of lithography and the comparative mass production of the later nineteenth century to eradicate the last remnants of graphic ambition. A comparison of J. S. Bach's handwriting with a modern print of any of his works shows how astonishingly mechanical and lacking in individuality music engraving has become, how Bach's vivid and picturesque writing has been turned into a 'dead letter'.

The impossibility of applying any artistic imagination to music script may have been what freed the music-publisher from any sense of aesthetic obligation. With the silhouettes on the title-page of Schumann's 'Kreisleriana' of 1837 we have reached the limit of what is acceptable. What follows goes far beyond that limit. No book-publisher would have dared to present to the reader a cover-drawing like that on the first edition of the vocal score of Gounod's *Faust*: a red devil on an emerald green background juggling with two hearts. Until quite recently the most precious and sophisticated music was disfigured by incredibly tasteless and cheap lithographs, bad lettering and bad spacing. Even the most demanding buyer seemed to accept it as necessary and did not object, in spite of the high price of all printed music. Indeed, all printed music always was and still is expensive in comparison with books. A thirty-two-page volume of music costs more than a book of a hundred and twenty pages.

This is due not to the rapacity of the publisher but, in the first instance, to the high price of engraving, a tiresome, slow process which requires much experience and knowledge and resists mechanization and simplification as strongly as music-writing itself. Every head, stem and tail, every dot and line, must be hammered into the hard zinc plate, every tie and slur drawn with a sharp stylo. The engraver also has to know more about music than the compositor does about literature. Not only are composers generally less conversant with the correct spelling of music than writers with the spelling of words, but a difficult handwriting sets greater problems in music than in any literary manuscript—particularly today, when guesses are hazardous. No typewriter comes to the engraver's assistance. Many attempts to design one have been made over the years, but only the simplest music submits to regular spacing. A good engraver needs four working hours for a quarto page of piano music of medium difficulty, and the best engraver cannot complete more than three pages of a difficult orchestral score in a working week. No wonder that publishers are always on the look-out for cheaper methods—and a further deterioration of the graphic qualities of printed music. Pessimists are convinced that music-engravers are a doomed race.

Today the tasteless lithographic covers have disappeared—only the title-pages of pop-songs still look more like posters than titles—but even the greatest musical masterpieces must be content with a modest presentation, while their relations in literature and art enjoy great luxury. Particularly now that the windows of music shops are resplendent with the highly coloured sleeves of long-playing records, it needs a careful and patient search to discover a copy of printed music in its drab and uninviting dress.

Poor appearance is not the worst consequence of the inadequacy of music script. Mistakes are the true scourge of music—of composers, copyists, engravers and publishers alike. In books, and even in the hastily set-up newspapers, printing mistakes are comparatively rare. Anyone who finds such a mistake is rightly angry or amused. Only exceptionally are such mistakes of any consequence, and in most cases the reader can easily guess the correct meaning. But there are very few if any music copies or prints without a host of mistakes, and this has always been so.

Even in the old days, when music was so simple that the script seemed to be entirely adequate, mistakes were the rule. First editions of Handel's works published by Walsh in London are full of grotesque examples. In Breitkopf & Härtel's 'Oeuvres complettes' of Haydn, probably published in 1804, there is hardly one correct bar. Nobody seemed to mind, no ungracious word from Haydn or Mozart has been recorded. Beethoven, with his dreadful handwriting, fought manfully for correct editions, but it was Brahms who, seventy years after the first publication, discovered a whole series of mistakes in the violin sonata Op. 12, No. 2, which to this day appear in some editions in all their old glory. Fifty years after its publication Clemens Krauss found a completely wrong clarinet passage in the full score of Strauss's *Salome*.

On the occasion of a new revision of Stravinsky's *Rite of Spring* in 1952 about seven hundred mistakes were found and corrected. Among other errors the horn parts on one page had slipped into the trombone parts, where there should have been rests—but in thousands of performances no conductor had ever noticed it. The *Rite* is in fact one of those works which seemed to have been cursed in the cradle. From Stravinsky's own manuscript onward through half a century it had not been possible to establish a correct text. When, after the revision in 1952, another errata list of about four hundred mistakes had accumulated I decided to break the spell with the strongest and most dangerous formula and ordered a complete re-engraving.

It is easy to drag those responsible before the tribunal of outraged conscience; particularly the composers, with whom the evil invariably starts because they make mistake after mistake in the first place without checking their manuscripts before handing them over to the publisher. I have come across only two composers who wrote their manuscripts with great care and read proofs with untiring punctiliousness: Bartók and Webern. But I would not be so bold as to say that even their works are entirely free from errors.

Thus the devil who slips misprints into books and journals is a trivial malefactor compared with the fiend who disfigures music and not only blinds composers, engravers and proof-readers but also sends a host of voluntary hunters in search of mistakes. They are usually the sort of people who triumphantly bring in every misprint as if it were a long-wanted bank-robber. One of them caused quite a stir by claiming that he had found tens of thousands of misprints in Verdi and Puccini scores, and some people said that this was due to some diabolical, though admittedly inexplicable, intention on the part of the publisher. These voluntary helpers seldom realize that they are reading texts which have already been cleansed of numerous mistakes.

Quite often their inconsiderate puritanism leads them astray. Once I was sent a list of more than a hundred alleged misprints in Bartók's *Mikrokosmos* which had been found by a comparison of the printed edition with the manuscript. The usual unfriendly letter accused the publisher of unpardonable negligence. A check against the manuscript used by the engravers—a photocopy of the original—showed that all the 'mistakes' were actual changes made by Bartók in the proofs and marked meticulously in the photocopy in red ink. At the time, in 1939, he had already sent the original manuscript with others to the United States prior to his own emigration, and with all the worries and troubles that awaited him in the New World he apparently never thought of correcting the manuscript. I do not know whether a note has been made in the New York archives. If not, the same discovery may one day be made again, and if by then the publisher's files have been lost or destroyed a 'revised' version of *Mikrokosmos* will be brought out which Bartók himself would condemn.

The same may happen to Brahms. The former librarian of the Society of Friends of Music in Vienna, Eusebius Mandyczewski, a friend of Brahms, used to show me printed copies of Brahms's works from his library which contain many corrections in pencil. Brahms never passed them on to his publisher, and Mandyczewski was quite sure that he eventually preferred the printed versions to these afterthoughts. But Mandyczewski has long been dead, and the archives of Simrocks in Leipzig no longer exist. Perhaps one day a sensational discovery will be made!

The insistence on unadulterated texts is a sign of the new dignity music has assumed in our time. The apparent carelessness of former days is now regarded as scandalous, not to say criminal. I have never heard of new editions of old literary works causing such heated controversies as have been raging around musical texts, with demands that the sanctity of the original should be guaranteed by law, and a body like UNESCO pressing for legislation which would oblige every owner of a musical manuscript to make it freely available for research.

This is where the comparatively new scientific pursuit of musicology comes into its own. While the theory and philosophy of music have been the subject of profound study and innumerable treatises since the days of Pythagoras and even earlier, the historical aspect only came to prominence in the last quarter of the nineteenth century. This is rather strange.

When the historian first entered the musical scene there was still a general passion for new music, with nothing to indicate an impending change in public taste and preference unless it was a premonition that 'old' music was to rise to an importance it had never had before. The other arts—literature, painting, sculpture, architecture—have always had a lasting message, an unalterable validity, and have therefore acquired historians to recognize and explain both message and validity, however unfashionable the appearance of the old masterpieces might have become. It was this indestructible meaning of the 'old' arts which justified and, indeed, demanded such study and research. But similar endeavours in music seemed rather pointless.

Music is—or was for thousands of years—essentially different from the other arts. As I have said before, it had no staying power, it did not last, but this cannot have been due to the absence of historians and historical research. In fact, 'old' music never had a message for either the composers or the audience of the new music. Every generation created the music that suited it and regularly took it to its grave, as the pharaohs did their retinue, and the next generation saw it disappear without regret. There was no inducement to historical research. It had no place in the whole realm of music, and if a man undertook a review of the music of the past, as Padre Martini did in the middle of the eighteenth century, his contemporaries were duly impressed but made no use of his achievements. It took another century for musicology in its present-day sense to establish itself, and I myself owe much to one of its most outstanding pioneers, Guido Adler. A great change had to come about before a legitimate place in musical life could be assigned to historiography. Against the background of the past this seems a bizarre contradiction, but, as we shall see, it is both the condition and the consequence of an era which threatens to lose contact with its own and clings to 'old' or 'historic' music.

The immediate application of historically orientated musicology is the editing of old music and unadulterated texts: the new musical philology. The editors of the nineteenth century were musicians to a man, and very often eminent ones, such as Liszt, Bülow, Tausig, Wilhelmj and even Brahms. The new editors, in contrast, are men of letters. The musician-editor transplanted the music he edited into his own time. The piano for which Mozart wrote was not suitable for *legato* playing, but Moscheles's piano was and he eliminated Mozart's *'non legato'* and drew long slurs above whole staves which not only look strange to us but make the music sound different. When, in 1802, Breitkopf & Härtel published Mozart's arrangement of Handel's *Messiah* they could proclaim in their announcement that, with due respect to Handel's genius and the grandeur of his work, the original lacked the more agreeable charm of new music. Carl Czerny inserted one bar in the first prelude of Bach's 'Wohltemperiertes Clavier' because the original did not conform to his 'classical' sense of balance. Hans von Bülow could add in a footnote to his edition of Chopin's Impromptu, Op. 36: 'These few bars [94–7] incline a little towards the commonplace. Anyone who concurs in this opinion may skip them without interfering with the flow of the piece.' All this seems quite absurd to us. But it was not done out of ignorance. There was a sincere attempt to prevent music from getting 'old', historical, a knowledge—perhaps unconscious—that music must live in order to exist, that a new generation must either appropriate or abandon it.

The modern men of letters who carefully copy old manuscripts and first editions must have the idea that music possesses the same objectivity, the same invariable validity, as the other arts. They require the performer of an *Urtext* to be as much a historian as they are themselves. Unfortunately for them, but fortunately for the art, every performance will deviate individually from the text and will be in some peculiar way 'modern', the first and original performance having been lost for ever. Quite a few works by J. S. Bach have lost a good deal of that former self-explanatory quality which enabled Bach to omit all indications of tempo, phrasing and expression. It is still an open question whether Bach's music is to be treated as black or white, loud or soft, without any crescendi and decrescendi and, of course, without any variation in tempo except for the ritardando at the end. Artur Schnabel was renowned for the absolute fidelity of his rendering of Beethoven's piano sonatas, but when he sat down to edit them in print an incredible number of markings slipped in which are not to be found either in Beethoven's manuscripts or in the first editions. On the other hand, when I once asked Pablo Casals to edit for me the unaccompanied cello suites of Bach he replied with a surprised smile, 'Hasn't Bach done that himself?'

How have the other arts withstood the passage of time, the change of purpose and taste? Not much could be done to literature. Editors of older literary texts (for example, Shakespeare or Milton) do not generally go as far as editors of older musical texts by reproducing the old orthography, but this slight modernization remains on the very surface of the works. Beautiful thoughts are like beautiful women and every fashion suits them. In architecture, however, it has often happened that Renaissance façades have been added to Gothic buildings, and Baroque façades to Renaissance, without invalidating the older structure. Was this not precisely what the high-handed editors of older music did in the nineteenth century? Or what such a truly modern mind as Stravinsky's did with Pergolesi, Tchaikovsky, Gesualdo and Bach?

Insistence on fidelity to the original has undoubtedly done much good to musical practice, particularly in the opera-house, where unwarranted editing used to be rampant. It is strange that Rossini should have agreed to the substitution of an aria by some utterly insignificant Maestro Pietro Romani for his own in the *Barber of Seville*. I remember from my own early days performances of Mozart's *Figaro* with spoken dialogue instead of the *recitativo secco*; *Don Giovanni* ending on the D-minor chord of the first part of the second finale because the second part was not considered to be in keeping with high drama; the *alla turca* from the A-major piano sonata, K. 331, orchestrated by Johann André, and played as an introduction to the third act of *Die Entführung aus dem Serail*; unpardonable cuts (it was only after the First World War that I heard Don Giovanni's 'Metà di voi quà vadano' for the first time); and other things of a similar kind which would no longer be tolerated—although the 'Leonora No. 3' Overture is still played before the last scene of *Fidelio*, and one wonders whether Beethoven would have approved of that.

Nor does faithfulness to the original stop here. In the last twenty years it has become not only the fashion but almost a point of honour to perform songs and operas in their original language.

As far as songs are concerned, the case for the original language is strong enough. The poems are often—though not always—of a high literary standard, and the double requirement that the translation should be of equally high quality and fit the music, which means not only right stresses in the right place but also the choice of the right vowels, is rarely attainable. But the amateur singer had to disappear before the argument in favour of the original text could acquire its full force, for the amateur singer insisted on singing in his own language and successful songs were regularly published in three or four languages. The professional singer, on the other hand, is expected to sing in any of the principal languages of the world, which is all very laudable. Whether he or she and the listeners do not miss the finer points of contact between words and music is another question; better understanding may often be sacrificed for the sake of the *Urtext*.

On the operatic stage insistence on the original language can easily lead to absurdity. To begin with, the critics (certainly) and the public (probably) are nowadays much concerned with clear enunciation by the singers. How clear can the enunciation be if the singers sing in a foreign language which they cannot speak? When, a few years ago, *Boris Godunov* was sung in Russian at the Royal Opera House, not even Russians in the audience could identify it; which did not prevent the artists and the administrators from being very proud of their achievement.

Arias in older operas do not really matter. The listener can guess with some accuracy whether their subject is love or hate, drink or revenge, or just a moonlit night. But these old operas have recitatives both 'secco' and 'accompagnato' which are essential for the action and therefore ought to be understood by both singers and audience. Later operas, unfortunately, do not even have arias in the proper sense, and one can never tell exactly when the listener will be lost. Would every non-German listener listening to a performance of *Götterdämmerung* in German know precisely what Brünnhilde and Hagen are talking about in the second act? Yet the events of the third act remain largely unintelligible if one misses that discussion in the second. It is sad that Ernest Newman should have wasted years of his life on a translation of the *Ring* into English which in places is preferable to Wagner's original. Of course, in the opera-house we have reached the point where most of the operas performed are supposed to be so well known that the words are of no importance. But the uninhibited pleasure of former days seems to be lost. I remember glorious performances at the State Opera in Vienna in the twenties when the famous tenor Koloman Patáky and the even more famous soprano Maria Németh sang in Hungarian while the rest of the cast sang in German. For anyone who knows an Italian opera very well, it is certainly fascinating to hear it sung by a native cast in its native surroundings, for the reaction of a native audience is just as interesting as the performance itself. But there is little to recommend Italian performances by non-Italians. True enough, English or, for that matter, any Germanic language would slow down the tempo of a work such as *The Barber of Seville*. But unless he is a linguist no English singer could sing in Italian at the same speed as his Italian colleague. When it comes to Mozart, whose operas are now almost invariably sung in Italian, even in Germany, his Italian was no more than a fashion. In his manuscript score of *Figaro* he himself translated into German the one sentence in the last finale which raised his music to the highest and most un-Italian level: '*O Engel, verzeih' mir!*'—O angel, forgive me! for da Ponte's platitudinous '*Contessa, perdono!*'.

The late Sir Thomas Beecham used to say that opera could not be sung in English because the two most important words of the operatic vocabulary, 'love' and 'death', were unsingable. If there were any serious doubts about the singability of the English language, Benjamin Britten must have dispelled them.

Moreover, singing in the original language must of necessity be confined to languages of which a smattering can be expected from a few singers and listeners. But very popular operas have been written in other languages, too. Could it seriously be suggested that one should forego *The Bartered Bride* altogether rather than hear it in a translation?

It is one of many contradictions in our musical life that the apparently laudable desire for the *Urtext* coincides with the ascendency of the producer, once a humble servant but now as important as the conductor and the prima donna. It is this mighty man who offends most frequently and most unscrupulously against the clear directions and intentions of composer and librettist. The late Wieland Wagner's productions, not only of his grandfather's works but also of Debussy's *Pelleas and Melisande* and Richard Strauss's *Salome*, were as remote from the *Urtext* as anything perpetrated by the editors of the nineteenth century. While many older critics and members of the audience were duly scandalized, many others found in these productions the additional sensation of 'modernization', which aroused their waning interest in the works themselves.

Worse things happened in the olden days, which cast their long shadow as far as our own time.

When Fritz Kreisler, the violinist, once published a little piece of his own in the style and under the name of Gaetano Pugnani it may have been a practical joke to test the wisdom of musicologists. To his surprise the law and its administrators showed little sense of humour, and when he later claimed both authorship and royalties he was refused. The forgery, once accepted in good faith, was irrevocable and unalterable.

But the case of Anton Bruckner became a *cause célèbre*. I was one of the onlookers: I knew the prosecutors, who had kept their discoveries secret until Bruckner's works entered the public domain, though one would have thought that truth can brook no delay; and I knew the surviving greybeards in the dock who seemed strangely paralysed and would neither admit nor deny the charges. The ring-leaders, however, had long since thrown themselves upon the mercy of the Eternal Judge. The allegations were fantastic: under Bruckner's eyes his symphonies had been altered, rearranged, reorchestrated by well-meaning friends and pupils who remained anonymous. For thirty years after his death these adulterated versions were in circulation under Bruckner's name, while his manuscript scores were lying in the National Library in Vienna, until a sentence in Bruckner's last will was re-read and seemed to hint at his disapproval of what had been believed to be the final versions. It was well known that Bruckner kept changing his symphonies after he had finished them—there are two 'original' versions of the First and Eighth symphonies and three of the Third. But who could have suspected that the printed versions were massive forgeries? Or that Bruckner was so frightened by his friends that even in his last will he dared not say in as many words that the published scores were forced upon him? Now the malefactors have been unmasked and the *Urtexts* established, and the files are closed.

There remains, however, another major secret to be unravelled. Several years ago a musical called *Kismet* was performed on Broadway, which used almost exclusively—and openly—music from Alexander Borodin's opera *Prince Igor*. *Kismet* did not become an international success, but some songs, particularly one, 'Stranger in

Paradise', based on a tune from one of the Polovtsian dances, made their way round the globe. This roused the displeasure of the guardians of the original, but Borodin, as a Russian, never enjoyed copyright protection in the United States and effective steps could only be taken when *Kismet* appeared on a London stage. The Belaiev Foundation, owners of Borodin's opera, represented by a committee of dignified old gentlemen who belonged to the first generation of refugees from the Revolution, at once instituted proceedings. They were not concerned with money. *Kismet*, being an act of sacrilege, was to be unconditionally prohibited and utterly destroyed. This action provoked a closer examination, probably for the first time since 1889, of the circumstances in which Borodin's opera was first published and performed.

The facts are notorious: inspired by Wagner's *Ring*, Vladimir Stassov conceived the idea that the Russians ought to have a national opera which could stand up to or even surpass Wagner's work. Stassov, literary and music critic and historian, was a formidable figure. One only has to look at Rjepin's portrait of this large, long-bearded man in order to appreciate the terror he inspired in the musical and literary circles of his time. He chose the subject from a 'mediaeval' Russian heroic poem, which was a forgery, as was another Slav poem 'discovered' in Bohemia at about the same time. And Stassov also chose the composer, Alexander Borodin, illegitimate son of a Russian prince, councillor of state, chemist, genius, involved equally in music, science and society. Borodin agreed and undertook to write the libretto himself. But years went by and to Stassov's despair the opera made little progress. Once a 'Polovtsian Dance'—allegedly from the opera—was performed at a concert.

In his memoirs Rimsky-Korsakov describes how, in the early morning of 28 February 1887, Stassov came in great distress to his house: during the night, at a party, Borodin had suddenly died, aged only fifty-two. Rimsky goes on to tell how he and Stassov went to Borodin's house and took away all the sketches for the opera which he, Rimsky, and his young pupil Alexander Glazunov completed in two years.

Rimsky was a punctilious and self-satisfied diarist. He left very detailed accounts of his salvage operation on the works of Mussorgsky, whom he considered a great genius but a hopeless amateur. At the end of his account he says, more from conceit than modesty, that he had deposited Mussorgsky's manuscripts at the Public Library in St Petersburg, where everyone could compare the originals with his versions and decide for himself. This was in fact done after the First World War and the Revolution, and posterity proved ungrateful to Rimsky. It preferred Mussorgsky's uncouth roughness to Rimsky's smooth routine, and a complete edition of Mussorgsky's works in their original form was published by the Russian State Publishing House. As regards Borodin and his opera, however, Rimsky is much more reticent. He left no word about the state of the sketches and the nature of his and Glazunov's work, no mention of the fate of the sketches themselves.

Late in 1889, Mitrofan Belaiev published both the full and the vocal scores. (Belaiev was an enormously rich timber merchant who had started a music-publishing business out of sheer enthusiasm for the new Russian national music. When he died in 1904, he left three million roubles to a foundation for the furtherance of Russian music, which still exists today.) One might have expected some circumstantial explanation from Rimsky, but he had nothing to say. Only Borodin's name figured in large letters on the cover and title-page of both orchestral and vocal scores, and a short preface by the publisher informed the reader that the opera was left unfinished by Borodin and that Rimsky and Glazunov completed it 'from the available material'. For many years this cryptic notice seemed to satisfy public curiosity. For a long time Stassov had prepared the public for the great event. Now that it had happened, nearly three years after Borodin's death, nobody was inclined to raise awkward questions.

Musicologists did not overlook it altogether. In the early 1920s the Russian writer Assafiev cross-examined Glazunov, who hesitatingly admitted that the publisher's foreword was neither quite right nor quite wrong; nothing existed of the fourth act, neither music nor libretto; the overture contained the tunes which Borodin had played to Glazunov without writing them down and was really Glazunov's work; there was not one bar in the whole opera which had not had to be revised and rewritten. Assafiev could not push him any further and shortly afterwards Glazunov escaped from Russia. Those were the ascertainable facts.

The American authors of *Kismet* pointed out in their defence that they had used the tunes only, not Rimsky's or Glazunov's harmonization and orchestration. The tunes must undoubtedly have been Borodin's and Borodin was no longer protected in Britain either. But how did Borodin's tunes look originally? Only Borodin's sketches could prove or disprove the Americans' case. An expert suggested that Rimsky would have deposited them at the Leningrad

Library, as he had done with Mussorgsky's manuscripts. Through an influential intermediary an inquiry was sent to the Library, but it drew a blank: the sketches were not there. Not even the score or the parts of the one 'Polovtsian Dance' which had been performed under Borodin's own direction could be found. Indeed, no attempt has ever been made in Russia to publish the sketches, although a comparison with the completed work should be one of the most rewarding tasks still left to musicology.

The parties in the *Kismet* affair agreed on a settlement, as is usual if neither can prove its point, but the matter remains mysterious. There was no material motive such as prompted Mozart's widow to have the Requiem Mass completed without disclosing the circumstances; to this day this has the musicologists guessing as to what is Mozart's own and what is Süssmayr's addition. Rimsky's credit was high enough to justify a clear account of his interference with Borodin's own contribution. Belaiev could have had no sinister intentions; he was too rich and too enthusiastic. But Stassov? Vladimir Vassilievitch Stassov, director of the Department of Fine Arts of the Public Library in St Petersburg, promoter of Borodin's national opera, instigator of the libretto, in possession of the sketches at some time at least? One wonders . . .

Musicology has disturbed many a grave that should have been left untouched. It is true that the classical and romantic repertoire which dominates our musical life is wearing thinner and now tends to be restricted to the most perfect masterpieces. Whole categories of once popular works have disappeared in the last fifty years. Not only does Schumann's piano music seem to have fallen from grace, but today his oratorios are never heard. Liszt has practically vanished from the programmes; even Mozart and Beethoven are reduced to their most accomplished and most intimately known works. In the operatic field the massacre has been even more widespread. Out of about two hundred and fifty immensely successful operas of the last two hundred years, hardly fifty have survived to this day. This is no peculiarity of our time but the natural process of withering and vanishing which distinguishes music from the other arts, always beginning with the weaker plants and gradually spreading to the stronger ones.

There is a new field here for the historian of music: reviving and reconstructing old works which should not have been lost. Thus Monteverdi has been rediscovered. Yet, while there are more than half a dozen new editions of his *Vespers* on the market, and the *Combattimento* has been performed again, little of this has achieved lasting success. Heinrich Schütz has perhaps fared somewhat better, though he too has remained an exotic and rare figure in the repertoire. Yet both, in their own time, were great masters. Nor should the Handel renaissance after the First World War be forgotten. This seemed to give a new lease of life to his operas with all their pompous splendour and much magnificent music, but within a few years they had lapsed again into obscurity.

The tendency to turn to forgotten music becomes more doubtful if works are resurrected which were considered even in their own time to be of second rank. When the fiftieth anniversary of Verdi's death was celebrated in Italy a leading critic said to me, 'You know how this is done? None of his masterpieces is being played. In Turin they do *I due Foscari*, which makes the Milanese wonder whether they could not find something worse and so *they* do *I Masnadieri* which, in turn, makes the Romans very cross because they know an opera which is worse still and *they* do *Il finto Stanislao*. And so we are reminded, on this festive occasion, that Verdi could be a very bad composer too.'

Nor is it only the lesser works of great composers which have been revived; lesser composers too, such as Albinoni, Johann Christian Bach, Stamitz and so forth have been re-edited, and in the last forty years publishers have been flooded with offers, many of which have been accepted. Only the French seem to have withstood the onslaught. Among all the discoveries only one, Bizet's C-major symphony, has come to stay; and that was discovered by a practical musician, not by a historian.

Musical life today is full of contradictions, and the historical approach is one of the most characteristic. We are searching and fighting with ever-increasing desperation for an adequate musical expression of ourselves in our new world. So can it help to hark back to a time which, despite every effort, remains irretrievably lost? There is no wisdom, no lasting perception in music, only the mood of a single period, a single generation, which cannot be recaptured by a different generation in different circumstances. Musicology, whether devoted to the re-establishment of the pure texts of old music or to the exhumation of music long forgotten, achieves the opposite of what it intends by carefully exposing every wrinkle and every grey hair. It has been the most endearing charm of music that it is young and remains young; it is a melancholy undertaking to prove that this goddess, too, can age.

5. THE MUSIC PUBLISHER: II

O nce the drab, misprint-ridden copies leave the press the publisher starts his real task of distributing them and making the work known and, if possible, famous. It is a noble purpose, beset by problems and obstacles.

Generally, the publisher is still thought of as the purveyor of printed sheet music. Indeed, selling music and no more has been his traditional business since the day in about 1503 when Ottaviano Petrucci of Venice offered the first printed sheets of music for sale. It was early days, music was a small art, and music printer-publishers with their small trade were accordingly small and insignificant people. It was only when music grew in stature and size during the seventeenth and eighteenth centuries that its public also grew and the trade began to flourish.

The public which brought this about was composed, as it had to be, of non-professional music-lovers and performers. Then, as today, professional musicians could not alone sustain a trade as such. The amateur performer was the principal customer; the fate of the musical art and of all those who served it, composers, publishers, dealers and instrument-makers, was in his hands. It is well known how music-making spread from *collegia musica* to the palaces of kings and noblemen and from those palaces to the humbler dwellings of a prosperous bourgeoisie; how the comparatively few professionals became, as it were, demonstrators who taught the amateur to sing or to play an instrument.

While minor composers were usually careful not to overtax the ability of the amateur who was to buy their works, great composers showed no such consideration. Not surprisingly, perhaps, the technical capabilities of the amateur grew to meet the demands made upon him, and he kept well abreast of the development of the art. Amateurs throughout the nineteenth century could sing the most difficult arias and play the most difficult sonatas and concertos and therefore bought the music. Only in rare and special cases in the late eighteenth and early nineteenth centuries did the publisher or the composer safeguard himself by opening a subscription and printing the names of the subscribers as a kind of roll of honour at the head of the published copies.

In the other arts the amateur is often an object of disdain and derision. But it was to him that music owed its real life. His history ought to be written in greater detail and the memorial which he deserves erected to him.

In the first half of the nineteenth century all this was at its best. Instruments were greatly improved—none more so than the piano, which had risen from the ranks to become the favourite of the time, soon to be found in every better-class home. Chamber music, too, was widespread, while singing was a natural part of the education of well-bred people. It is characteristic of the growth of the trade that in 1837 an aria from one of Albert Lortzing's charming, trivial and highly successful operas sold 20,000 copies. The population had only to grow, as in fact it did, to make the music trade a major field of commerce. The nineteenth century was its golden age. My London printer used to tell me how he opened his printing-plant with a first order for 5,000 copies of the English vocal score of *Pagliacci*. And the boom spilt over into the first years of this century: at an exhibition in Vienna in the early 1920s the publisher of *The Merry Widow* could show statistics of the trainloads of vocal scores, piano scores, separate pieces and arrangements of all sorts which had been sold during a few years.

Those days are past and gone, as if they had never been. As usual it was a variety of causes which began to undermine the music trade after the First World War. Broadcasting, which left the book trade unharmed, struck the music trade a heavy blow. The still imperfect but much-improved gramophone record was another contributory factor. But it was the part played by music itself which, in the end, proved decisive. It slipped out of the hands of the amateur. He had grappled successfully with the mounting difficulties of music throughout the nineteenth century and had even mastered Wagner. Now, in the early 1920s, it became too much for him. The new music, whether atonal or twelve-tonal or even traditional, was too highly professional and offered him little or no access. In the nineteenth century it was contemporary, new music which kept enthusiasm for the art burning. But after the Great War the amateur was thrown back on older music, receiving no fresh encouragement from the music of the day. It is not difficult to sympathize with this today: the uncertain beginnings of the 1920s have become the stark reality of the 1960s.

The music trade soon felt the pinch. Sales began to drop, though the drop was at first selective. There were still plenty of children starting music lessons in the traditional way, and easy music for beginners did not immediately suffer. Even Chopin's mazurkas and waltzes held their own but his ballads, scherzi and rondos did not. The day came when publishers of 'classical editions' had the greatest difficulty in deciding whether to reprint the second volume of Beethoven's piano sonatas. Chamber music, the greatest treasure of European music, became a real dilemma for the publisher. Within a few years wide gaps opened in the catalogues which were never to be filled again. Today only a handful of the once numerous 'classical editions' survive, and catalogues are markedly reduced.

Quite recently it has been said that the music-publishers are failing in their moral duty by allowing old masterpieces to run out of print. The works quoted as examples were Bizet's *La Jolie Fille de Perth*, which Sir Thomas Beecham wished to perform; Rossini's *Otello*, which was revived in Rome after being ousted by Verdi's mighty opera three-quarters of a century ago; Schubert's complete *Rosamunde* music and even Mozart's *Il rè pastore*. In none of these cases were vocal scores available, while full scores and orchestral parts could be obtained only with considerable difficulty.

Though this was certainly sad the responsibility rests not with the publishers but with the public. All these works are 'in the public domain'. They have by no means disappeared: scores can be found and copied in every important public library and parts can be written out by anyone, although by no means cheaply. But some publisher somewhere would surely reprint them if there were enough customers to buy copies. To pretend that the 'original' publisher has an obligation to keep in print works which have lapsed into the public domain and thence into disuse is foolish, and the accusation that by not reprinting them he is abusing his monopoly is even more so, because this monopoly comes to an end with the copyright. The hard fact must be faced—and it is harder for the publisher than for the few enthusiasts still buying music— that the once very large number of sheet-music buyers has dwindled to the few who for one reason or another need it: professionals, teachers and students. Gone are the days when, at Christmas, music-publishers issued splendid volumes beautifully bound in linen or leather which were favourite gifts. In music-publishing Christmas now passes unnoticed, and records have taken the place of printed music.

If the music-publisher, whether serious or popular, still had the dignified composure which he once shared with the book-publisher, simply selling music and leaving it to its fate, both he and his composers would end up in the workhouse.

There was a time, between the wars, when it was believed that publicity could halt this process. Posters were printed extolling the pleasures of 'music in the home'. 'Days of Home Music' were arranged, with lectures and model performances, and much money was spent by both publishers and dealers in exhorting people not to abandon the old methods of music-making. It was all in vain.

It was not only the technically difficult works of the classical and Romantic masters which went out of print; there also disappeared from the market other categories of works which had made great contributions to the livelihood of composers, publishers and music-dealers.

Foremost among them was the enormous literature of 'salon' and 'recital' pieces of the type of 'The Maiden's Prayer' by a Polish lady called Badarzewska, the disappearance of which roused no regret. But this treasure-house of cheap melodies and fake brilliance served to keep the less erudite amateur in close touch with music. It was by no means confined to Germany, although composers such as Brinley Richards, W. V. Wallace or MacDowell were certainly anxious to have their works published in that promised land. I should perhaps apologize for including MacDowell, but there were quite a few otherwise more ambitious composers among the contributors: Wieniawski, Anton Rubinstein, Tchaikovsky. I remember myself playing Rubinstein's 'Trot de Cavalerie' and Tchaikovsky's 'Troika', which were 'salon' pieces par excellence, and also 'The Silver Brook' by one Fritz Spindler— Op. 254, no less. Indeed, the most popular composers had a truly phenomenal output, which indicates the distribution of this kind of music. I possess a fair collection of that gigantic literature, which, although mostly published in Germany, had a marked preference for French titles and advertisements. *Nouveautés!, Grands Succès*: so run the bold-type legends on the back pages of pieces like 'La Chasse aux papillons' by Nicolai von Wilm, Op. 198, No. 6, or O. Hackh, 'Le Chant de la fileuse', Op. 104, or Theodore Oesten, 'Bocage de roses', Op. 404.

Victorian and Edwardian art and craft seem to have been rediscovered lately. This music belongs to that period. It is a chapter in the history of musical culture which found its purely Anglo-

Saxon manifestation in the equally enormous quantity of ballads published at the same time in Britain and the United States. It was an ominous pointer to the decline of everything which had made music a great art.

If nobody regrets the utter destruction of 'salon' music, I for one deplore the loss of another large genre which fell a victim to the changes in musical life: the many arrangements of symphonic and chamber music for piano solo, piano duet and two pianos which were an essential part of the catalogues of classical and romantic music. They provided the amateur with an intimate knowledge of works which were otherwise beyond his active participation. I myself owe much to these arrangements, and so must many others of my age. Now that they are no longer available they are scorned by puritans and historians. People, they say, should not tamper with the originals. And only the originals will do.

Yet such arrangements have a perfectly respectable ancestry, of which fact the historians at least should be aware. Beethoven was a diligent arranger of his own works, arranging or transcribing the Piano Trio, Op. 1, No. 3, and the Octet, Op. 103, for string quintet, the Piano Sonata, Op. 14, No. 1, for string quartet, the String Quintet, Op. 16, for piano quartet and the Second Symphony for piano trio. He also approved many arrangements, particularly of the Septet, for a variety of combinations and for no other purpose than to make these works accessible to the widest possible circle of amateurs. In his Paris days Richard Wagner too made a living from arranging such things as the overture to Donizetti's *La favorita* for string quartet.

The desire for such practical arrangements, and the better knowledge derived from them, continued up to the beginning of this century. The symphonic poems of Richard Strauss and the symphonies of Gustav Mahler were still issued arranged for piano solo or duet and for two pianos. That marked virtually the limit of what was reasonably playable on the piano. But after the First World War all this came quickly to an end. New music did not lend itself readily to transcription. Even professional coaches had great difficulties with the vocal score of *Wozzeck*. But the existing transcriptions of classical and romantic music also vanished for lack of interest: remaining copies were pulped, existing plates melted down. It was the end of a whole epoch of musical culture.

Gradually, however, new forms of sheet music began to appear which to a modest extent made up for the losses of the music trade.

The most respectable of the newcomers was the pocket- or study-score. While the amateur could still play chamber music and symphonic works in practical arrangements he had been little interested in scores, which were regarded as the tools of the professional. In 1866 an Englishman, Albert Payne, invented the pocket score and established himself—characteristically—in Germany rather than in England. It was not his intention to replace any existing full scores by small-size reproductions designed not for conducting or playing but for reading. He only printed scores of chamber music, which had traditionally never been published in score form but only in parts. It was certainly both interesting and useful to see Beethoven's Great Fugue in score for the first time. The success of these little yellow books was so encouraging that Payne's successors introduced orchestral works into the series, the purpose and usefulness of which was not immediately apparent. But as the popularity of live music in the home waned, so the demand for pocket-scores increased, and the original publisher now finds himself up against a large number of competitors, both in Europe and in America. Old and new music is now issued in study-score form; musical erudition has replaced the dexterity of the amateur musician of yesterday.

I wish I could welcome this change as enthusiastically as others have. How many non-professional music-lovers can really read a score? Even professionals such as Sergei Prokofiev had their troubles with 'transposing' instruments and wrote their scores 'in C', with each instrument as it actually sounds, though they were not so printed because conductors insisted on 'transposing' instruments being engraved in their proper pitch. For the amateur score-reader this can be most confusing. He will be able to cope with J. S. Bach, Handel, Haydn, Mozart and Beethoven, but where the orchestration itself is of special interest, as with Berlioz or Wagner—not to mention Debussy, Richard Strauss or Stravinsky—he will have to be content with following a melodic line. And if, in still more modern music, there is no such line, I wonder what real benefit he can derive from the score. There can be little doubt that the man who could play Siegfried's Journey to the Rhine from Klindworth's piano arrangement knew infinitely more about it than the imperfect score-reader of today. Yet it remains true that the score is the only publishable—and saleable—form of serious and, particularly, new music.

If the pocket-score brought some relief to the ailing music trade, another way of making music between the wars contributed more to mitigating the loss of sales: the accordion. For the old-fashioned amateur of the nineteenth century music-making was a matter of comparative solitude. In the changing world after the First World War solitude was no longer desirable, and as music can serve the most diverse needs it helped the headlong flight from solitude as much as, in different circumstances, it had promoted seclusion. Mass music became a slogan and the accordion became its champion. It was like an infectious disease, spreading within a few years over the whole world. Cleverly sponsored organizations, clubs and groups created a passionate interest in the instrument, which had to be both cheaper and easier to play than the instruments built by skilled artisans in and around Ancona. Accordion manufacture became a major industry, and the whole Black Forest resounded with the din of machines producing hundreds of thousands of these instruments, in all sizes.

The accordion had its idealists, who believed that it was capable of artistic achievements. In Trossingen I heard quite an impressive performance of a Bach fugue by the Hohner Concert Orchestra, a large assembly of accordions. Hindemith, Richard Strauss and Stravinsky were among those asked for original compositions, which they did not supply. The instrument was obviously destined by providence to remain in the cosier regions of entertainment and, removed from the interest of puritans, could enjoy transcriptions which were beneath the dignity of more noble instruments. New publishers and a large, new and inexpensive literature sprang up and kept the trade busy.

Even after the Second World War it seemed briefly that the accordion was still with us, and always would be. But, mysteriously, it lost its hold and vanished. The young took to the guitar—again, not the venerable, beautiful Spanish instrument as played by Segovia but a poor and cheap relation which supplies the 'beat' and does not even require printed music at all. In the last ten years millions of these guitars have been made and sold, with no benefit to music proper or to the music trade.

Between the wars a movement began which aimed at introducing music into schools as a regular subject. This movement increased greatly after the Second World War and is no longer a matter for debate but an accepted fact of life. It could not make up for everything the music trade had lost, but it opened up a new field to publishers and dealers which holds out great promise.

Much is expected of music as a part of the curriculum of compulsory education—Zoltán Kodály, in the preface to one of his educational works, expressed his belief that the harmony of music would one day produce harmony between peoples.

As far as school was concerned, my generation grew up without music. There was some primitive and unorganized singing in the lower forms of the grammar school I attended. The teacher, who also taught such optional subjects as shorthand and calligraphy, was about the least respected member of the staff, as we boys soon found out, and this was one more reason for us not to take singing seriously. During our last four years at school, after our voices broke, there was no more mention of music. Our teachers behaved as if it did not exist at all. We heard much about Homer and Sophocles, Shakespeare and la Fontaine, Goethe and Schiller, but the names of Bach and Mozart were never mentioned. Incidentally, I do not remember having heard the names of Leonardo or Michelangelo in school either.

My generation has not acquitted itself well. Two world wars and the monstrous atrocities that accompanied them do no credit either to the perpetrators or to their victims. It is, therefore, understandable enough that the new educators of a new generation should look for new and better ways of education and should choose music, assuming that an average gift for music is no rarer than a similar gift for mathematics, which every child must learn. It is a laudable purpose partly to tempt and partly to coerce children to make music, although music has never shown itself apt to improve either mind or character. If mankind could really be bettered through music a generation of archangels should now be growing up. Yet juvenile delinquency seems to be rampant in spite or because of the boom in music. I say this with no intention of disparaging music or of discouraging its introduction into the syllabus, but one should not expect something from an art that is not in its nature. Music is neither moral nor immoral, but *extramoral*. Until quite recently it was considered a valid expression of every kind of emotion, good or wicked. Verdi's Iago is musically as important and perfect as his Desdemona. And our new music has discovered—not for the first time in history—that music can with equal validity express complete emotional indifference. This inherent versatility should never be forgotten by those who pin great hopes on music as an educational medium.

But music is certainly as worthy a subject as any other taught in schools, and the school music movement has made great strides. In the United States there are 71,000 school orchestras and high-school bands, with more than 5,000,000 active members. Music plays a similar part in Scandinavian schools and in other countries. An international organization, *Jeunesses Musicales*, has sprung up, which aims at a natural contact between man and music. While all these new developments are unable to soften the frightening impact of 'pop' music and groups on the young, they at least educate a few of them in serious music.

This great movement, however, suffers from one major disadvantage: the prominent composers of our time seem not to be interested. Their mistrust of the accordion was understandable, but the recorder, the school orchestra and even the school band deserve contributions from the best composers to give them a sense of importance. The sporadic attempts of Hindemith and Britten are too few and too insignificant. In the main schools live on second-rate music of the seventeenth and eighteenth centuries, on transcriptions and arrangements far worse than the discredited piano versions of chamber and symphonic works, or on irrelevant original compositions by composers of no standing.

The only exception, and a most notable one, is the work of the late Zoltán Kodály, who devoted the greater part of his active life to the musical education of the young. His principles, though, do not quite conform to those of the school orchestra movement. He was primarily concerned with singing rather than with instrumental music, and his views and methods have spread far beyond his own country. He sacrificed much of his own creative talent in this cause and wrote hundreds of exercises and part-songs to implement his ideas of musical education. But apart from this one solitary effort school music has been neglected by the outstanding composers of our time and, with an artistically poor repertoire at its disposal, it cannot fill the gap left by the disappearance of the knowledgeable and technically efficient amateur of yesterday.

*

Neither pocket-scores nor school music could prevent a sharp decline in the sheet-music trade. If the new methods of listening to music had not come to his rescue with records, record-players, radio and television sets and tape-recorders the dealer might have disappeared altogether. There are already countries where one has to travel far to find a man who bothers to stock sheet music.

As a consequence, print numbers are much smaller than is generally realized. Although printers are busy they are printing more titles in smaller quantities than fifty years ago. The publisher's problem then was to print large quantities economically and offset printing came as a welcome aid. The problem now is to determine the smallest quantities which can still be printed at a price which will not be prohibitive.

This applies to popular as well as serious music. Before the Second World War, when sales had already declined seriously, hit songs still enjoyed a wide circulation. If the amateur could no longer cope with Brahms he could still deal adequately with 'Valencia' or 'The Lambeth Walk'. Prints of half a million copies of a smash hit were not unusual. A few thousand records were sold, too, which was welcome if financially unimportant. This situation has now been reversed. A top hit today sells a million or more records, while only a few thousand printed copies find their way to the public. Orchestrations of hits, which were once in great demand, are now hardly ever printed. In most cases a 'conductor' part is enough for any dance-band to use as a basis for improvisation. There can be no question of any sale. Dance-bands have no standard composition which would make printed orchestrations useful. Broadcasters employing a considerable number of bands insist on variety of sound and style to such an extent that the same pop tune played by two different bands is hardly recognizable. Therefore no more is needed than a hint, in the shape of a conductor part, which is usually given away free by the publisher.

As far as serious music is concerned almost all the music destined for music-making in the home has become unsaleable. Songs, instrumental and chamber music are to all intents and purposes dead. There are few editions of the most famous classical and romantic works still in print, and new works in these categories have no hope of becoming known. A few years ago French publishers approached their Ministry of Fine Arts for a subsidy for the printing of contemporary music. Enclosed with their application was a list from which one learnt with dismay that an outstanding piano work by one of the most prominent composers of our time had sold only eight hundred copies in seventeen years, a piano sonata by a young and very promising composer only a single copy in one year, and the vocal score of an internationally successful opera only twenty-four copies. The Ministry declined any subsidy, and, I believe, rightly so. It would have made printing easier, or at any rate possible, but would have contributed nothing to the sales. This music could not be sold at the price of a bus-ticket. One has to realize that a wide and once highly cultivated and fertile area of musical life has been laid waste. Songs, instrumental and chamber music were the happy children of very personal and widely practised music-making. With the disappearance of this practice they, too, inevitably disappeared.

Orchestral scores of works by prominent composers are printed in quantities of 200 or 250 copies, and this is usually sufficient for many years. If the composer is not well known 50 copies will often suffice, the majority of which are given away. Pocket- or study-scores of new works by well-known composers are printed in quantities ranging from 500 to 1,000 copies, and some even enjoy a reprint of 500 copies, which in most cases marks the virtual end of their career. But even pocket-scores of the established old master-works drag their feet and the publisher is often tempted to let them run out of print.

This, I believe, is one of the most momentous changes within the art itself. I have mentioned before that the amateur musician of yesterday has become the passive listener and, to a lesser degree, the passive reader of today. It is a grotesque thought that this listener or reader will never comprehend a work of music on his own account; that an interpreter will always stand between him and it. Until the turn of the century or thereabouts it was the glory of music—of *every* type of music—to become the personal property of those who loved it. Now it has become a large inanimate object to be exhibited to an enormous, passive audience. And if, for lack of personal contact, the knowledge of older music becomes more and more superficial, new music hardly ever penetrates to the public consciousness at all.

Masterpieces have been written in the last fifty years which receive more performances than Beethoven's symphonies could boast in their time. Stravinsky's *Rite of Spring* or Bartók's Concerto for Orchestra are played hundreds of times every year in every corner of the world, and every concert-goer must have heard them over and over again. Thousands of records and study-scores are in circulation. Should the present-day music-lover not know them as well as his predecessor fifty years ago knew the symphonies of Brahms? Yet how many are there who could whistle even one motive or play it with one finger on the piano? If, on hearing it again, they recognize the work they can be truly proud of themselves. Again, is the general knowledge of Berg's *Wozzeck* comparable with the knowledge of Wagner's *Ring* at the beginning of this century? It is certainly true that music has become very complicated. Yet I wonder whether *Wozzeck*, forty years after its première, is more difficult for us than *Tristan* was at the beginning of this century. Contemporaries always found new music too difficult. There were a confusing number of notes in Mozart's *Entführung*; Beethoven's Violin Concerto was considered unplayable; it was said that *Parsifal* could not be learnt by heart and, therefore, could not be performed. Has new music really become more complicated than modern science, which is understood by its students as readily as our generation understood the simpler physics of Newton and the chemistry of Lavoisier?

Complication is not the real trouble; this lies in the fact that the average cultured man or woman looks not for knowledge but for information, quick and comfortable information which is the true purpose of mass education. It is information and not knowledge which broadcasting scatters abroad over countries and continents; and for such information new music, like new science, is too complicated. On average we are much less educated than our fathers were half a century ago. They knew more about the technicalities and physical principles of the telephone and telegraph than we know about sound broadcasting and television, or about biology and chemistry, which today have become almost inaccessible to the layman. This ought not to apply to any art, and particularly not to music.

But it does. In spite of the omnipresence and fantastic quantity of serious music flooding our daily life it recedes to the periphery of our consciousness. How music, removed from living re-creation by the millions for whom it is destined, can flourish only the future will show. The absence of personal participation, however, uncovers one of the roots of the problem which threatens our serious new music today.

Since the disappearance of the amateur musician and, with him, of the sales of sheet music, public performance has become the principal purpose of music—performance in the theatre and concert-hall, on sound and television broadcasting, in dance-halls, restaurants, bars and night-clubs, live or from discs and tapes, as background in films, as salesman for a wide range of non-musical objects such as food, detergents, drink and cigarettes. Indeed, this most 'useless' art has developed an astonishing usefulness, and it is for the publisher to find—within the limits of respectability—all the wide gaps and the little crannies through which music flows or oozes into daily life.

Though music can no longer provide its creators and their agents with a living in the old legitimate way it has become capable of great commercial achievements. No other art has, in fact, been so commercialized. Money is the yardstick by which its success and, occasionally, its value are measured. Once created, published and publicized a work of music, whatever its nature, must make money or it fails utterly.

Popular music, indeed, has no other purpose. This has become one of a few types in which the individual work means as little or as much as the individual ant in an ant-hill. The directness, bordering on effrontery, with which it pursues its commercial purpose and demands money for its not inconsiderable services must fill every publisher of serious music with envy. Between the 'popular' publisher and his authors—and there are many authors, sometimes half a dozen for a song of two and a half minutes' duration—there is an admirable agreement about their hopes and ambitions: they all want to make a lot of money and they want to make it quickly. Anyone who thinks otherwise is badly mistaken, and, whereas the mistakes of serious composers and publishers are occasionally overlooked, in the world of popular music they are unforgivable. But anyone who believes that he need only write a pop-song in order to make a fortune is also mistaken. Every profession requires its own standard of perfection, however high or low that standard may be. This requirement is even more ruthless than usual in popular music, because only the immediately successful song really registers. Being ephemeral, it is given no time to prove its worth as a work of serious art is. The life of a song—and only one of the best songs, at that—is the hectic, golden life of a day-fly. In a few weeks it must complete its life-cycle, from its launching to its arrival at the top of the charts and thence to ultimate oblivion—leaving a trail of money behind it.

Therefore the publisher must be extremely quick off the mark, and must not lose an instant. In a matter of days the work is 'produced', usually in the form of a conductor part which indicates no more than the intentions of the composer. These are then interpreted by the various band-leaders with complete disregard for the composer, who in turn is sincerely grateful for their indifference. Then the publisher's 'pluggers' go to work. They are the men who have all the contacts, who know the singers, the band-leaders, the programme producers on radio and television, the places of entertainment, night-clubs and restaurants with music or floor-shows. The plugger must first of all find a prominent singer, male or female, who likes the song. These singers are specialists—in sentimentality, in suggestive humour, in calculated indifference or in sensual rhythm—and the good plugger must know whom to approach. A good pop-singer is by no means a hack, incapable of singing in the conventional sense. A tormented, hoarse voice requires talent and much hard work, and there is more 'interpretation' in the rendering of a pop-song than in that of a symphony.

The singer is the most important contact. If he or she is sufficiently well known he or she has an exclusive contract with a record-manufacturer, and that manufacturer, too, is in a breathless hurry. Any serious music which may at the critical moment be ready for recording or pressing is ruthlessly shelved to make room for the popular arrival. In a few days the record is 'on the market' and the plugger begins the second phase of his task. The bands and the disc-jockeys are his next 'plugs'. Here, ethics and morality become somewhat loose. The habit of bribery has grown to such proportions that some European broadcasting organizations have had to introduce a system of control in order to limit the abuse of an abuse: the band-leader with an engagement on radio or television receives from the publisher a certain amount as a fee for the special arrangement of the music which suits his band best, and undertakes to perform the song a certain number of times. It is all well designed and calculated.

The disc-jockey, on the other hand, is an important link in the radio chain, riding his disc as a jockey rides to win the Derby. He must be very knowledgeable in the field of popular music, he must know the latest fashions and trends, the successful composers, lyric-writers and record issues anywhere in the world, and with the enormous stream of popular music being thrown 'on the market' it is no mean task to keep the recorded programmes up to date. And the fate of a new song largely depends on his benevolence.

When all this is done—the singer found, the record on sale, the band-leaders engaged and the disc-jockey won over—the engine starts running at full speed. If the song is a hit authors, publisher and record-manufacturer never have to wait long for their customers. The publisher, in particular, starts the foreign exploitation. He usually has permanent contacts in the most important countries, and within a few days of its birth the song appears abroad in the versions of the sub-publishers. Though music is international pop-songs are international only with considerable reservations. They cannot simply be translated. They have to conform to other tastes and temperaments, they must be adapted, a process which starts with the title. There is nothing sacred about the 'original', if indeed an original exists at all. The adaptation requires the same knowledge of the public in a foreign land as the original publisher possesses in his own country—and that, in nine cases out of ten, means the United States. Questions of an author's 'moral right' do not arise. Anything which helps to create success is welcome. There are quite a few cases where it is the adaptation and not the original which makes its mark—a cleverly chosen title, clever new lyrics, perhaps a lucky chance—so many imponderables surround the success of a pop-song. And everywhere the same hurried procedure is followed that brought the precious original into being. The number of people involved grows to a sizeable crowd— authors and co-authors, adaptors, publishers and sub-publishers— and the material benefits spread far and wide. Within a few weeks the new hit is heard from the North Cape to the South Pole, from Oklahoma to Yokohama, and all the new means of communication around the globe are put to work. A few weeks later all is over, and the song is forgotten. Hardly one in a thousand survives to become an 'evergreen'. For the crowd at the gates is tremendous. The popular publisher has to produce several hundred songs a year if he is to have a reasonable chance of finding among the flock of wild geese the one that lays the golden egg. In 1964 for instance British record-manufacturers issued about 4,000 pop-songs, of which only 34 climbed to be number one in the hit parade. The great majority died in the cradle.

I do not understand this type of music and I do not know how well the experts understand it. Perhaps it is not so very different from serious music, where the bad can be recognized with a fair measure of certainty while the good is less easily detectable. Occasionally I watch a BBC programme called 'Juke Box Jury' where a panel of experts—singers, disc-jockeys and experienced teenagers—listen to the latest records and decide which will become hits and which misses. I find it most reassuring that they rarely agree among themselves.

How different it all is in the case of the serious music-publisher! There is no need for this headlong haste. Serious works are created *sub specie aeternitatis*. Untouchable as they are, they look much more delicate than their popular relations, but they are, in fact, much more robust. Serious composers share the general impatience of the time and cannot let their new works rest. To wait three years for the first performance of a new piano concerto, like Beethoven, or fifteen years for that of an opera, like Wagner, would seem impossible to them. In his most productive years Benjamin Britten fixed the first-performance dates of his operas before he had started composing them and said that this stimulated

his inspiration. It is, in fact, seldom possible to delay a first performance until the work is really ready.

The public performance of a dramatic or symphonic work is the
first step in its career. Performance on the radio does not really
produce the same result. The Press usually takes little notice of
broadcasts, and for the listener the performance remains too
impersonal and anonymous to arouse his interest as it would if he
met it face-to-face in the concert-hall. The records which so
greatly smooth the path of popular songs do not come into the
picture, for no power on earth could persuade a manufacturer to
record an unknown and unperformed piece. Even a new work by
Stravinsky has to earn its laurels in performance before it is considered worthy of recording. The risk is the publisher's alone.

It is not, however, as difficult to obtain a first performance as is
generally believed. The idea that a new work of serious music is
beset with difficulties from its birth is not quite correct. It is true
that star performers, conductors and instrumentalists guard their
own popularity jealously and usually care little for new works
because they do not wish their names to be associated with possible
failures. This was not always so; certainly not in the nineteenth
century nor even between the wars when conductors such as
Koussevitzky, Ansermet, Kleiber and Klemperer were little concerned about their reputations. Nowadays new works have to be
satisfied with the patronage of lesser conductors, but these lesser
conductors are more than keen on first performances and are not
easily discouraged even by musical absurdities. A work which
cannot find a first performance today must be bad or extravagant
beyond all belief.

This is a considerable advantage. Forty years ago when the
conspiracy against all tradition in music began and aroused widespread opposition, there were a few conductors who joined the new
composers in storming the barricades. But this was of little avail.
The great majority of conductors, concert promoters and critics
and, of course, the public were quick to dismiss the unusual as
bad and to have nothing to do with it. So an International Society
for New Music was founded, which, with much enthusiasm and
little money, arranged annual festivals so that the composers and
their friends, at least, could hear the new works. These festivals
were not very festive, lacking as they did the material opulence
that festivals require, and the public, by avoiding them, fortified
and confirmed the beliefs of the promoters. But as a narrow back
door to musical life they were important, and many names which

appeared there for the first time have become household words in contemporary music. The Society still exists and still arranges its festivals, and the public continues to show the same indifference. But the Society's services are really no longer required. The lesser conductors and opera-houses, with their better financial backing, are always on the look-out for first performances and are numerous enough, and even when a new work fails there are always a few words of faint praise for the man who first had the courage to present it in public and so entered it in the official register of musical births.

The first performance, then, presents no undue difficulty; but the second is a much rarer and much more decisive event. Now the work no longer has the distinction of being a discovery, which camouflages many a failure at the first performance; after the first performance of the work it has taken off its baptismal robe and is expected to make a good impression, so to speak, in its working-clothes. It will be more thoroughly and more severely examined and people will want to know what the experts and the public thought of it when they first heard it. For between the first and second performances stands the menacing figure of the critic. He has not been consulted before the first performance, but with the second he has had his say, and often enough his verdict has been the kiss of death.

The busy world of popular music hardly knows him. Popular songs are sometimes criticized in specialist papers, and in a jargon comprehensible only to the expert, but the public at large is not interested in the critic. It needs no recommendation or explanation, but reacts to a new song instantly, expertly and irrevocably.

But with serious music the layman looks, for instruction and advice, to a man whose profession and task it is to listen to music day by day, to study and analyse it, and so to acquire if not a superior judgement at least an incomparable depth of experience.

The institution of *regular* music criticism is not very old, not much more than a hundred and twenty-five years. Music itself had to grow in importance and size in order to justify public verdicts. But the critic has been a man of prominence, inseparable from musical life, for more than a century. Composers, performers and publishers meet him in an atmosphere of love-hate and few of them remain unruffled by bad notices or unflattered by good ones. To the end of his life Wilhelm Furtwängler used to read, with pride or fury, every line written about him. Even such a warrior as Stravinsky, bearing the scars of innumerable critical attacks, allows himself now and then to be drawn into skirmishes with the Press, which, by virtue of its commanding position, always has the last word. Richard Strauss in his best years used to say that he always had a bad Press but wrote good music. But in the last years of his life he, too, could lose his temper.

There have been critics of various kinds: laymen such as Bernard Shaw, who were more securely guided by their instinct than many an expert; composers such as Robert Schumann, who said the nicest things about music generally but suffered from bias and prejudice; and learned music critics like Fétis or Hanslick, whose misjudgements could be quite monumental. It is the Hanslicks who eventually have held the field, while the laymen and the practising musicians have withdrawn.

What useful function does the critic perform and how important is it?

Those immediately concerned, composers and performers, are inclined to deny that the critic is either useful or important. They never forget any mistake a member of the profession may have made in the past if it will serve to prove their point. This has given rise to much inconclusive discussion. It is indeed not easy for the critic to be fair in his judgement, nor is it easy for the criticized to be fair to the critic. It is taken for granted that the critic is a fount of all available knowledge and experience, but complete objectivity is beyond human capacity. The critic is no computer throwing out an entirely impersonal answer to the question fed into it. There were, and perhaps still are, critics who guarded their independence carefully. Ernest Newman, one of the most prominent critics of his time, refused to make the personal acquaintance of any composer. But even that did not prevent him having his musical preferences and idiosyncrasies, like everyone else.

The critic is also an individual man or woman, not *vox populi*. He is not representative of the public, and often enough is in open conflict with it. The public, for example, liked Wagner's music from the outset, but Hanslick did not. On the other hand, when it came to Brahms the public and Hanslick were in complete agreement.

There is, however, an undeniable air of authority about the writings of a music critic (though the writer often remains anonymous) in the distinguished periodicals or daily papers, and it is this unfounded authority which concerns his heroes or victims. But the music-lover likes to compare his own impression with that of an expert. Although periodicals have only a limited circulation, and while only a fraction of the readers of daily papers may read the music column, music criticism constitutes part of the cultural duty of any reputable paper and no editor could afford to do without it.

As for the usefulness of music criticism, there is no question that it affects the careers of composers and performers; in the case of performers it may even have a decisive influence. As far as new works are concerned, however, that influence should not be over-rated. Certainly the critic who cannot make up his mind whether to call a work good or bad is failing in his critical function. But the best notice cannot make a work better than it really is, even if, for a limited time, it provides it with an undeserved aura of success. Conversely, a bad notice may delay a second performance but will not, in the end, prevent it. The assumption that the critic informs and guides the public is quite misleading. Whatever the critic may write, the public is the supreme judge and can be neither influenced nor confused by expert opinion. One need only recall what the critics, or the great majority of them, wrote about Stravinsky's *Rite of Spring* in 1913. But the work came to stay, and to be accepted as a masterpiece. There was a time, in the 1880s, when the critics thought that Joachim Raff's symphonies were as good as those of Brahms. And where is Raff now? All this has been proved over and over again. From experience, and with a touch of cynicism, I can say that a really destructive notice is as good for promotion as an enthusiastically good one. As a publisher I cannot do without the critic. He is more often a help, however involuntarily, than a hindrance.

But the profession of the music critic could well be improved, to the benefit of all concerned. He is very often in a much worse position than his colleagues in literature and art. A literary work can usually be understood at a first reading or hearing; a work of the visual arts can be studied as long as necessary and in every detail until the critic can form a considered opinion. The music critic, however, often meets a new work only at a fleeting first performance. Very seldom does he have an opportunity to study a score beforehand. Particularly with new music, an unprepared hearing conveys little information. One should not blame the publisher. In the general rush to give new works their first performance, he only rarely has time enough to print a score and distribute review copies. Many composers, among them Stravinsky, want to hear their works before they will allow them to be printed. Many months often elapse after the first performance before the critic can see a printed copy.

Moreover, the critic is subject to certain journalistic rules which, though they may be good for the local reporter who has to be on the heels of every robbery and every fire, are harmful to music criticism. The critic frequently has to rush from the concert-hall or opera-house to his office or to the nearest telephone-box so that people next morning may be certain of reading his assessment of a new work. Curious things sometimes happen. When Benjamin Britten's *Rape of Lucretia* was first performed in New York, the leading music critic of the time, Olin Downes, declared the following morning that *Lucretia* was a masterpiece and probably the best opera of the century. This pleased the composer, his friends and his publisher so much that the article was at once duplicated and distributed all over the world. But three days later, in the Sunday issue of the *New York Times*, Downes wrote another longer and more elaborate article recanting everything he had said. On examining the vocal score—which had been in his possession for some time, but which he had not had a chance to study—he found that, far from being a masterwork, *Lucretia* was a second-rate piece. How embarrassing!

Critics should have time to think. On the morning after the performance of a new work they should simply report on the facts, so discharging the journalistic part of their task. The criticism of the work itself would not come too late if it appeared a few days later, assuming that a good critic also has a good musical memory. But the facts are often neglected. The performers always receive the attention due to them but the public hardly ever does. This is regrettable from the point of view of both publisher and promoter. Anyone who has to decide whether or not a second performance should be given would certainly be interested in the opinion of an expert (while the quality of the performance is of little importance to him), but he would also want to know how the public reacted. This the critic seldom tells him, and perhaps that is the point at which he oversteps the mark and sets himself up as sole arbiter. At the end of a bad notice one sometimes reads that the public applauded the performers and not the work. How could the critic know this? If a work fails completely there are usually no ovations for the performers either. I feel that in such cases the critic should have the courage to admit that the public does not share his opinion.

Criticism is also found where it does not belong, in dictionaries and reference-books, which should confine themselves to data and lists of works, being bought and used merely for information, not for evaluation. It is amusing to find in Riemann's famous lexicon of

1919 the following sentence about Schoenberg's *Treatise on Harmony*: 'The author's naïve admission that he has never read a history of music gives the clue to this unparalleled piece of dilettantism.' Richard Strauss fares no better, being called 'a colossus with feet of clay'. Stravinsky did not seem worth much ink and paper. After giving an incomplete list of his works performed up to that time the editor simply adds, 'Stravinsky lives at Morges, near Lausanne,' and so unwittingly did the right thing. This bad example, however, has not prevented later editors of encyclopaedias from making the same mistakes: in the second of the fifteen or sixteen volumes of the largest musical dictionary ever undertaken in Germany, one can read the utterly ill-conceived and, at best, absurdly premature comment (the volume was published in 1952) that Benjamin Britten was 'the Saint-Säens of British composers'.

Despite all this it must be said that music criticism has lost much of its old vitality and courage. Past mistakes, and particularly the experience with twelve-note music after the Second World War, may have disheartened it. When it comes to modern avant-garde music one seldom finds a clear-cut pronouncement; the critic prefers to shelter behind theoretical discussions which avoid the decisive question of whether, above and beyond technicalities, a work is good or bad. This more than anything else again raises the problem of the usefulness and importance of music criticism in our time. Where does the critic stand? Is he the representative of the public, of the listener, or is he the advocate of the composer? Should he simply explain a composer's intentions or should he also praise or condemn them, as interpreter or judge? The distinction of critical achievement, a famous German critic once said, is measured by the distance in time by which the critic is ahead of public opinion. But only the most courageous have a chance.

Once the publisher has succeeded in obtaining a second or even a third successful performance a new work can make its way through the concert-halls and opera-houses. But only a few do. Again and again it happens that a work acclaimed by Press and public, on which high hopes have been set, disappears after a few performances, while another of which little was expected achieves a resounding success. Although the works of serious music are in general sturdier than the most enduring popular hits quite a few of them suffer from a fragility that is difficult to understand. While the public never seems to tire of listening to the same works of Mozart or Beethoven, Brahms or Elgar, it is one of the greatest problems of our musical life to keep even the most successful new works in the repertoire.

In the field of opera, organizational and administrative reasons often prevent the carrying-over of a new work from one season to the next. There is hardly an opera-house left anywhere which can keep together an ensemble of principal singers and conductors for more than one season, so that if a new opera is to be repeated in the following season it will require studying and rehearsing all over again. Such works thus compare unfavourably with those of the old standard repertoire which every singer, conductor and orchestral player knows virtually by heart and which can be staged with the minimum of rehearsals. And so it regularly happens that a new opera is played half a dozen times within a few weeks, only to disappear—at best for a number of years, occasionally for ever. What a waste of time, effort and public money when, after nine months of exhausting rehearsals, Schoenberg's *Moses and Aaron* is given three performances and then not performed again! There are undoubtedly many members of the public who may not want to listen to a new opera two or three times in quick succession but would like to hear it again a year later in order to check or correct their first impression. They hardly ever get that chance. How, then, can a contemporary repertoire be assembled, as it was in the nineteenth century? Then there were many avenues by which a new and successful opera could become intimately known and popular: not only were vocal and piano scores in wide circulation but orchestras and bands in places of entertainment played selections, and singers included the favourite arias in their concerts. There was a general desire for close acquaintance which was not easily deterred by musical difficulties such as those presented by Richard Wagner and, at the end of the era, by Richard Strauss.

These avenues to popularity are now closed by the music itself. There are no selections or arias to be extracted from today's new operas. The symphonic repertoire has benefited in a few instances— Hindemith's *Mathis der Maler* symphony, Alban Berg's symphonic pieces from *Wozzeck* and *Lulu*, Britten's Interludes and Passacaglia from *Peter Grimes*. But these symphonic extracts tend to lead their own lives independent of the operas. New operas can be heard only in the opera-house, and there perennial casting difficulties prevent the frequent and regular revivals any work of new music, and new opera in particular, would require in order to become familiar to the opera-goer.

But does the opera-goer or the public in general *want* to become familiar with new works? There is some inexplicable hesitation on the part of the listeners to become closely involved in works unknown to our fathers. Even if an opera-director could and would keep a new opera in the regular repertoire he would find little support from the public. Benjamin Britten's *Peter Grimes* was one of the greatest operatic successes since Strauss's *Rosenkavalier*. After its sensational première in London in 1945 the opera was played from 1946 to 1948 in every remaining opera-house in the world, and was everywhere acclaimed with the same enthusiasm. If this had happened fifty years earlier I believe the work would have established itself as an indispensable item in the operatic repertoire. But it petered out. There were and still are isolated revivals, but the reception is much cooler than it was in the beginning and tickets are not easily sold.

This strange aloofness on the part of the public is no less apparent in the concert-hall, where no organizational problems stand in the way of regular repeat performances. Here too the most superficial acquaintance seems to satisfy the listener, and out of many excellent works written after the First World War only a comparative handful have found a permanent place in musical life. To quote only one or two outstanding examples: in the 1920s Ernest Bloch's 'Concerto Grosso' was one of the most outstanding successes but it has disappeared and attempts at reviving it have failed. Honegger's *Roi David* or *Jeanne au bûcher* are practically forgotten. A long list of similar works could be compiled which were neither common-place nor unduly demanding, yet though they once appealed to large audiences they could not be kept alive.

Superficiality and oblivion are brother and sister. In most cases the composer has only to die for his works to be soon forgotten by public, conductors and concert-promoters alike. Exceptions such as Bartók rather confirm the rule.

And so it happens that even the thirtieth performance of a new work is no guarantee of lasting success.

Old friendships, on the other hand, are unshakable, both in the opera-house and in the concert-hall, although the dividing-line between real affection and comfortable habit is not clearly defined. It may be idle to speculate why new friendships are so rare and so difficult to achieve. But one of the basic reasons is, I believe, the disappearance of the amateur musician, of the man or woman who not only listens but makes music himself—and the same type of music which he hears from the professionals; that is, new music. But new music is not written for the amateur.

The prevalence of old and familiar music does more than the comparatively rare appearance of new music to bring the performer into the centre of musical life. When the same works are performed over and over again it is not so much a question of *what* is performed as of *how*.

I have mentioned the ancillary rights of performers, and said that they provide a profound insight into present-day musical life. Indeed, the most contradictory attitudes exist here side by side. Historians and purists today insist that there should be no 'interpretation' in the true sense, that the original and unadulterated texts sufficiently express the composer's intentions and that the performer, far from being an interpreter, has to do nothing but follow the composer's instructions. Performers themselves tend to agree with this new but nevertheless sacred principle. But as soon as they do so they waive any claim to a creative contribution and therefore to any right of their own, however 'ancillary' it may be.

As so often in life, facts are stronger than theories. The idea that there should be no interpretation in music does not apply in the popular variety, where interpretation is not only permissible but essential. This is not the limited improvisation of the *taille* in old scores or of the *basso continuo*, which could vary from simple chords to an independent interpolation according to the capability of the player. In popular music the composer gives the interpreter no more than a cue, and he is welcome to any interpretation he likes, so long as it is effective. The composer, therefore, is almost insignificant. The millions who buy pop records buy them because of Bing Crosby or Duke Ellington or Sammy Davis, Jr. Popular songs are identified with their interpreters and not their composers, and fidelity to the text becomes absurd. In such cases the neighbouring or ancillary rights are well justified and closely connected with the primary authors' rights. The performer of a pop song does make a creative contribution of his own which demands and deserves recognition and remuneration.

The composer of serious music, however, found no support for his claims to an exclusive right. It is strange that a legal detour had to be made to establish that even the most carefully written musical text requires some mysterious ingredient to bring it to life, even if every detail of the performance corresponds to the indications of the score and no wilful addition or omission can be discovered. Stravinsky insists that there should be no 'interpretation' of his music. In recent years he has suppressed all tempo indications in his scores, replacing them with metronome markings to avoid any misleading 'expression' and to emphasize that performance is a mere technical process, independent of any mood, understanding or personal involvement on the part of the performer.

At this point the tyranny of performer and composer change places. Where once the performer could successfully pretend that he knew better than the composer, he is now reduced to doing as he is told. Fortunately or unfortunately, the human mind is not a mechanical device like the metronome, and accuracy in musical matters is unattainable. The simplest things are indeterminable. How loud is *forte*, how soft *piano*? And is it the same wherever it occurs? Is Schumann's 'as fast as possible' at the beginning of the G-minor Sonata followed by 'faster still' in the coda, really nonsensical, or Beethoven's *'con una certa espressione parlante'* in Opus 33, No. 6, an unmistakable, certain indication of speed and expression? Whatever composers or theorists may say, in the International Convention on the ancillary, or interpreter's, rights it is laid down in black and white that every performer must necessarily make a creative and personal contribution which is worthy of legal protection. Ernest Ansermet, himself one of the outstanding interpreters of serious music in our time, defends what the lawyers have formulated: that the mystery of musical creation extends to the re-creator.

If the law has reasserted the importance of the performer it has not given him back the panache of his more romantic—and, perhaps, less efficient—predecessors. Paganini's 'devil' and Liszt's bravura are no more, nor are singers what they used to be, famous for their voices and the scandals around them, like Pasta and Malibran, Nourrit or Lablache. There were still some survivors of those halcyon days a few years after the First World War: Eugen d'Albert, Moriz Rosenthal, Bronislav Huberman, Tetrazzini and Toti dal Monte, Caruso and Chaliapin, Arimondi and Baklanov. But what once seemed almost black magic has turned into mere technical excellence. Perhaps it was the professional superiority of Artur Schnabel or the perfect naturalness of Adolf Busch which introduced the new type of soloist, who is no longer called virtuoso and despises magic, leaving all the responsibility, as it were, to the composer. It is not easy to say whether today's violinists, pianists, cellists and singers are better than or as good as their famous predecessors. The virtuoso of former days with his long hair and fluttering tie was anxious to show how difficult the piece he was playing was and how he mastered it. The modern soloist seems not to notice the difficulties and avoids a whole musical literature written for virtuoso display; Paganini's 'Streghe', Liszt's 'St Paul marchant sur les flots', Sarasate's 'Gipsy Tunes'. Such music has fallen into disrepute, and solo recitals, particularly by instrumentalists, are rare. They all prefer to play concertos with an orchestra, even two in one evening. It has all become rather dignified and rather dull.

The orchestras, however, are undoubtedly better than they were before. Human beings are now more efficient: the runners, the high- and long-jumpers, the tennis-players, the acrobats in their dinner-jackets—and the orchestral musicians. There are always some old people who like to dwell on bygone glories such as the world will never see again. But I well remember the days of wobbling horns in the minuet of Beethoven's Eighth or scratching violins in the prelude to *Traviata*. This hardly ever happens today, and if it does happen the public takes great exception. The instruments may be better, but the musicians are certainly much better educated both musically and generally than they were at a time when it was the general view that music could prosper with no more than elementary schooling. And when one thinks of the versatile gentlemen in dance-bands, each of them playing three or four different instruments, and remembers the miserable men in old dance orchestras fiddling away at their waltzes and polkas, one can only stand and admire: it is an astonishing change, both musically and socially.

Like the famous dance-bands the great orchestras have only recently acquired a virtuoso reputation. Before, and for a long time after, the renowned Mannheim Court Orchestra amazed listeners with its precision and discipline, its measured crescendi and ritardandi and its surprising sforzandi, history ignored the orchestras and also the conductors who had to indicate the tempo from the *cembalo* or mark it with a foot- or stick-beat on the floor, a service that earned them no public recognition. Nobody has troubled to tell us whether Mozart and Haydn were good conductors. Music had to become more personal and individual to provide the conductor and the orchestra with an individual task. People noted that Carl Maria von Weber or Mendelssohn were better conductors than others; Spontini's ivory baton became famous; Berlioz and Liszt demonstrated that conducting was a creative or at least re-creative occupation demanding exceptional qualifications. With Bülow, Richter and Hermann Levi there arrived the conductor-virtuoso, and with him the virtuoso orchestra. Toscanini, Furtwängler and, more recently, Karajan; the Boston Symphony and the New York, Vienna and Berlin Philharmonic orchestras—these are as famous today as the great singers and instrumentalists were in former times. They dominate the musical scene and rule our musical life.

The excellence of the modern performer has quickly become a matter of course, and the public at large is often unaware of it. Particularly where the mass media of communication, broadcasting and gramophone records, take possession of music, performances of the highest standard now reach every village and hamlet where professional performances of similar quality were previously unknown. Once upon a time simple folk could enjoy their own simple music-making. But the new professionalism discourages them; even to them amateurism has become intolerable.

There will be quite a few who welcome this change as advancing the level of musical culture. But it leaves no choice; it means perfection or nothing. And the art of music, which has become so common, becomes also more remote.

All this is the music-publisher's joy and sorrow. As printer and promoter, patron and exploiter, he has to meet all the problems, deal with them and find encouragement and at times consolation in the thought that it is the art itself which creates and solves them.

6. ECONOMICS

xperience has established certain wise rules which govern
the way in which the right price of goods and services results
from the interplay of supply and demand—in which, with
a good measure of exactitude, jewellery and potatoes, bank-
managers and chimney-sweeps, find their market. Such reliable
methods do not apply to the arts and their products, which have a
pretium affectionis that can never be 'right'. Affection is often an
extravagant spender, and indifference an incorrigible miser. If one
tried to analyse the total (and fantastic) expenditure on music and
find where it all went, one would discover that there is almost
mindless generosity where no real value and lasting benefit result,
and great and often ill-tempered economy exercised where money
could buy something precious. It could, therefore, be said that the
whole economy of music is misdirected. This is not altogether new,
but it is more obvious now that music really brings the money
rolling in. There is an unprecedented boom in music, but the price
asked and paid for it is still the most sensitive point in the nervous
system of our musical life.

In the noisy world of popular music the problems are not quite
so acute. This is felt by all concerned, the entertainers as well as
the entertained.

Musicals, to start with, are an important business proposition.
The authors and owners of a successful musical often impose
extraordinary conditions: such a musical—which on the Continent
has not yet supplanted the old operetta—is, for a long period, the
private perquisite of the Broadway theatre and of the original cast
which first staged it; on a day often determined several years
ahead it must be presented with the original cast in a large London
theatre, and remains reserved for a further long period during which
nobody else can acquire any rights in it. Authors, publishers and
promoters form a natural consortium which sees to it that in the
first five or six years all the available money flows into their pockets
alone. Only when the cream has thus been skimmed off does their
grip loosen enough for other theatre-managers, sub-publishers
and singers to be allowed a share in the proceeds. There is amazingly
little opposition to this quasi-monopoly, and no complaint is ever
raised, for the expectation of eventually channelling at least a

tributary of the mighty stream of money into one's own till silences all the objections which would be raised if such ruthless exploitation was tried with serious music.

Earlier successes of musicals or their equivalents seem rather modest compared with those of our days. In its own day, when the difference between opera and operetta was hardly known, *The Magic Flute* was the greatest draw of the musical theatre. On the stage of its original performance it achieved the sensational run of a hundred performances in thirteen months, from 30 September 1791 to 31 October 1792. More than a century later, when opera and operetta had definitely parted, operetta being recognized not as a short opera but as a dramatic musical entertainment of lesser artistic ambition and lower purpose, Lehár's *Merry Widow* ran for four hundred performances between 1905 and 1907 at the theatre where it opened. But Rodgers and Hammerstein's *Oklahoma* was played in the same Broadway theatre from 1943 till 1949, for five years and nine weeks, 2,152 performances in a row. This was no isolated case. *South Pacific, Annie Get Your Gun, Kiss Me Kate,* not to mention *My Fair Lady,* beat all the old records. This boom far exceeds the equivalent growth of population and wealth. It is sad and almost frightening to see how public pleasure in *The Magic Flute* turned into the passion for *The Merry Widow* and her Viennese successors, and how this passion has become an obsession with the musicals of today. Small wonder that the money pours down on the lucky authors like Jupiter's golden rain into Danae's lap. Even if the sale of sheet music is but a fraction of what it was in the days of *The Merry Widow,* stage performances (already an important source of income in Lehár's day), the sale of millions of records, broadcasting, television and sound film, all unknown in 1905, provide a revenue which far exceeds anything popular works could earn before. Not even the American tax-collector and his colleagues around the world could give an exact estimate of the total revenue of any of the great musicals of the last twenty-five years—certainly quite a few million dollars, of which on average two-thirds go to the authors and one-third to the publishers and sub-publishers. This, however, takes no account of what is lost in those costly failures which rub shoulders un-obtrusively with the successes.

Popular songs are much smaller affairs than musicals, but their capacity for making money is in comparison no smaller. As I have explained, the interpreter is the vital key to these hidden treasures. It is estimated that, in the last twenty-five years, 300,000,000 of

Bing Crosby's records have been sold—and not all the songs were good in themselves, without his inimitable rendering. The authors whose product catches the imagination of a singer of Bing Crosby's calibre can consider themselves very lucky indeed. Among the groups of long-haired young men who at present dominate the world of light-music entertainment, the Beatles are selling 15,000,000 records a year. These are figures which were never reached by the old light or popular music, even in the great years between about 1860 and 1914 when such immortal melodies as 'The Blue Danube', 'Les Pâtineurs' or 'O sole mio' were written, played, printed and sold all over the world.

It is only natural that the happy inventors of new noises and new ways of making them are not satisfied with their shares as authors and performers. They have turned publishers as well, and so corner all the available revenue; and this has caused much resentment among legitimate publishers. But how legitimate is the publishing of pop-songs? There is little if anything to preserve for posterity. The performer reigns supreme, and next to him comes the record-manufacturer. And he, too, tries his hand at publishing, not being satisfied with the profits from the sale of his records but wanting the publisher's share of mechanical royalties as well. The game is well worth the candle. A number-one hit may earn a hundred thousand dollars in a few weeks, which for a piece of music of two and a half minutes' duration is no mean commercial feat. But, again, this does not happen every day. The number of the lucky ones is small, the failures are legion and if anyone, writer or publisher, believes that Tin Pan Alley is paved with gold he will soon be disappointed.

The serious music-lover is easily inclined to frown upon the disproportionate profitability of musicals and pop-songs and to say that fortunes are made without any visible effort by exploiting the unstable nervous condition of the young. To send millions of teenagers into a frenzy is not an art in any sense. But this popular music does not pretend to belong in the category of 'art'. It is a tonic mixed from mysterious ingredients that causes the excesses which only music can cause, excesses which provide an outlet for the aimless rebellion of a dissatisfied young generation without bringing it into physical conflict with the law and the police. For such useless but profitable purposes a lot of money is spent, but no more than it is worth to the consumers. There is a market level in operation which does not differ essentially from the trade in other and often similarly doubtful goods.

The howling musical entertainment of today has necessarily displaced the more dignified light music of our parents and grand-parents. Only the best works maintain a somewhat uneasy existence, though more of this unfashionable music can be heard on the Continent than in faster-moving England and America. But sometimes the new ways of utilizing music open up unexpected commercial channels, even for this type.

The publishing company which I served used to publish great quantities of band music. In the good old days when soldiers marched on foot and fleets consisted of battleships and cruisers, each with large guns and large bands, there was an almost insatiable demand for marches, and one of these was 'Colonel Bogey'. The composer was musical director of the Royal Marines and one of the most successful of all composers of marches. 'Colonel Bogey', written and published in 1916, quickly became *the* military march of the British, Canadians and Australians and has remained so to the extent that modern armies and fleets have any use for marches; it provided the composer and his successors with a modest but reliable yearly income.

One day, fifty years after the march was first played, a miracle happened: a film company made the epic *The Bridge on the River Kwai*, about British soldiers in Japanese captivity, and in it used this very march, which has nothing of the hollow pomp of military ceremonies but, with its unusual rhythm and melodic lift, is a perfect expression of simple optimism. In the film a group of British prisoners-of-war whistle it when they go to work on the bridge, knowing that some of them will never return. The film became a world success and the march a hit. It was 'discovered' where before it had been unknown—in Europe, in North and South America, and even in Japan. Millions of records were made and sold, and a French wine-merchant played it in his vans around France to advertise his '*vins du postillon*'. The financial result for the composer's family was a sum larger than all the money the march had earned in the preceding fifty years.

The success of another march, which did not have quite such a brilliant history, was even more remarkable as it had been forgotten soon after its publication in 1921 and taken out of the catalogue. After the Second World War a BBC producer happened to find a copy and discovered something special in the march which had until then escaped everyone. He made it the signature tune of a programme series, and for more than ten years sixteen bars were played from a tape five times a week, thus providing the family of the long-departed composer with a very comfortable living.

So even in old-fashioned entertainment music there are some hidden gold-mines waiting for the lucky prospector.

Economically, the great gains of popular music complete the picture of a happy state of affairs. Some eyebrows may be raised when one reads that some clever young men in their early twenties are making the kind of fortunes which could not be made by any serious work of any nature and could not be amassed even after long years of hard study. It may be bad for morale and health. But nobody really feels robbed and the economy is nicely balanced.

Serious music, on the other hand, squeezes itself rather painfully into the market. It is not designed as entertainment for the paying public. It educates, stimulates, appeals to idealism and the higher flights of imagination, to the mysterious inner self; all nebulous, intangible values which cannot easily be translated into cash—values, it may be argued, which the creative mind owes to mankind. Education, after all, is or should be free, the doors of museums and galleries open to all, and every distinction between rich and poor banned from the world of the spirit. In such an atmosphere serious music becomes an intractable piece of merchandise. The more widely production and consumption of serious music spread, the deeper seems to become the resentment that serious music, too, costs and needs money. It is the old idea of the incompatibility of music and money, which plainly does not arise in respect of popular music. Fame is always legitimate, but money contaminates art, and the brutal requirements of modern life cannot coexist in peace with loftier human purposes. Therefore, neither the promoters of serious music nor its public adopt what would otherwise seem quite a natural attitude: those who cannot afford a first-class ticket travel second class, and those who cannot afford a Rolls-Royce drive a mini-car without accusing the railways or the car-manufacturers of discrimination against them. But when it comes to serious music, they both claim a Rolls-Royce as of right. It must not be withheld because of money.

It is a strange situation. We are outraged when we read of Mozart's financial troubles, but we do not really approve of a successful serious composer living today in very comfortable circumstances. Though romanticism is no longer accepted, there still lingers on the old romantic idea of the hungry genius creating his masterworks in an attic warmed only by his inner fire. There are few composers left in attics nowadays, but their average—if an average is at all admissible—modest affluence does not go unchallenged.

The main challenge comes from the interpreters with whom
they have to share what money is available for serious music.
Indeed, promoters are infinitely more generous to interpreters than
to composers, on the often correct assumption that it is the interpreter—conductor, soloist or orchestra—who fills the concert-
halls, rather than the works he interprets. From the great stars to
the organized orchestral musicians, interpreters demand and receive
the lion's share of all the money which is spent on serious music,
and the fortune of a great conductor or singer far exceeds that of a
similarly great composer. There are some who possess town houses,
villas in the country, private planes and yachts, but, apart from an
occasional sarcastic aside, nobody seems to begrudge them their
opulence, while a similarly wealthy composer would without fail
be the subject of many stories about greed and commercial acumen
as opposed to dignified poverty.

It is there that the economics of the serious-music business seem
to be misguided. For, in the midst of an unparalleled boom, serious
music and its promoters are constantly fighting against financial
loss and for bigger subsidies from the public treasury. In every other
trade a boom fills every pocket, and *popular* music is no exception.
But serious music cannot make ends meet. Opera-houses have never
seemed to be able to balance their budgets since the days of the
legendary impresario Barbaja, who could run half a dozen *stagioni*
at a time without losing money. Later opera-houses became 'court
operas', the hobby, the privilege and the duty of emperors, kings
and dukes who lacked the courage to spend taxpayers' money on
singers, orchestra, decors and costumes but covered the deficits of
sumptuous opera-houses out of their private purses. But when
most of them disappeared after the First World War democracy
took over, the court operas became state or municipal undertakings
and the taxpayer was thereafter the victim of the growing annual
losses.

Orchestras, on the other hand, have only joined the ranks of
the loss-makers fairly recently, most of them having been able,
until the Second World War, to balance their budgets. This, too,
is no longer so. Now opera-houses are nearly always full, orchestras
play more often than before to full houses, all of them benefit from
broadcasting, television, records and films—and all of them lose
more and more money every year. There is a general clamour for
serious music, but it is an accepted fact everywhere, in rich and
poor countries alike, that the price of opera- and concert-tickets
must be lower than the true economic cost, or else the public may

discover that serious music is not, after all, a necessity of life. In fact, on an average, not much more than half the costs of opera-houses and concert societies are covered by the sale of tickets and normal commercial principles cannot and do not apply. Public bodies, the state and municipal authorities must come to the rescue with public money, and they subsidize the ailing mass-production and consumption of serious music as unwillingly as they maintain homes for the old. Where serious music does not belong to the spiritual needs of people, loud complaints are heard about the waste of taxpayers' money on 'minority tastes'. And if the subsidizing bodies were to close their tills, all the hectic activity around serious music would be reduced to a trickle, while the roaring flood of popular music would continue to provide its makers with uncontested riches. What a contradiction! One would like to believe that serious music too is dear to the hearts of millions who, according to the rules of economics, would be prepared to pay the right price for it. But serious music is grotesquely underpaid; or, to put it quite brutally, from an economic point of view it is bankrupt.

Though the ordinary opera- and concert-goer, provided with expensive productions and excellent performances, may never become aware of the poverty behind the glittering façade, it does influence the composition of orchestras and their repertoire. Generally speaking, orchestras today are smaller than they were fifty years ago, when every composer owed it to himself to write for quadruple woodwind, six horns, four trumpets and a correspondingly large number of strings. Such large orchestral forces are today an expense which would normally be justified only if the work in question was old and famous enough to attract a large public. A young composer or untried work could hardly expect the sacrifice involved. Equally, solo concertos and oratorios require an outlay on the part of the promoters which only established works can warrant. Bartók's violin concerto of 1938 is about the last to have been accepted into the regular repertoire; no piano concerto since Ravel's has been so honoured. It would be difficult to think of an oratorio since Stravinsky's 'Symphony of Psalms' (1930) which is regularly performed. But excellent concertos and oratorios have been written since those of Bartók, Ravel and Stravinsky. Names like Britten, Honegger, Frank Martin spring easily to mind, but for them the money is not available. If a soloist is to be engaged he must play the concertos of Beethoven, Mendelssohn and Brahms, two in one evening if possible, to give full value for his *cachet*, and a choral work must be by Bach, Handel, Beethoven,

Verdi or Brahms in order to be sure of general acclaim and a full house.

Indeed, the finances of promoters are so delicately balanced that after they have received the subsidy and sold all the available tickets, paid the fees of soloists and the salaries of the orchestra and administrative staff, nothing remains. There is no bargaining with star conductors and soloists, no bargaining with organized orchestral musicians; but the composer and the publisher—as the weakest partners in the business—are held responsible for all the financial worries. This leads to a great deal of argument and sometimes to angry exchanges. Even the broadcasting organizations, with their enormous budgets, point to the composer—and to the publisher as his representative—as the real culprits. In the richest country in the world so-called 'non-profit-making' institutions are being founded for no other purpose than to avoid paying the composer. All other participants are paid, and well paid at that—musicians, administrators, instrument-makers and tailors. But the composer must generously supply his wares free of charge. There would be a storm of indignation if he asked to be paid on the same scale as the others, or if he withheld his work.

So is it really the composer and his agents, the performing and mechanical societies and the publishers who, by constantly upsetting the economics of musical life, dig their own graves? Mechanical rights are the least contested so long as they are paid by the manufacturer as a royalty on the selling-price of every record sold, though composer—and publisher—have to make certain concessions in respect of the costs of expensive sleeves which they neither choose nor want. While the standard sheet royalty on literary and musical works is 10% of the selling-price, the royalty on records is only 8% on the Continent, $6\frac{1}{4}$% in Great Britain and the British Commonwealth, and even less in the United States.

But broadcasting organizations making records and tapes have to pay mechanical royalties too, and dislike doing so intensely. In 1948 the Brussels Conference for the revision of the Berne Convention expressed the view that mechanical reproductions made for the purpose of broadcasting should not give rise to an additional income for the composer and, therefore, should not require his consent, provided that such recordings be destroyed after twenty-eight days. Some countries incorporated this recommendation in their new copyright laws, and some extended the period to one full year. The result is that broadcasting organizations pay a derisory amount under the heading of 'mechanical fees', a fraction of one per cent of their total expenditure. And even this seems to worry them out of all proportion. Opera-houses and orchestral societies never have occasion to pay mechanical fees.

Performing fees, on the other hand, are a general tax payable by anyone who publicly performs music. Opera-houses in Europe pay a standard rate of 10% of their takings—that is, of the actual sale of tickets. That seems fair enough, except for the fact that ticket-prices are notoriously low and cannot keep pace with the inexorable rise in the cost of living. The increasing deficit of the opera-house is covered by an annual increase in the subsidy, but the composer has to wait until the administrator or 'intendant' of the opera-house summons the courage to increase the price of the tickets again. Opera-houses in the United States will not accept the hallowed principle of paying a percentage of their takings and prefer to pay instead a lump sum which is well below 10%. As a result, and taking into consideration that most of the operas performed during a season are in the public domain and therefore free from royalties, total average performing fees paid by an average opera-house in the Old or New World hardly ever exceed two per cent of their total expenditure.

Conditions with orchestral societies are very similar: low ticket-prices, large subsidies and performing fees varying from one to two per cent of the total expenses. Broadcasting organizations, with their enormous consumption of music of every type, are more difficult to assess. They pay an annual sum to the performing rights society of their country, a sum which bears little relation to the music actually broadcast but is a fixed fee per licence issued or—in the United States, where no licences are required and the number of viewers or listeners is guessed at rather than known—based on probabilities, which remains well below two per cent of the total running-costs of the organization.

Still, the managers of serious music will say that these small percentages indicate the margin between carrying on and abandoning serious music altogether. They certainly mark the battle zone wherein the publisher has to register his claims on behalf of his composers. 'Music-publishing is no business for cowards,' a famous publisher once said to me. 'One has to have guts to demand money for music, because nobody gives it gladly and voluntarily.' Indeed, it requires courage and tact. I trust I will not be suspected of advocating usury. Among my publisher colleagues I have acquired the unenviable reputation of being too accommodating towards 'music-users'. With a stubbornness that has seldom been rewarded I have tried to find the compromise which leaves all parties without any feeling of injustice. However, courage and tact are a rare combination even in quiet times. A boom such as serious music—no less than its popular sister—is now experiencing may make rabbits courageous, but it cannot make lions tactful. When the music business grew to its full stature after the Second World War it was not at first easy to find the middle way between exaggerated demands and ill-intentioned resistance; there were wild arguments, and these the publisher had to meet, for the composer rightly kept out of the ring. It is, after all, the publisher's task to fight for his composers. But the composer involuntarily becomes a court of appeal, inclined to listen to the exhortations of promoters more readily than to his hard-boiled, businesslike publisher.

Although an uneasy armistice was achieved between the parties in the end, it remains one of the most regrettable features of our musical life that serious music cannot prosper in peace and quiet. It is the performers who dominate musical life, not only artistically but also economically. They are indispensable and, consequently, demanding. In a curious way, all parties are linked together: professional music-making, ruthlessly claiming its reward; passive listening, unwilling to spend enough to keep music going; and the composer and publisher, who between them are the great spoilers of an otherwise happy game. Perhaps some composers are unaware of this state of things; perhaps some publishers find in the endless quarrels some sporting pleasure which has eluded me. This situation has to be seen in the context of the most recent development of the art of music itself if the problems of the future are to be assessed.

The serious composer may not be highly paid by modern commercial standards, but his earnings are none the less more than adequate. Some time ago the British Composers' Guild published a statement that the British composer of serious music earns on average less than he would on National Assistance. This is quite absurd. In other walks of life the idea of an average has some validity; it is even possible to calculate an average national income-level. But in the arts there is no average. Ability is the only and absolute criterion, not only for the success of the work but also for the well-being of the artist. There are in Britain, as in every other country, serious composers earning next to nothing because their works are neither published nor performed. Even modern copyright legislation and modern applications of music have been unable to make failure lucrative—this goes for serious music as much as for popular. But the successful composer—and his publisher—have their share of the treasure that is constantly being dug from the soil of music. Not that riches suddenly come pouring in as they do in popular music. But over the years Puccini's *Bohème* or Strauss's *Rosenkavalier* have earned more money than all the *Oklahoma*s and *My Fair Lady*s put together, while Bartók's 'Divertimento' and Britten's 'Variations on a Theme of Purcell' leave all the number-one hits far behind. However, while pop songs and even musicals reach the summit of popularity—and profitability—with enviable frequency, commensurate successes by serious works are admittedly rare, and seem to become rarer as time goes on.

Serious music shares in the benefits of technical progress, particularly those of broadcasting, which multiplies performances beyond anything that could have been expected fifty years ago. Prominent performances at prominent festivals, which now fill the once quiet summer days with the most expensive noises, are relayed by most European and some American broadcasting organizations, each of which pays performing fees and so substantially increases the revenue of the composer for the single live performance.

On the other hand sound film and television, which are of inestimable value to popular music, are disappointing media for the true art. When the sound film came into being some enthusiasts forecast the arrival of a new art, and they did so again when television arrived upon the musical scene. But it has happened with neither. Both are so wedded to easy popularity that serious music is seldom admitted, producers having little confidence in its entertainment value. They have made films of the most popular operas, but even *Madam Butterfly*, *Rosenkavalier* and *Don Giovanni* could never compare or compete at the box-office with the films of *South Pacific* or *My Fair Lady*.

The music of an opera obviously stands in the way of any such successful adaptation. Even if the composer could be persuaded to collaborate (a very rare event) it would be discovered over and over again that the most important moments musically, when all action ceases and music alone takes possession of the stage, are quite unsuitable visually. In Benjamin Britten's *Billy Budd* the wicked master-at-arms Claggart has a long and important aria which, in purely musical terms, describes his character more convincingly than words could do. When Canadian television made a film of the opera, primarily for broadcasting but also in the hope it might be suitable for showing in cinemas, this aria—together with half the opera—was cut. 'Why, for God's sake, have you cut this too?' I asked the producer. 'Oh,' he replied with disarming frankness, 'we have made this Claggart up to look such a monstrous devil that we don't need the aria.' Benjamin Britten was, understandably, very cross and refused to see the film, which, in spite of all the cuts, was not a success.

Symphonic music was found a modest and not altogether legitimate place in all the new applications of music. To start with it has been discovered by choreographers. Since ballet as an art form— not easier to perform than opera, but easier to look at and to enjoy— has captured a much larger public than before the Second World War, the repertoire of ballets proper has become too small, or rather choreographers have developed a dislike for them, preferring to use symphonic pieces which seldom have an obvious choreographic 'argument', such as Mahler's 'Song of the Earth' or Mozart's 'Sinfonia concertante'. George Balanchine started it all, but he is an exceptional musician who finds something danceable even in Webern's Symphony. Other, less musical, choreographers simply misuse the music because the great majority of ballet-goers do not listen to the music at all (ballet critics hardly ever even mention the music, so subordinate is its role). Furthermore, the music is usually badly performed, not only because ballet does not command the best conductors and the best orchestras, but because the music has to consider and adapt itself to the dancing, be faster here and slower there than the composer would have it. However, such ballet productions often enough result in whole series of performances which the symphonic work could seldom achieve in its own right, and this entitles the choreographer to some measure of gratitude from the composer.

Occasionally it is a film which provides a windfall for the composer. For the exclusive use of Rachmaninov's Piano Concerto No. 2 a fee of $80,000 was paid. Such use is just as illegitimate as its use for ballet purposes, and Stravinsky for one will not allow his music to be used for purposes other than those for which it was written.

Naturally, the gramophone record plays a considerable part in the earnings of a successful serious composer. Sales are incomparably smaller than those of popular music but the price and, therefore, the royalties are higher, and sometimes a serious recording reaches a respectable place in the hit parade. When the recording of Benjamin Britten's 'War Requiem' first appeared it climbed, in bad company, to fourth place. Serious music also enjoys an advantage which only exceptionally comes to popular music: a standard serious work is recorded over and over again. New interpreters make new recordings which find new customers, so that recordings, like perform-ances, become a permanent source of revenue. Moreover the long-playing record, which has caused many a headache for the makers of the two- or three-minute products of popular music, is a real blessing for the longer works of the serious art.

But it must again be remembered that only the most outstanding serious works are recorded at all; others can only be recorded with the help of subsidies, and their sales are negligible. Therefore the additional income from mechanical reproductions principally benefits those composers who already draw an important revenue from performances. This, in economic terms, conforms to the disheartening rule that money always seeks the company of its own kind.

All this has made serious music lucrative too. The composer who has provided the concert repertoire with half a dozen sizeable standard works can count on well over a thousand live or recorded performances every year, and three or four repertoire operas have a few hundred performances every season. The composer of such works achieves a six-figure annual income which compares well with the income of a substantial industrialist. Music had to travel a long way to arrive at this point.

However, one does not need to write works like *Madam Butterfly*, *Till Eulenspiegel* or *Petrushka* to make quite a com-fortable living out of serious music. More modest, more local, success and recognition also express themselves in the shape of money. There are only a few serious composers with really large incomes, but then genius is a rare quality. The number of those who have an annual—if not absolutely regular—income of between $20,000 and $50,000 is not as small as may be generally believed. Half a century ago they would have had to teach or play in an orchestra, and their compositions would have made only a small—though very welcome—contribution to their standard of living. Even now their works have little staying-power, and unless they produce new provincial successes at regular intervals their revenue sometimes drops very quickly. Their heirs in particular cannot expect much; the death of the composer is usually the end of his music too.

As I have said before, none of this quite follows the rules of ordinary commerce. Even with a total estimated expenditure by the public on music in all its forms—tickets for concerts and opera, records, musical instruments and licence-fees for radio and television sets, not counting the many places of entertainment where music is but one of the attractions offered—of several thousand million dollars a year, the share of composers, librettists and song-writers remains well below the normal commercial level. But the change in their financial situation is no less momentous than in the art itself. If art and commerce are still not entirely reconciled, the '*amour des lettres*' and the '*esprit des affaires*' have at least found a method of living reasonably well together; even Beaumarchais would be satisfied.

When writing of copyright I made the point that many great works of art and literature were created long before the idea of protectable intellectual property was even conceived and that the absence of protection did not stifle creative genius nor its introduction promote it. So it is worth observing that the comparative affluence of the serious composer today, resulting from the complete protection of his works and the equally complete organization of his material interests, has done no harm to the art. If hunger was once a stimulant, opulence has not blunted the spirit of adventure in seeking new ways, a new art altogether. On the contrary it is during the last fifty years, the very period when conditions have been created to assure every successful work of its material reward, that serious composers have shown most indifference to the public and its taste—and to the financial benefit that could be derived from satisfying both. There is no sign of ideals being lost and sights lowered. On the contrary, it is reassuring to see music going its own way, unperturbed by any extra-artistic consideration.

However, those who expected the art itself to be better off may feel disappointed, for no benefit can be observed here which could be attributed to the protection and profitability of intellectual property.

7. AN UNHAPPY RELATIONSHIP

I have stated that the publisher has to stake the composer's claims and fight for them, first for the principle and then for the money which follows the recognition of the principle. With popular music this is purely a business like any other, with no reservations of a moral nature, no appeal to ethical consideration. The rules are well defined, the game needs no umpire.

With serious music the whole climate is entirely different. All claims are unpopular, resented and resisted, and the publisher, whose task it is to register and pursue them, is himself the most unpopular figure in musical life. His alleged greed is contrasted with the hypothetical selflessness of the composer, who, it is believed, would be content with a more modest way of life and a lower income from his works than the publisher is trying to obtain for him—and, which is the most aggravating aspect, for himself. For the publisher lives on a share of the composer's income; not just a commission, like a mere agent, but a real share, as I have shown, because he has not only to act as an agent, writing letters, paying visits, making telephone-calls and distributing publicity material, but also to print and publish, sell and hire and keep stocks and books. Whatever the publisher achieves financially benefits the composer too, by virtue of the existing contract. Composer and publisher are, in fact, bound by common interests with only one subtle difference: the composer wants his works performed; so too does the publisher—but *not* at any price. This is the point where 'music-users' never tire of separating the two.

Some years ago the Council of Europe convened a commission of legal experts in Strasbourg to advise on ways and means of facilitating exchanges of musical programmes between European broadcasting organizations. (One of the impossible demands made on music is that it should promote and strengthen the spirit of European co-operation generally by such programme exchanges.) Among other bodies the Music Section of the International Publishers' Association was invited to take part in the deliberations, and I had the honour and displeasure of representing it. Among the fifty experts from more than twenty countries there were no musicians, only jurists of some prominence, chosen by their respective governments. From the very beginning of the proceedings I found myself in the dock. Far from demanding any financial gain, it was said, composers were glad and grateful for any work performed in Paris to be heard in Zagreb and Stockholm, and I was told in no uncertain terms that publishers were acting neither in the interests of composers nor on their instructions when they tried to make exchanges difficult by their financial demands. The representative of one of the smallest, though by no means poorest, European countries went so far as to say that publishers prevented the spread of learning and culture and, indeed, the entire progress of humanity.

While I had not expected a particularly friendly welcome this outburst of hostility came as a surprise. I tried patiently to explain that it was not fair either to the composer or to the publisher that one single actual performance should be sufficient to satisfy the whole of Europe without any supplementary payment to the copyright-owner. Surely, I said, if Radio Stockholm could relay a work from Radio Paris without cost to itself, it was not likely to put on a performance of its own for some considerable time. The assembly listened silently, unconvinced. It was in marked contrast that at the afternoon session the demands of the musicians and the technical staffs were discussed with great restraint. They all demanded much heavier supplementary payments for their services and insisted on restrictive conditions which made the free exchange of programmes practically impossible. But no accusation was made and regret was expressed in very careful terms. In my closing speech I could not help comparing the two attitudes, and an agreement was eventually reached; but it left a bitter taste.

This incident is an example of a fairly widespread campaign against the music-publisher, characteristic of the change in the organization of our musical life and of the art itself. There is a belief that in present-day circumstances the publisher of serious music has become a hindrance rather than a help, and that composers and music-users would be happier without him.

Indeed, there are great changes which have affected both the position and the function of the publisher. Before the establishment of the authors' societies the publisher was the only intermediary between the composer and the organizers of performances. The material existence of the composer depended entirely on him, all the composer's income went through the publisher's hands and if the composer found himself in financial difficulties the publisher was the first and often the only person to whom he could turn for help. The authors' societies have now become a new and considerable power, which looks after the composer's worldly needs with much greater authority than the publisher ever had. To the composer they must appear his most powerful protectors. It is true that they have no incentive to economize on their expenses, they do not know the difference between a genius and a freak, and they cannot produce any publicity for any of their members. But all this contributes to their reputation as entirely objective administrators of their composers' temporal substance.

So it has happened that the income the composer receives from the publisher in the shape of sheet royalties and shares in hire fees is but a fraction of his total revenue. In France not even the royalties from dramatic performances are administered by the publisher; in fact the publisher is excluded not only from the administration, which hurts his pride, but also from any share of the takings, which hurts his pocket. And, as I have explained before, where the publisher participates in the rights administered by the authors' societies it is the author who allows him a share, not the other way round. All this makes the composer feel much more independent of the publisher than before and reduces the latter's importance and usefulness. That all the royalties collected and distributed by the societies are to a large extent the result of the publisher's activities is never admitted without reservation. It is significant that in the years since the Second World War the publishers have lost the leadership of the authors' societies which they had held since their foundation, when their experience in organization and business made them indispensable. No performing rights society in Europe still has a publisher as president.

One must not be sentimental about this change. The traditional right of the publisher is the graphic right, the right to print and to distribute the works he publishes. Only fifty years ago both composer and publisher could make a living from it, and in the heydays of music sales they could both put something by. This graphic right, which remained most valuable in popular music at a time when serious music could no longer be sold, has now become almost worthless for both types; tradition has departed from music publishing so far as serious music, the publication and promotion of which was the glory of the profession for more than a century, is concerned. Even the most hard-headed among publishers must occasionally stop to think about the change which, to many people, makes him look like a remnant from a bygone age, fighting to keep his place with methods which are not justified morally by being justified economically. It is indeed a valid question whether, as far as serious contemporary music is concerned, music-publishing has outlived its day or whether it still has a function to perform.

No legislation or organization has been able to solve the problem of the beginner. This problem hardly exists in popular music, where names mean very little and technical study nothing. The young composer of a pop-song finds the door of any pop publisher far enough open to give him a chance unless his work is too obviously bad. But if he has merit he usually has luck also, and, once lucky, he can wait in comfort until the muse, or whatever deity may be concerned, knocks again. If he is unlucky, nobody would dream of encouraging him to try again. For such as him there is no mercy; he must find another trade to earn his living and nobody pities him. These are very clear, very reasonable conditions.

Serious works, however, are neither written, accepted nor rejected as quickly as popular ones. Even the most gifted, ingenious beginner needs ten years to accumulate a sound basis of successful works—not every work is successful—and to reach a reasonable income-level. It may even take him this long to come to the conclusion that his talent is not fulfilling its initial promise. The organization of musical life has never provided for those years of developing and maturing or failing. Authors' societies can do nothing for their young members. There are grants and commissions, usually for impractical works which disappear into the archives after their first performances. All these quasi-charitable opportunities are too small and too irregular to provide the young composer with a secure living, however modest.

Former generations bore this cross with dignity. It was a matter of course that the young composer had to have a regular job as an orchestral musician, coach, teacher or small-time conductor until the income from his works was large enough for him to devote himself exclusively to composing.

Great masterpieces have been written in this way. Gustav Mahler could compose only during the summer months. If one reads the letters the young Richard Strauss wrote to his parents one is amazed to discover what a rather frail young man was capable of seventy-five years ago. On 12 March 1892 he writes:

On Tuesday night *Tristan* [in Weimar], at 11.30 p.m. travelled here [to Leipzig], Wednesday from 10 a.m. until 2.30 p.m.

first rehearsal for the Liszt-Verein concert, in the evening back
to Weimar. Yesterday, Thursday night, conducted *Lohengrin*
in Eisenach, at 1 a.m. again to Leipzig, today from 10 a.m. till
1 p.m. and from 3 p.m. till 6 p.m. second rehearsal. Tomorrow
10 a.m. main rehearsal, in the evening concert. . . . I am feeling
a little groggy now but otherwise well and happy. . . .

Strauss was then twenty-eight years old and had finished his own
Opus 26! He used to admit with a sigh that composing was hard
at the end of a busy season, but he knew no self-pity and continued
this life for thirty more years.

The present generation of composers is physically fitter than all
its predecessors: taller, healthier and more robust. But who would
dare to expect from them what Strauss and many others before him
did? In fact mental strength does not seem to keep pace with
physical fitness, and young men today cannot do two things at a
time. If composing, they can do nothing else, and as serious composing does not immediately produce a livelihood somebody has
to keep the young man's head above water. In the present circumstances this is of decisive importance for the art in all its aspects.
After all, even popular music has its roots in the art, however ill-
bred an offspring it may be.

As there is no systematic authority for or source of such assistance at the beginning of a composer's career, the task falls to the
publisher. I, like many other serious publishers, have not only
printed immature works in order to encourage a young man but
also paid fixed salaries or guaranteed incomes to real or presumed
talents; like many other publishers, too, I have often been disappointed. Some only half fulfilled their promise, others not at
all. One, of whom I was not alone in expecting great things and
for whom I procured a ballet commission, absconded on that
occasion with a girl from the corps de ballet and was never heard
of again. But the few who fulfil or exceed expectations compensate
for all the failures and mistakes, for the wasted labour and money.
One feels oneself confirmed in one's task and, rightly or wrongly,
believes one has rendered a service to the art, perhaps even to
mankind.

However, such satisfaction is very personal and very solitary
and few are inclined to recognize it, least of all the composers
themselves. The older generation of composers felt, and still feel,
closely associated with their publishers. I found this feeling with
Richard Strauss, Igor Stravinsky, Béla Bartók and Zoltán Kodály,

although none of them needed or received from the publisher the
kind of beneficence that the younger generation needs and receives.
Shortly before his death Richard Strauss told me that he could
never forget that his publisher paid him a large sum for the publishing rights in *Salome*, at a time when the best-informed people
were convinced that the work would never be performed. There
is no question of such gratitude or recognition with the younger
composer. Once he is successful and feels firm ground under his
feet all his respect for his publisher is quickly gone. Like Beethoven,
he can find six or seven publishers for every new work, men who
print and distribute his music, account for his royalties and do
similar menial jobs for him. For at a certain point in a brilliant
career promotion itself becomes a mere formality. Particularly
today, when really successful composers are rare, all eyes are upon
them, and it only needs an announcement that a new work is available for it to be accepted and performed. Yet at the start of the
composer's career, this would have required many advertisements,
leaflets and letters, much personal persuasion and, above all, faith.
That it was his first publisher who had, and did, all this and gave
the young man the opportunity to make mistakes and to survive
them means very little. With the profit the publisher eventually
makes all accounts are considered settled. There is no room for
sentimentality.

However, I cannot blame the younger composers for not feeling
so attached to their publishers as their older colleagues, who had
known different times. The whole development of music and
musical life tends to push the publisher into a kind of parasitic
secondary role. Who then can complain if the composer himself
discovers this and turns to those who, unwilling and unable to help
the beginner, associate themselves all the more eagerly with
success?

So, in the guise of prosperity, a slow change has crept into the
profession and is beginning to darken its horizon. We shall have to
confront the publisher with the new problems of a new music and
shall have to consider the time which is left to him: for the day is
not far off when most of the great successes of old music will cease
to provide the resources with which to finance the new. When
the works of Wagner, Brahms, Bruckner and Dvořák lapsed into
the public domain they left a painful gap. Now Verdi has become
public property. Debussy is about to follow, Puccini has not long
to go and by the year 2000 only a fraction of the former wealth
will be left with, so far, no adequate replacement in sight. This is

not a question of individual publishers, who may come and go with their successful composers, but of the profession as a whole, its place and function in musical life. Will it be replaced by another institution? Perhaps it was never so much the composer as the performing public who needed the publisher, just as the reading public needs the book-publisher. Is not redundancy looming ahead, with the development of a music unsuitable for a performing public and the ascendancy of a public more and more given to passive listening?

Art is a phenomenon not of biology
but of history—*R. G. Collingwood*

I. INTRODUCTION

In the niches of the façade of Garnier's Académie Nationale de Musique in Paris, the Grand Opéra, are placed four busts of composers who, a century ago, must presumably have been regarded as the worthiest representatives of opera or of music generally: Mozart next to Spontini, Beethoven next to Auber. It is always a desperately difficult task to choose just four names from the multitude of acknowledged masters. But surely the selection at the Place de l'Opéra is particularly strange. Who made the mistake: experts or public?

The answer is that, while the public was not directly consulted, it misled the experts by heaping successes on both Spontini and Auber, at one time even preferring Spontini's *Vestale* to his neighbour's *Don Giovanni* and Auber's *Muette de Portici* to Beethoven's *Fidelio*. And the same public afterwards calmly stabbed the experts in the back by consigning Spontini and Auber to oblivion. Now the reminder in golden letters is as ineffective as it seems irreparable.

Those were the days when the public, the generality of uncommitted music-lovers, ruled the musical scene, passing judgement or revising it, unconcerned with the opinion of experts but guided by an instinct which corrected every initial mistake as surely as the needle of the compass always corrects itself.

Those days are over. Public judgement and public rule are suspended. The material changes of the art, transportation and preservation, protection and profitability have gone hand in hand with a revolution, inside the art, the speed and thoroughness of which far exceed all the known changes of the past. All that happened before in music was evolution, transition from style to style, from intention to intention; through the last three hundred years we can follow music from erudition to beauty, from beauty to expression. Wagner and even Richard Strauss felt indebted to Gluck as their spiritual ancestor, despite the vast difference between his music and theirs. But in the last fifty years there has been a break which has left no spiritual kinship between old and new music. Music now strives to cut itself off from its past, indeed from its most glorious past, from its Golden Age. This would be painful even if the results were more manageable.

If a similar revolution has taken place in painting and sculpture, it has been mitigated by the fact that no comparable Golden Age preceded it, and that this revolution has found itself a label by calling its works 'abstract'. A label is reassuring; it creates a category and defines a direction. If one has a label one knows, or believes one knows, what one is doing. But new music will not accept a label or submit to a heading. Whatever one calls it, dodecaphonic or serial, structural or indeterminate, it will not allow itself to be nailed down. It still seems to scatter in all directions away from the solid and great achievements of the recent past.

This is bound to irritate and disorientate the uncommitted music-lover, to whom new music generally has become strange and remote. 'Is it right,' he must ask, 'that Beethoven, who has been dead for almost a century and a half, still means so much to me, while Boulez, living next door to me, means so little?' The answer to this simple question would be equally simple if one were to assume, as quite a few people do, that the revolution in music was the inconsiderate vandalism of a few wayward rebels. But half a century of destruction and experiment without apparent new purpose, or with so many conflicting purposes as to obscure any clear line of development, indicates some deep-seated disturbance.

This is why this strange and remote new music deserves and requires to be taken seriously. If one cannot live with it as one still lives with all the earlier music from Bach to Debussy, one must at least try to find out where one stands and how the present confusion fits into the context of the past. In life as well as in art there have been good and bad times, which have not been welcomed with the same enthusiasm and have not left posterity with the same sense of admiration. But bad times, too, have their relevance and cannot be dismissed. Nothing is as tantalizing as the feeling of having lost contact with the times. Assessing the time, measuring what it can create, comparing and contrasting the present with the past, may supply no guidance for the future, but may still restore the confidence which the uncommitted music-lover has lost. Anxious questions will have to be asked and answered, questions which have been avoided in all the writings about new music. They are useless for the composer working under the compulsion of forces of which he is unaware. They are vital and inescapable for those who cannot find consolation in their bewilderment.

In these fateful years of change and revolution many musicians have crossed my path, from the greatest of my time to the undernourished and underpaid young proof-reader whom I successfully recommended as conductor of the Viennese performances of Brecht–Weill's *Beggar's Opera*—to his eternal gratitude. Poor fellow! He never looked as if he could weather the storm.

If one spends a lifetime at the foot of Olympus one might hope to meet the Olympians, superior beings enjoying their own genius and fulness of life without ever looking over their shoulders, without resentments, sure of themselves and of their mission. I must confess that I have never met such an Olympian. Perhaps he did not exist in my time any more. Or has music always been incapable of breeding such Olympians?

Music is curiously enclosed within itself. It seems to know nothing but its own creator. The visual arts and literature must take note of the world around them and assume an attitude towards it, but music is impervious to any knowledge and wisdom. Whatever the composer wishes to be, apart from being a composer, his work will not disclose it. Nor does music meet with the other arts; it collides with them. Poetry, in particular, is crushed by it. Whatever has been written about it in the last two hundred years, it remains unalterably true that music sucks the marrow from even the sublimest text. This anonymity and cruelty are bound to be reflected in the character of the musician. Musicians generally may not be evil but they certainly are not good—Liszt being perhaps the only notable exception. (Beethoven may have dreamt of an ideal human race but he hardly counted any of his contemporaries among it. And Richard Wagner was almost evil.) To do good is not the task of music, nor of its creators. Music has no vocabulary for it, no words for love of mankind and for selflessness. And where there is no vocabulary, there is no awareness of the object. There lies a thorny contradiction. No other art gives itself away so freely, receives its re-creator with such open arms as music does— or did, until fairly recently. It makes the man in the musician all the more fascinating, the man who knows and feels only himself and still scatters his riches among the people, friends and strangers alike.

And this brotherhood of envy and selfishness has been faced with the most formidable artistic and human problems. How did they stand or lose their ground? There is a human side to the whole struggle for and against a new art in the midst of a changing world which must not be forgotten when talking of music. For one of the major issues in our time is the personality, the individuality of creative man.

2. 'LA MUSICA A' MIEI TEMPI'

E very generation sings, with Rossini's Bartolo, '*La musica a' miei tempi era altra cosa*,' trying to justify its preposterous veneration of old or dislike of new music. This is and remains one of the strangest phenomena of music—at least, of European music. One is somewhat surprised to hear American-type pop-songs from Japanese singers and marching songs after the Russian model from Chinese demonstrators. At school we were told that in Korea, more than in any other part of the Far East, life and customs had remained unchanged for two thousand years, yet this did not prevent both North and South Koreans from having all the planes and tanks and guns to wage war in its most modern form. In Europe things did not happen with such unexpected suddenness, but life changed again and again, sometimes for reasons which seemed obvious and sometimes inexplicably. Nothing gave more convincing evidence of such changes of thought, mood, enterprise, fashion or food than the arts; but no old art fell into such disrepute as music. If the artists of the Italian Renaissance despised the barbaric gothic style of the North, their reverence for the older Greek and Roman classicism was boundless; if we do not now build as Kallikrates built or paint as Raphael painted or write poetry as Homer or Milton did, the old masterworks have none the less lost nothing of their validity. They are a constantly re-valued and upgraded asset in the balance sheet of mankind. Who could seriously pretend that Bramante's light was dimmed by Le Corbusier, or that Leonardo's stature has been reduced by Picasso? Yet in music not one artist has arisen who, over the centuries, has added to our patrimony. One becomes more painfully aware of this strange mortality of music in an age which is again turning away from the past, with all the old radicalism. When the symphony of the eighty-year-old Zoltán Kodály was first performed in Lucerne he said, as if to excuse it, 'This is the music of *my* time'—*la musica a' miei tempi.*

The latest music is not 'the music of my time'. I must try to find, amid all the stormy changes of the last fifty years, the point where I was left behind, a point not so easily determined that I can say without hesitation which precise work at which precise date was still just within my range. One has to be honest with oneself. In my case I am following the phenomenon of ageing with a certain critical curiosity; I disapprove of my inclination to halt the world at a particular moment and to dread any change because, unwillingly, I believe that everything that follows must be inferior to what has gone before. This applies not only to music but to many minor and major habits of daily life, to places, to people. I can therefore still understand the latest developments in a technical sense, and regret their necessity, but I no longer take part in them.

This does not mean that one has to return to one's first love, like Otto Klemperer or Ernest Ansermet and many other former champions of the new, much less try to prove, for merely biological reasons, the exclusive validity of the old and the invalidity of the new. This is especially true if, instead of attempting to assess the value of the new, one is content with a comparison, leaving any verdict to the public in the widest sense which, without consideration of new gods, their prophets or detractors, is the only competent architect of the temples of the arts.

When I made my first acquaintance with music, electric tramways were not the only astounding innovation: Richard Wagner too was the subject of violent debate. There were serious experts who insisted that Wagner had destroyed all musical form and that his 'endless' melody was a contradiction in itself because form was definite and a fundamental requirement of all melody. I seem to remember that the harmonic freedom of Wagner's music was much less debated. The 'Tristan sequence' certainly sounded strange but it was not yet accused, as it is today, of corrupting our whole tonal system. I remember a summer holiday spent with my parents and the family of a schoolfriend of mine in a house buried amid the enormous forests of Northern Bohemia, when in ten weeks my friend's mother, an able pianist with a small but expressive voice and also an enthusiastic Wagnerite, took me through every bar and every note of the *Ring*, playing, singing, explaining, to persuade me that music had not ended with Mozart and Beethoven, as I was inclined to believe. I can still hear her singing 'Des seimigen Metes süssen Trank wirst du mir nicht verschmähen . . .' and her quiet insistence that no sweeter or more beautiful tune had been written before or since. She did not, in the end, make me a Wagnerite, a blind admirer of everything Wagner wrote and of how he wrote it, but perhaps I was not made for any kind of blindness.

Brahms too was 'new', but he presented no problems. One could like his music without getting into arguments with one's friends. Tchaikovsky, no less new, was labelled a barbarian—apparently synonymous with Russian, more of which language was heard in Prague, where I grew up, than anywhere else outside Russia. Balakirev and Rimsky-Korsakov were often played, not so much for their music as for their political sympathies and opposition to Austro–German domination. But the musical revolution really came from Debussy and Richard Strauss. Of the two Debussy was, in Prague, more a rumour than a living person. I remember vaguely 'L'Après-midi d'un faune' at the Czech Philharmonic, and the irritation it caused me afterwards when I found that I could remember no more than the very first phrase. On the other hand Strauss's symphonic poems were often played. Conductors loved them and we, the young audiences, were enchanted with them. This, for us, was new music, harmonic freedom, springy rhythm, ravishing sound and harsh clashes, and all this without demolishing all the notions of the glorious past. One could hear in the same concert Beethoven's Seventh and Strauss's *Till Eulenspiegel* and one could see the bridge spanning a century.

In 1909 I heard *Elektra* (*Salome* had been performed too but was presumably considered unsuitable for a schoolboy). That new music was indeed more violent, and more dissonant. With Mozart and Haydn it had been a lovely little angel, now smiling, now weeping. Beethoven had introduced a brutality which Haydn found abhorrent, but now, in unguarded moments at least, the little angel had become a raging fury. *Elektra* was easily the most dissonant-sounding piece of pre-war years, not excepting Stravinsky's *Rite of Spring* written five years later. What a change from Donna Anna's 'Vendetta ti chiedo!' to Elektra's 'Vater! Agamemnon, dein Tag wird kommen'! Two years later, though, there followed the sensational success of *Rosenkavalier*. I well remember the white and green posters with Roller's figurine which could be seen on the hoardings in Prague and, strange as it may sound today, there were special trains which took music-lovers from Prague to Dresden, 150 miles away, across the border in Saxony; but in those blessed days one needed no passport and Austrian crowns were as good as German marks. I was surprised to hear the experts—among them my music-teacher, who was a simpleton— say that with *Rosenkavalier* Strauss had withdrawn from the ranks of the avant-garde and returned to the security of big royalties and small objectives. For me, certainly, the work did not have the cyclopic grandeur of *Elektra* but it had instead a fragrance which no other music had and which has not diminished with many years of close acquaintance.

Looking back, I can understand better the disappointment of the young. The break seems to have occurred some time between 1908 and 1911: in 1911 *Petrushka* was first performed, in 1912 *Pierrot lunaire*, in 1913 *The Rite of Spring* and *Ariadne auf Naxos*. The ways had divided. Some said that the end of music had arrived—which they had not said of *Elektra*—while others, such as Florent Schmitt in Paris and Alfred Kerr in Berlin, spoke of 'new steps of listening', whatever that may have meant. Those who relied on their ears, which until then had exercised supreme authority in music, could only observe that in evil times music, too, had to sound dissonant—although in 1913 there was as yet no conclusive proof that the times were really evil.

Dissonance has a long history, and it is not easy to find a clear connection between its development and that of the times. Before J. S. Bach, chromaticism was considered cacophonous; even at the time of his death conservative musicians still looked upon it as a symptom of disease. But composers became used to using all the twelve notes of the chromatic scale, and dissonances stole in like thieves at night. The introduction to Mozart's string quartet in C major, K. 465, of 1785 is intriguing not because of the dissonances themselves but because of the still unrecognizable intention behind them. Twenty years later Beethoven combined a sustained dominant seventh with the common chord. People called it one of Beethoven's frequent extravaganzas and were reconciled when the dissonance ruefully resolved itself and returned to the beloved E flat major. In the Seventh such comfort was not easily to be had, but 'Not these sounds,' said Beethoven later, rejecting his own violent discord.

Yet this did not prevent younger composers from rattling at the locked doors of the harmonic edifice wherein they felt themselves more and more closely confined. Schubert experimented, not always happily and not always with restraint, in getting from one key to another, distant one without walking the long corridors of the usual modulations. Chopin heard hidden enharmonic relationships which loosened the fabric of tonality so much that Wagner, with an ear not perhaps naturally sharper but sharpened by new circumstances, could advance from *Lohengrin* to the *Tristan* sequence; for in *Lohengrin* tonality had already breached its banks. One only had to continue in this way, adding more and more vehemence in keeping with a world that became noisier every day, and one arrived at Strauss and Debussy—and Gustav Mahler, too, though Mahler's works were then so rarely played that they could not be regarded as a characteristic feature of musical life. It was all an apparently consistent development or progressive change, leading up to Schoenberg's *Pierrot* and Stravinsky's *Rite*.

One would not get very far in trying to relate the progressive change in music to the progression of extra-musical events. The period between Bach and Mozart was comparatively quiet in Europe, though one might say that it was then that the seeds of future troubles in politics, economics and music were sown. Mozart and Haydn, the fathers of the French Opéra Comique, Cimarosa, Paisiello, to name only the most outstanding musicians of the time, all witnessed the French Revolution, but their music was unaffected. It had already gained a large measure of that freedom which, in other contexts, led to great social and political convulsions. Beethoven, however, was affected by both the spirit and the letter of the new era. His music had an earthy or democratic quality as distinct from, or even opposed to, the more aristocratic attitude of Mozart's or Haydn's; it had what his contemporaries, with a mixture of shock and fascination, called vulgarity. But Beethoven, like Mozart and Haydn, is called a 'classic', though musical classicism has little or nothing in common with literary or architectural classicism except in its formal perfection. Something was stirring within life and within the arts, of which Beethoven may be regarded as a forerunner.

The industrial revolution, a reality in England, a distant fear on the Continent, may have sparked off the Romantic movement, with its nostalgia for a vanishing dream-world. At this point there is a much closer resemblance between the arts, between Schumann and Eichendorff. It was the same flight of fancy in each case, trying to escape from reality and knowing nothing but its own jubilant or aching heart. 'Programme music', Berlioz and Liszt, belong spiritually to Victor Hugo and all of them to Wagner and to his *Gesamtkunstwerk*, the 'total' work of art embracing all the arts in one and the same aim, a thing that had never and could never have been thought of before. Music had indeed joined company with the other arts, reflecting as they did in some half-conscious way the coming of the greatest change in European life and temper.

In the last decade before the Great War there was no need for apparently far-fetched theories. The kinship between Renoir and

Debussy was obvious; that of Schoenberg–Stravinsky and Picasso–
Braque–Derain's 'analytical cubism' even more so. Together music
and the other arts conspired against all tradition.

Friedrich Nietzsche once wrote that music was the last blossom
flowering in the autumn of the relevant culture, a language of a
bygone era arriving too late; and that 'all truly significant music
is a swansong'. This has certainly been true of the past. Gothic
music was much less complicated than the finely chiselled stone
decorations on the windows, walls, portals and towers of the cathe-
drals where it was sung, but, more important, it had nothing of
their grandeur, nothing of the mystery of their dark, high vaults.
Music, indeed, missed the great movement of the Renaissance
altogether. What we know as Renaissance music is really gothic in
the feeling of its polyphonic tracery, unaware of the clear, straight
lines of Renaissance art. Up to that time Nietzsche was obviously
right.

Then, quite inexplicably, music caught up with Baroque art. It
is difficult to understand why Nietzsche thought Handel's music
was the true expression of the Lutheran spirit. With its coloraturas
and fiorituras, with its ravishing beauty of sound, Baroque music
seems to come from the same intellectual climate as the large
canvases and painted ceilings with their exuberant colours and
movements, the fantastic, gilded interiors of Baroque churches
and palaces. Music suddenly found its rightful place and became
as pompous and stilted as the fashion, the style and the language—
and often as hollow. And from that moment—about 1650—music
followed close on the heels of the other arts. The musical equivalent
of Racine or Claude Lorrain was not Mozart, not *Figaro* or *Don
Giovanni*, but the *opera seria*, the *tragédie lyrique* which was
finally interred with *Idomeneo* and *La Clemenza di Tito*. Far from
being a swansong, Mozart's music was a premonition and we have
seen how, in the nineteenth century, it could never again be left
behind.

How music springs from the unconscious will perhaps never be
explained. But it has acquired an almost prophetic quality, it has
become a most sensitive seismograph which records every tremor
of emotion. There is some consistency in this development: music
had to become up to date as Baroque music had done. It had to
possess itself of all its means, as the music of Mozart and Haydn
did, it had then to become individual and personal as Mozart had
already foreshadowed and Beethoven then consummated; and
from there it found its way into the greater mystery of the

human mind. It was the end of a long road from a craft to an art.

It was this new quality of music which, in the nineteenth century, drove the stormclouds of coming change across its once serene skies and led inexorably to the crisis of the years before the First World War. By then it was no longer concerned with external problems of composition alone, but with the convulsions of the time itself—with the soul.

Looking back at those pre-war days, which seem now as far away as the days of Charlemagne, I cannot help wondering how and why the arts alone were driven to warn the world of the impending catastrophe. I am not using this strong word lightly: in 1914 mankind left its secure dwellings to wander into the wilderness of half-imagined, half-formulated new ideals and has not settled again to this day. Up to that fateful summer day in 1914 life was indeed secure, to a degree that seems almost unbelievable to us: diplomats, though as dangerous as ever, were proverbially polite; currencies were reliably stable; the greater part of the world was open and travellers needed no passports but could settle where they wanted and take all their money and possessions with them; summers were hot and winters cold, the rich were rich and the poor were poor, and everything was in its proper place. True, there were some incidents, wars in Manchuria and in the Balkans, which fertilized the toy industry but did not disturb the prevailing sense of satisfaction

Only the arts were nervous, upset and uncomfortable, as if they had the animal's instinctive awareness of an approaching storm. There is a passage in the Klytemnestra scene from *Elektra*, easily the harshest piece of music before the *Rite*, which mirrors the whole situation: in the midst of the most violent harmonic clashes there comes (at figure 168) an almost honeyed phrase in thirds and sixths: 'Wenn einer etwas Angenehmes sagt'—'If someone says something agreeable'. Many agreeable things *were* said, but the arts did not believe them. For the people, the public, there was still much consolation to be found in Verdi, then almost contemporary, in Puccini, whose sun shone brightly, and in Viennese operetta and its sweet, illusionist tunes.

It is an intriguing thought that the statesmen of the last decade before the First World War could have consulted not only their diplomatic files but, perhaps with the help of psychiatrists, the arts as well. They might have gleaned there some wisdom no other visible fact could provide, a warning that something was stirring in the human mind which might escape their control and set the whole world on fire. But the outraged conservatives would not look for enlightenment, nor could the radical innovators spell out the reasons for their malaise. So fate had to take its course, as in a Greek tragedy, and everyone professed surprise.

War broke out, suddenly and, as it seemed, senselessly. So tenuous was all the elaborate security that a few shots in a far corner of the Balkans unleashed a conflagration without parallel in European history. War came not as a hollow-cheeked fury with a flaming torch, running howling through the land, but as a paper ghost, pasting with remarkable composure large posters on walls calling men to arms for reasons which were either unintelligible or, if intelligible, unconvincing. This was particularly true in the old Austro–Hungarian Empire, composed as it was of a dozen nations who were determined never again to live together in peace. But, for the present, their uniforms were still the colourful affairs we had seen at school in pictures of the capture of Belgrade by Prince Eugen.

Like all wars, it did the arts no good. Gold went for steel and pens for rifles. It was like a change of scene on a darkened stage. When, five years later, the lights went up again nothing stood where it had been before. We came home from the war like Enoch Arden: the world had taken to new ideals.

Music, in particular, broke out of its stable like a wild horse and became atonal. How all the good old rules went with the wind! Atonality was not just a new light. It was a bomb, threatening to blast the once luxurious palace of music to the ground. That fitted well into the general mood of destruction, which had priority over every thought of reconstruction. We had not freed ourselves. Time and circumstance had done it for us, by an inexorable process. For six hundred and fifty years Austria's destinies, according to the old National Anthem, had been united with the Hapsburg throne, a much more ancient union than that of music with tonic and dominant. If the one was dispensable, why not the other? Those were great days: the days of *collages*, of Dadaism and Surrealist manifestos. All this was atonal, intended to destroy the past root and branch. The futurists of the past had become the artists of the present, and if the general political and economic confusion made the new world less desirable than the old had been, the arts at least seemed to enjoy the new paradise.

But musicians had to think of the future. Complete freedom is a fickle friend. If a new art was to arise from chaos it had to find shelter in new rules.

3. THE VIENNESE SCHOOL

W hen I entered music-publishing in Vienna in 1922 music, like everything else, including the minds of people, was in an unbelievable state of confusion. With the exception of the Hungarians all the other nations of the old monarchy had something to celebrate: independence for the Czechs, Poles and Yugoslavs; return to their motherland for the Italians. But the Austrians themselves did not quite know what to make of it. They did not feel liberated, the new democracy meant little to them, for they had loved the splendour and the thought of old Franz Josef aimlessly reading his papers and reports. Vienna in particular, the old imperial city, had fallen low beyond belief. It was difficult to realize that the landlords of the Hofburg and Schönbrunn would never return and that anyone could now loiter in the state apartments on payment of a modest entrance-fee. Much had been lost and no compensating gain was in sight—except music.

Vienna had a well-founded musical reputation of long standing, from the Emperor Leopold I, who saw the Turks at the gates of his capital and was himself a composer of more than average gifts, up to Brahms, two hundred years later. There could be no doubt that the interest of the Imperial House in serious music made Vienna a metropolis of the art and attracted the best Austrian (though non-Viennese) composers such as Gluck, Mozart and Haydn, and foreigners such as Beethoven and Brahms, not to mention the ubiquitous Italians from Niccolò Porpora to Antonio Salieri. The Hapsburgs may have had many unpleasant characteristics but they were genuine music-lovers—and not of the cheap variety.

This created a climate in which musicians felt at home in spite of disappointments. If one runs through the list of Beethoven's dedicatees, from the Archduke Rudolph (why, by the way, 'Emperor' Concerto, a nickname unknown in Austria? Archduke Rudolph was the twelfth son of Emperor Leopold II and never had any chance—nor, presumably, any desire—to become emperor) to such impecunious generals as Count Browne, one of many catholic Irish refugees in Austrian service, one can see how the example from above inspired and encouraged society. Some historians have doubted this, seeing architecture and painting as the real hobbies of the Austrian nobility. Hobbies they certainly were, and expensive ones at that. But music, and especially new music, was cultivated with great enthusiasm both in the imperial palace and in humbler dwellings, and up to the last days of the Empire the royal boxes at the Opera and in the Musikverein were never empty.

This desire—or curiosity—for new music was finally saturated with Brahms. The Vienna Court Opera did not care for the first performance of *Tristan* and let Gustav Mahler go, while concert-goers did not like Bruckner. The famous Vienna Philharmonic Orchestra viewed new composers with suspicion and hostility. The taste of the public was uniquely subtle and discerning. 'We cannot even play Beethoven's Fourth,' the secretary of the Gesellschaft der Musikfreunde told me, when I wondered at the almost complete absence of all new music from the programmes—Richard Strauss's symphonic poems were the only notable exceptions. Every public has the music it deserves. And the Viennese who, despite food-rationing, shortages and inflation, congregated on Sunday mornings at the Musikverein did not come out of curiosity or with the intention of gaining new experience. They came to forget their troubles, to be lifted briefly out of their everyday misery, and they found new music quite unsuitable for this puspose.

Before the war, in the midst of imperial opulence, and afterwards, in the midst of republican poverty, one could hear in Vienna the best performances of all the uncontested masterpieces. The palace on the Opernring had been degraded (or so the older subscribers felt) from a Court to a State Opera; its annexe, the Redoutensaal, previously inaccessible to ordinary mortals and still hung with precious tapestries, was used for 'chamber operas' such as Pergolesi's *Serva padrona* or Boïeldieu's *Jean de Paris*. The Opera clung to the old custom on its bills and posters of calling the singers *Herr Kammersänger* or *Frau Kammersängerin*, as if nothing had happened.

In the pit sat the same Philharmonic Orchestra, which gave its concerts on those memorable Sunday mornings, a worthy assembly of ageing professors who knew all about their craft and refused to learn what they did not already know. Younger, less experienced conductors were really given a rough passage by those grey-bearded experts. 'What is he going to conduct?' somebody asked when a new conductor was to make his first appearance.

'I do not know,' replied Professor Ruzitska, the first viola, 'I do not know what he is going to conduct. *We* are going to play the Seventh.' But when Felix von Weingartner, impeccably elegant, stood in front of them and slowly and deliberately opened the door from the Scherzo to the Finale of the Fifth the listeners felt that there was no other place on earth where one could hear it so perfectly played, and the performers knew that there was no other place where it was more appreciated or savoured with more delight by greater connoisseurs.

It was in this same Vienna that an entirely new music was hatched, and a school for it founded. Seldom can a school of revolutionary ideas have received so little encouragement from its environment or have existed in unfriendlier surroundings. The *genius loci* favoured it with no more than a disapproving grimace. The public, critics and writers ignored it. This was not like post-war Berlin, where political and economic collapse had brought all tradition into disrepute and created a hot-bed for everything that had not been done before, good and bad, decent and obscene. This was Vienna, which looked to the past for consolation. Indeed, the fact that the new school was founded in Vienna was nothing but a geographical coincidence. Heralded in 1922, the manifesto of the 'composition with twelve notes' appeared in 1924. It was a strange and, in its own way, courageous document, which offered a new and respectable home to atonality. Arnold Schoenberg brought the new teaching to composers, as Moses brought the tablets of the law to the Israelites; initially he had no better success.

I do not know whether Schoenberg and his disciples would have welcomed quick and easy victory. It may have been the inimical atmosphere surrounding the school which moulded its character. For this was not like Raphael's 'School of Athens' where wisdom was freely offered, where believers were fortified in their belief and the incredulous persuaded by reasoned argument. That was a closed shop, a sect which cared nothing for proselytes and demanded unquestioning devotion to both the teacher and his teachings. It was proud of being a small number of the chosen in the heart of general Philistia.

My own temperament has always kept me away from factions and cliques, political or otherwise. Also, I was afraid of the unavoidable conflict between duty and conviction. My relations with the members of the school therefore remained generally friendly but superficial.

I did not meet Arnold Schoenberg very often, but whenever I did he was full of sarcastic witticisms and biting remarks about others: composers, critics, writers, performers and publishers. He despised Richard Strauss and hated Stravinsky no less than the great masters of the past, with very few and curious exceptions. Even minor figures were not too small to be attacked. His resentments were monumental and perhaps deprived his own work of monumentality. He was always in opposition, sensed opposition everywhere, revelled in the idea of stirring up the whole world against himself and then hurling all his disdain in its face. This kept him always ready to pounce on something or somebody and constantly sharpened his razor-edged intellect.

Schoenberg was certainly far from being the ideal Olympian. He was worried and bothered by many things and many people, by the very existence and success of others. He could be breathtakingly overbearing, and I could never be sure whether his superciliousness was his real nature or a protective wall around him. He must also have had his happier moments, which I could not discover myself. Among his disciples he walked like a prophet. They believed in him as in the Revelation; they were even prepared to bear the cross of poverty, for which the Master himself had no liking. I believe he was a good friend to them, and when National Socialism scattered those stalwarts of the school still in Vienna he diligently wrote letters of recommendation to help them find new homes and work. I have read one of those letters in which he praised all the merits of his protégé but remembered also to mention his shortcomings, which, in such a desperate situation, seemed superfluous.

So the source from which the new teaching sprang was not as pure as one might have wished. But the harbinger of new music mellowed with age, and in the end his work was able to achieve its true stature.

The other two members of the 'trinity' were, each in his own way, very different from their master.

Alban Berg, tall, handsome, perhaps a little effeminate, was always polite, lovable, open-minded, with no display of fanaticism. In the somewhat sinister clique which surrounded the school he looked like a good boy from a good family who had fallen into bad company. He had no resentments and probably no personal enemies. He did not enjoy the hissing and whistling which accompanied every performance of any of his works, and the furore surrounding *Wozzeck* particularly grieved him. Indeed, when *Wozzeck* was first performed at the State Opera in Vienna it looked like a popular uprising, with police on foot and on horseback surrounding the whole area, ready for battle.

Berg regretted that people did not like his music; he would much rather have pleased them, but he could not betray the principles which he felt were right. Nor would he allow his own judgement of what he believed to be good music to be corrupted by the prejudices of the school, which accorded full honours to Bach and Brahms, tolerated Mozart and dismissed all the rest as worthless. His analysis of Schumann's 'Träumerei' is a little masterpiece.

In many quarters Berg's music is now considered to be decadent, the end rather than the beginning of an epoch. Unassuming men are more easily taken for decadent than fire-eating rowdies. It was said that Berg wanted to 'break the spell of twelve-note music' by preserving the human element and making his music an expression of feelings. But Schoenberg himself would not have disputed that, insisting that twelve-note, like any other music of the preceding two hundred years, was melodious and expressive. This may later have been the starting-point of further development and change. With all his unswerving devotion to his master, Berg was never dogmatic. Neither his 'Lyrische Suite' nor *Wozzeck* nor the Violin Concerto nor *Lulu* slavishly follow the official recipe. But in his time he was the most successful member of the school and *Wozzeck* was its 'prize song'. It was a pity that Berg did not set to music Gerhart Hauptmann's *Und Pippa tanzt*, a play full of poetry, fancy and colour. Gerhart Hauptmann was the greatest living German poet and Berg was advised that Hauptmann's demand for half the income from the opera was unacceptable. So this quiet man chose the outmoded sexual atrocities of Wedekind, and *Lulu* has never achieved the fame of *Wozzeck*.

I saw Berg for the last time a few days before Christmas 1935, at the first performance in Vienna of the symphonic pieces from *Lulu*. He looked pale and complained about pains in his leg— 'toothache in the wrong place', he called it. The next morning we went away for a few days in the snow. On Christmas Day I received a telephone call: *Alban Berg is dead.* The friendliest light of the school was gone. Some weeks later Berg's wife, Helene, came to talk about the work he had left. 'Tonight Alban told me . . .' she began firmly.

The third star was Anton von Webern—he did not care for his particle of nobility, which dated from the sixteenth century.

Webern was neither eruptive like Schoenberg, nor amiable like Berg, but obdurate, merciless, unbending, the man who drove the new theory to its most extreme limits. His works were short and soft, often short and soft to the point of absurdity, a mere dissonant breath which provided ammunition for all the wags. At the first performance of his Symphony, Opus 21, under Otto Klemperer a wave of uncontrollable laughter seized the audience and ambulances had to be called. But Webern bore it as St Francis bore the stigmata. He never made any concession. The opportunism of the prophet Schoenberg himself, who made his entry into the United States with the harmlessly tonal Second Chamber Symphony, was entirely foreign to him. But despite this rigid orthodoxy he also lacked the venomous spirit of opposition which distinguished his master. Webern was a martyr at a time when martyrs were urgently needed but martyrdom was out of date, a martyr without mercy and without hate, with no consideration for himself or for others. One could not help feeling some restrained admiration for him.

Webern did not expect any material gain from his compositions and did not, like his master, ask for large advance payments, although he was certain that his time would come. He conducted a workmen's choir and workmen's symphony concerts and gave lessons, to earn the modest living without which, in those hard times, one could not even be a fanatic. It seemed impossible to find a proper place for him in this world.

Webern's disregard for his environment was bound to collide fatally with the world of reality and to result in tragedy. He survived all the adversities of the time: the occupation of Austria, the war of annihilation against all new art and finally the shooting war itself. And at the very moment when life seemed to smile on him and when all the obstacles which had hurt him most of his life were about to disappear a senseless, casual death took him away. He could hardly have guessed that he would one day be regarded as the purest spirit of new music.

The Viennese School claimed to be the supreme arbiter of all things musical. It held the key to the new music, and decreed what was still acceptable of the old. But, looking back, it is strange that the three great creative men were surrounded by men of such little significance. In fact, not one of the original disciples has made any mark on contemporary music.

Among the composers only Hanns Eisler had more than an average talent, but he was too much distracted by his rabid communism

LBM

to create a work of convincing importance and size. Others
such as Apostel or Schloss have never been able to attract any
attention and have long since disappeared. It seemed that they all
owed their acceptance by the school to their devotion and pugnacity
rather than to any real merit. And the unanointed were repelled by
the atrociously overbearing behaviour of the guardians or doorkeepers of the school. Ernst Křenek would have liked to be
admitted after having voluntarily accepted the new teaching—or,
as the school would have put it, having appropriated it without
authorization. By doing so he had disappointed all those who had
greeted him as the Mozart of the twentieth century. It had
escaped his many friends that Křenek was a speculative and philo-
sophical individual who gained little satisfaction from the facility
with which he reeled off his earlier works. His twelve-note opera
Karl V, the second ever written, did not have the blessing of the
school. Its failure could not atone for the cheap world success of
his *Jonny spielt auf* and he was left to fight and to think for himself.

Likewise Joseph Matthias Hauer was ignored, mainly, I
imagine, because he claimed to have originated twelve-note
composition. He was a tragicomic figure at the periphery of new
music, a teacher at a primary school in the Austrian provinces and
a self-taught composer. His simplicity of mind was of Brucknerian
proportions and this made the complexity of his writings and the
ugliness of his music quite inexplicable. But he lacked the quick,
sharp wit of Schoenberg and the guardians of the school, and so he
was doomed in advance. Although Schoenberg himself paid him a
half-sarcastic compliment in his treatise on harmony, the guardians
of the school treated him with disdain and derision. In his own
way he was a martyr, too, who knew how to forego the pleasures
of this world and serve his strange god. For the last picture I saw
of him after the war he had grown a beard and looked like a saint
on a Greek icon, unaware of the world around him but sure of his
solitary heaven.

The school seemed more efficient in rejecting than in attracting
young talent. One of the best of his generation, Luigi Dallapiccola,
had to find his way to twelve-note music alone and considerably
later.

But if the school lacked a younger generation of creative talent
which could make its way in the world, at least it was well provided with publicists. They were an aggressive, vociferous and
arrogant band, proclaiming the infallibiliiy of the doctrine and the
utter worthlessness of every other way of composing, manning the

guns and bolting the doors and creating, quite unnecessarily, the general atmosphere of a beleaguered camp. I believe it was their busy theorists and writers who, more than anything or anybody else, turned the school into a clique.

Erwin Stein held the position of official panegyrist and publicist. His 1924 article on 'New Formal Principles' had among the initiates almost the same standing as Albert Einstein's first few pages about relativity in physics. After he emigrated Erwin Stein could not maintain his exclusive loyalty, and had to find another idol in Benjamin Britten, applying the same exclusivity which made the unwavering old champions of the school regard him as a renegade. But at the first performance of Schoenberg's *Moses and Aaron* he suffered a severe relapse and came back from Zurich convinced that Schoenberg's was the outstanding work of the century.

In those pre-war days one preferred to turn to writers who lived outside the inner circle, like H. H. Stuckenschmidt or René Leibowitz, who seemed more reliable and independent and, perhaps, less single-minded.

Music, however new, must be performed—and the school needed performers. And again it had good, competent performers although none of them were outstanding.

There was the left-handed violinist Rudolf Kolisch and his string quartet. As far as technical accomplishment and beauty of tone was concerned the Kolisch Quartet could not compete with the famous quartets of the time, the Rosé, Brussels or Czech quartets and therefore did not have the same appeal to a wider public. But it was astounding how these four men not only knew the whole classical and romantic repertoire by heart but also played the music of Schoenberg, Berg and Webern as if it was the easiest thing on earth.

Similarly the pianist Eduard Steuermann was no more than a competent performer and thorough musician with no spark of brilliance. He, too, played Schoenberg's piano music with an amazing matter-of-factness but could seldom convince his listeners. When he edited Brahms's piano works for me I could see how his excessively strict theoretical schooling had tended to suppress all spontaneity and had created problems which unfettered musical instinct solves without even being aware of them. But competence rather than brilliance was the watchword of the school, even though it was lost on the public. A combination of the two such as was demonstrated by the pianist Artur Schnabel, who composed twelve-note music in his leisure time but preferred to play Beethoven in public, was within neither the reach nor the intention of the performers of the school.

Among conductors Hermann Scherchen was a member of the inner circle. (It must be realized that in the 1920s it was the conductor who needed courage, rather than the composer or even a pianist or chamber ensemble playing to small and rather select audiences. There was still a spark of fire left which could produce memorable musical battles, and the conductor at the head of his troops had to bear the brunt of public anger. The three great men of the school were not very prolific composers and performances were few, but each time there were brawls and demonstrations. In Vienna, there was one fair-haired lawyer who made every performance of a work by Schoenberg, Berg or Webern a dangerous occasion for the rest of the audience because he was always ready to assault physically anyone who raised so much as an eyebrow in disagreement.) Hermann Scherchen had both courage and skill, though like all other performers of the school he was more competent than brilliant. In his later years he seemed to believe less strongly in the ideals of his youth. When we last met in London he surprised me with a long, derogatory lecture about the music he had once admired.

Otto Klemperer, though not an inner-circle man, was certainly the most brilliant interpreter of the new music. I owe to him my first encounter with Mozart's *Don Giovanni* in the Old Theatre in Prague, where the first performance of the work had taken place, and to this day I am grateful to him for that unforgettable experience. As director and first conductor of the Kroll Opera in Berlin he was a very important man and a great asset to the school, though he was widely suspected of performing the new music rather to cause a sensation than because he believed in it. But it was most impressive to see how, at that memorable première of Webern's Symphony, he conjured up the sparse sounds from the orchestra with his overlong arms and powerful gestures, unperturbed by the commotion behind him. Today old age and illness have extinguished the memories of his youthful adventures, and he has retraced his steps to Beethoven.

But the enduring fame rests, I believe, with Erich Kleiber for his first performance of *Wozzeck* in Berlin in 1925, which proved that the work was both performable—which many people, and especially the coaches at the State Opera in Berlin, would not believe—and effective in every operatic sense. Kleiber did not belong to the Viennese School like Scherchen or to any other, nor did he care for Klemperer's extravagances. He was, therefore, more trustworthy than the other two, and one had the reassuring feeling that he conducted the new music not because of its novelty but because he honestly believed in its excellence. One does not talk of Kleiber in the same breath as Toscanini or Furtwängler; his performances may not have had the tension which the other two created when they stepped on to the rostrum. But his performances, whether of Berg or Mozart, Wagner or Strauss, were both brilliant and impeccable. He was one of the comparatively few who left Germany without being forced to do so; the Teatro Colón in Buenos Aires and indeed the whole of South American musical life benefited greatly from his emigration. When we met again after the war he was reluctant to accept a permanent position, 'At my age I should be free to conduct where and what I like,' he said. But a sudden death took him away.

After Schoenberg's departure and Berg's death the school was left deserted. No new light appeared, and when the ranks were decimated by emigration and the new powers of anti-modernism took possession of what was left they found little enough to destroy.

Those interested in the theory and technique of twelve-note composition as invented (or discovered) and practised by Schoenberg can read all about it in the sizeable literature on the subject. It is difficult reading for the most part and cannot be usefully undertaken without a good knowledge of the classical or traditional theory of harmony, counterpoint and musical form. It will teach the reader how to *write* music but not how to *hear* it. In fact unless he is himself a composer the knowledge of the new compositional technique will be as useful or useless to him as the study of traditional technique is for the appreciation of the music of Bach or Beethoven.

For our purpose here it is sufficient to say that, in the first place, twelve-note music is atonal, having no tonal centre or key. But while atonal music pure and simple dispensed with all restrictions the rules of twelve-note music are rigidly strict: stricter than the rules of classical or romantic music, stricter even than the rules of the polyphonic music of past centuries. But so it happens often enough in life: revolutions which set out to overthrow a tyrant have often ended in a new and harsher tyranny. After the Bourbons came the Terror; after the Tsars came Stalin. Similarly music, after a short spell of wild freedom, found itself in the straitjacket of an iron discipline. Once the 'row' of twelve notes—none of which must be repeated—is found or invented there is a much smaller area of freedom left than composers had in the nineteenth century when, for instance, Beethoven could write a sonata movement with five different main subjects or Wagner a continuous 'symphony' of nearly two hours' duration.

Within the small area of freedom, however, the degree of skill required is unprecedented in music. Every note and every interval is governed by the rule of the first 'row', its inversion, its mirror and the inversion of the mirror.

The mere listener, however, is seldom aware of the great art which goes into the writing of what is usually a short piece. Even if the row has a clear melodic profile, such as the ten-note fugal theme of the twelfth of Bach's 'Forty-Eight', often quoted by the school as a precursor of its own theories, the lines of this horizontal–vertical music soon become confused to the ear. Theoretically, the progress of a dodecaphonic piece is more logical and more com-pelling than any sonata movement, but the listener will not easily gain that impression. For him the piece will usually start hesitantly, continue without any clear aim and end abruptly. The old notion of a coda rounding off a piece of music has to be forgotten. Only the careful reader will discover the complicated formal principles, and it may be said that this discrepancy between the technical achievement and the acoustic result emphasizes the distance between composer and listener which, from Schoenberg onwards, becomes a feature of 'new' music.

The contrast within a single piece which was the great achieve-ment of classical music, somewhat uncertain in Haydn but fully developed by Mozart and Beethoven, is also abandoned. On the other hand the listener can hardly fail to hear the wide intervals and jumps characteristic of this new music. This is not altogether new. Such wide intervals are found in Fiordiligi's 'Com' un scoglio' where, some people believe, they are meant as a form of parody, and in Richard Strauss (for example, in the final section of *Don Quixote*) where they are written quite deliberately. But while they are not characteristic of any composer before Schoenberg they have become another unmistakable property of his music and of music after him.

It is also remarkable that certain conventional and fundamental requirements of traditional music have at least been obscured in twelve-note music, in practice if not in theory.

Every piece of music normally receives its basic character from the speed or tempo. Of all the uncertainties which surround older music the uncertainty of the tempo is the most painful. It extends to the music of J. S. Bach. Dodecaphonic music, strangely, knows only an indeterminate tempo which cannot easily be described as fast, slow or moderate. Even if the tempo indication reads 'fast' the flow of audible music is punctuated by so many rests that, apart from isolated fast phrases or passages, the overall acoustic result is a moderately slow or moderately fast pace, however fast the beat may be counted.

Besides the speed the rhythm is usually, or traditionally, regarded as the living pulse of every piece of music. But a healthy pulse, whether in the musical or the medical sense, requires regularity; it is not simply a sequence of long and short noises or notes but the repetition of a certain pattern of long and short noises or notes. There is nothing in the theory of twelve-note music to prohibit such a regular pulse, but the general ban on repetition may have led to the avoidance of regular rhythmic patterns. The result is not rhythmic in the customary sense.

All this is not meant as a criticism of twelve-note music. Its purpose is to indicate the difference between 'old' and 'new' listening, the fact that this new music is not merely conveying the traditional meaning by new means. But the following is an example of what can happen.

When Schoenberg's Violin Concerto had its first European performance in Venice—in 1948, I believe—I did not arrive until the afternoon before the concert. I sat that evening next to the critic of *Stampa*, the leading Turin newspaper, an extremely experienced man with a profound knowledge of every kind of contemporary music. There was no printed score available, but my friend had attended three rehearsals while I had come quite unprepared. In the middle of the performance he whispered to me, 'Do you know, they haven't played the second movement!' After the performance I asked the conductor, Arthur Rodzinski, why the movement had not been played, but he assured me that not one single bar had been cut. True, the three movements of the Concerto are linked together without a break and the second is, perhaps optimistically, marked *Andante grazioso*. But a mistake such as occurred with my experienced friend indicates the difficulties of the listener when confronted with an apparent uniformity of tempo and rhythm. Later, when I was able to study the printed score, I discovered a certain march-like character in the last movement, but I must confess that I could not hear it in the actual performance.

I have said that twelve-note music does not convey old meanings by new means, but this cannot be so easily applied to the music of Schoenberg and Alban Berg. Schoenberg, the teacher and guiding light of the school, insisted on the old function and purpose of music—that it should be an expression of feeling, laugh or weep, be tranquil or excited, in fact have all the properties which music had acquired in the preceding two hundred and fifty years. This was somewhat contradictory. Was it possible, with a new way of musical thinking, to preserve the essential character of traditional music? Schoenberg certainly revolutionized music, and revolutions usually have new objectives and no rules, but Schönberg's revolution had new rules but no new objective. Only Webern had the courage to face all the consequences of the new teaching. There is no remnant of the 'traditional' in his music or in its intention. His music does not mean what music before him meant.

But the 'meaning' of music is and always was a mystery. Professional criticism could do little with the anarchy of atonality. It could accept or reject it; like all anarchy, it was a matter of blind belief or blind objection. Schoenberg offered a thoroughly considered code of new laws that could readily be debated. Criticism then centred round the argument that diatonic music and its degenerate offspring enharmonic music had a psychological foundation in human nature. With greater assiduity than ever before music was not only compared with language but was even defined as one, one which developed according to its own laws; Schoenberg was reproached with having invented a musical Esperanto which could never replace the 'natural' musical language.

But music and language are two different things, and a comparison, let alone an analogy, between them must fail. Music lacks the most elementary requirement of any language: vocabulary. Though it is true that within a certain style and period certain turns have the same effect on the listener, such effects have changed almost before our eyes. The minor mode, for instance, was unknown to modal music and had no specific 'meaning' in that of J. S. Bach. But in classical and, still more, romantic music it became the expression of grief, despair, pain, sadness, although even this 'meaning' is not as inflexible as the meaning of words. Such sad pieces as Orpheus's lament over the loss of Eurydice or Constanza's 'Ach, ich liebe' in Mozart's *Entführung* are in major mode. Twelve-note music has done away with major and minor modes and, therefore, with whatever meaning they had. But it has firm rules, and if one pursues the comparison with a language one arrives only at the absurd conclusion that music is a language with a grammar but no vocabulary.

The reproach of artificiality was not therefore well founded. Twelve-note music is no more arbitrary or unnatural than any other musical form. The old forms of sonata, rondo or song, too, were invented rather than revealed. But the new fundamental element of this new music, and one which strikes the unbiased listener, is the avoidance of consonance and the merciless insistence on dissonance. All that the more modest music-lover needs to realize is that new and categorical rules have utterly destroyed all consonance and created a system of dissonance in keeping with the spirit of the times. Consonance being thus prohibited, with a kind of religious fanaticism, dissonance assumes a legitimate place in music and in life. It no longer serves as a contrast or warning, as it did with Beethoven or even with Richard Strauss and Debussy. Freed from anarchy as well as from bad conscience, it is the ruling principle of new music and modern life. This has been the purpose of every musical theory since its very beginning; and theory has always been as liberal or as authoritarian as the time that produces it. There is nothing in twelve-note theory which violates the pattern of the past. However one may like or dislike its practical results, the principle was unquestionably right. It was wrong only when it claimed that the 'tonal' system was exhausted. It was not the old system that was exhausted but the mind. The public could still enjoy the 'beautiful' music of a lingering past but composers could no longer supply it.

4. THE WORLD AROUND

Viewed from close-up the Schoenberg School seemed larger than life. In fact it played a rather modest part in the musical life of the years between the wars, despite its noisy propagandists. Of all its output only *Wozzeck* reached a wider public to become a musical sensation; the repertoire of contemporary music was dominated by great masters who, in their own ways, also trespassed on the old rules and on the experience of security and contentment but were neither atonal anarchists nor adherents of any new teaching.

Maurice Ravel was the most widely acclaimed 'modern' composer of the time. A piece like his 'Bolero' seemed to possess everything that could be expected of new music: rhythm, impetus, harshness, bravura. Orchestras, conductors and public alike revelled in it. I remember its first performance in Vienna, when it had to be played three times. Today people prefer the *Daphnis and Chloë* suites and *La Valse* which were also popular at that time; and everyone who could still play the piano played the 'Sonatina'. Ravel's operatic essays, however, were no more successful then than they are today.

After Ravel, Stravinsky had a harder passage. In his *Histoire du soldat* and even more in the Symphonies for Wind Instruments and in the Octet he seemed to be carried away by the atonal current; but he battled to reach the safer shores of neo-classicism which made more of a point of their distance from the past rather than their closeness to it. That was his real originality. *Oedipus, Apollon, Symphony of Psalms* and *Persephone* were no nostalgic recollections but overwhelming testimonies to the change of time, climate and mood. The unbiased public seemed to grasp this more easily than the learned critics, who expected every new work to be another *Rite of Spring*—not that they liked that either.

While all the rough edges of Stravinsky's 'barbarisms' were smoothed away in the stream of European influences, Prokofiev brought all his with him from Russia in their full and unashamed vigour. People listened with great pleasure to the Classical Symphony, although it was a by no means good-humoured skit on the most sacred elements in music. They even enjoyed the Scythian Suite and 'Pas d'acier' which had frightened the dauntless Diaghilev. When Prokofiev hammered out his Third Piano Concerto with his mighty hands the audience were in a state of frenzy. Though his operas had no luck, the March and Scherzo from *The Love of Three Oranges* had a resounding success throughout the concert-halls of the New and the Old Worlds.

I met Prokofiev on his last journey to Russia. He felt ill at ease and attributed this to the lack of his native air. He believed he had exhausted his inventive powers and expected to find in Russian surroundings either a fresh excitement in new music, or a fresh satisfaction in the old. In spite of his Herculean appearance he had none of Stravinsky's greatness and resolution. With a boyish laugh he waved his enormous right hand to bid me farewell. 'When I know how to write music again I will come back! The Russian Government has promised me full liberty: I can come and go as I please.' He did not come back, and he did not live happily. What he composed in Russia does not compare with the works he had written abroad. The furs belonging to his French wife are still with a Paris furrier; in a Paris cellar lies a large box with pro-grammes, newspaper cuttings, photographs and hundreds of little souvenirs of the years in Germany, France and the United States which he left behind, perhaps for fear that they might hinder his rebirth.

Russia had become a place of mystery. News about life and art there was scanty and biased. I remember a discussion with the Moscow correspondent of a leading Viennese paper who, for reasons unknown to himself, had been left in Russia during and after the purge of the early Thirties. Somebody asked him the inevitable question: 'Do you think that the Bolshevist régime will last?' 'Oh,' he replied, 'I have been living in Russia now for sixteen years and I cannot tell you. But if you ask someone who has made a fortnight's guided tour through the country with Intourist I am sure he will not hesitate to give you a definite "yes" or "no".' A few works and a few names attracted attention, though not the indefatigable Miaskovsky, writing symphony after symphony un-perturbed by the superstition that nobody after Beethoven could get beyond the Ninth. Mossolov's 'Iron Foundry' became a fashionable piece, but people really listened to Shostakovich. His First Symphony and the concert suites from his ballets *The Golden Age* and *The Nose* aroused expectations that the new Russia, like the old, would make a great contribution to new music.

'The Iron Foundry' was a good counterpart to Honegger's 'Pacific 231', a musical portrait of what was then the most modern railway engine. Music was finding new subjects indeed for onomatopoeic exercises. But Honegger, the pin-up boy of serious music, also wrote the beautiful 'Pastorale d'été' and the important *Roi David*.

The Spaniard Manuel de Falla preserved some of the rare exotic charm of earlier days. His works were few but they were all distinguished, colourful and justly famous.

It is remarkable that Italian music, which had animated and dominated European music for so long, was rapidly losing its momentum. The country which had invented opera and kept up the supply for more than three hundred years could produce no more. Italian opera did not fade out: it simply stopped dead in its tracks. Wolf-Ferrari, Zandonai, Montemezzi were, with their small successes, far behind Verdi and Puccini. Alfano (who completed Puccini's *Turandot*) and others failed utterly in the theatre. The younger composers took to symphonic, chamber and instrumental music, for which the Italian masters of the nineteenth century had had no time or use. Respighi's 'Pine Trees of Rome', with a real nightingale on a record, and his 'Fountains of Rome', a somewhat inflated sequel to Liszt's 'Jeux d'eau de la Villa d'Este', became fashionable successes. (When I revisited Rome not long ago, incidentally, the fountains were gushing with their old clear freshness but the pine trees were all brown and looked sick and I was told that the polluted air of the Eternal City was slowly but inexorably killing them.) Respighi's compatriot Alfredo Casella obtained some temporary success by harking back to the glorious past with works like 'Paganiniana' and 'Scarlattiana' rather than by searching for a better future. I was surprised at the reverence with which the Italians spoke of him after the Second World War. His operatic attempts failed, no less than those of Gianfrancesco Malipiero, whose ancestor had once thrown Venezia's wedding-ring from the Bucintoro into the sea. With experimental works such as 'Impressioni dal vero' he aroused more interest than applause. But the real genius among Italian composers was Luigi Dallapiccola, who, perhaps for that very reason, had to contend with artistic and political opposition. It is not easy to understand why his music is not heard more often. It is, for me at least, among the best written of our time.

Before we enter upon the German scene the strange figure of Ferruccio Busoni deserves to be mentioned. Italian by birth,

German by choice, he has to this day a reputation which seems disproportionate to the work he has left. He was an original thinker and speculated about a new aesthetics of music long before Schoenberg. But his music hardly reflects that originality and is strangely lifeless, inhibited perhaps by too much thought. He was a great pianist and his Bach transcriptions demand the almost impossible, even down to the haughty footnote that those who cannot span a tenth should not attempt to play them. He must have been a fascinating teacher, but only his pupils can bear witness to this aspect of the man and artist. He must also have been a great inspiration, perhaps one of those rare men who stimulate their pupils to give of their own best rather than to accept the ideas of their master. It is difficult if not impossible for those who never met him—and I am one of them—to appreciate all this, but it is reassuring that such personal qualities alone can erect a monument which, in the second generation after his death, still stands and commands the reverence of the musical world, unsupported though it is by tangible achievements.

Among the young Germans Hindemith was the most outstanding. I remember a hilarious evening in his company when, with Licco Amar, the first violin of his quartet, he improvised 'off stage' a funny Tyrolean yodel duet. His music had a modernity of a special kind. It avoided all recherché problems; it was music to be played and enjoyed and not to be thought about, driven by an impatient temperament, infectious in its *joie de vivre*. Hindemith had a prodigious output, and the universal popularity of his works made him the best-known of all German composers of his generation.

And the other German composers? It is most illuminating to step out of old habits and acquired prejudices while one is still capable of an open mind. In Britain Edward Elgar was still alive, Ralph Vaughan Williams and William Walton had had their first successes. Yet in Germany they were just as irrelevant as Reger, Pfitzner, Schreker, Mahler and even Bruckner were to the Anglo-Saxon taste. Neither group contributed to an international contemporary repertoire. In Germany, Elgar's 'Introduction and Allegro for Strings' was known, and in England I was surprised to find Pfitzner's overture to his opera *Christelflein* on the programmes. It cannot be said that the two were properly represented.

Differences in national temperament are often quite amazing and they express themselves in music more openly than in any other way. After the Second World War I persuaded Ernest

Ansermet to perform Vaughan Williams's Fifth Symphony in
Geneva. 'It is certainly an excellent work,' he said to me afterwards, 'but who wants to hear it again?' Equally, Elgar's 'Enigma
Variations' were, at my instigation, first performed in Zurich in
1948, but the critics wrote that they preferred Brahms. On the
other hand I remember Benjamin Britten telling me how bored
he was with Pfitzner's *Palestrina* after hearing it somewhere in
Germany. Before the Second World War the few attempts at
introducing Mahler into England failed lamentably. Experts and
public agreed that his music was too involved and too morbid. And
Bruckner, second only to Beethoven in the Germanic world, was
too German, pompous, long-winded, stodgy, elephantine. Strangely
enough, both were discovered in Britain after the war, while Reger
and Pfitzner remained for the Anglo-Saxons what Elgar and
Vaughan Williams still are for the Germans.

Seen from a distance of thirty or forty years the musical scene
between the wars was turbulent and disorderly, a curious mixture
of uncertain tradition and uncertain innovation. In the midst of
all the hue and cry about new music the Czech Jaromir Weinberger
earned a world success with his old-fashioned opera *Schwanda the
Bagpiper*, and Rachmaninov delighted audiences by playing his
piano concertos with a stony face and incredibly agile fingers.
Above it all towered Richard Strauss, imperturbably writing opera
after opera, undeterred by the bad press he invariably received after
Ariadne. But in fact he and Schoenberg were the only ones who
stuck to their principles.

Also unaffected by theories new or old was Béla Bartók. This
small, thin, taciturn man was not an easy person to deal with,
and his silences could drive a visitor to despair without his so much
as noticing it. He never looked you straight in the eye and his finely
chiselled face was like a mask, seldom changing beyond the occasional fleeting shadow of a distant smile or momentary anger. He
spoke with visible effort, he seemed embarrassed to talk of himself
or of his own or any other music.

Behind the unapproachable façade lay an extreme intolerance in
both artistic and human matters. I cannot agree with the romantic
descriptions of him which insist that he was the kindliest of men
but was ashamed of himself and took refuge behind a wall of
reserve. His reticence and intolerance were no deliberate protection
from a world which would not understand him. They were his
very nature and only in his music could he escape from it. Did this

trouble him? Bartók was not an unhappy man in the usual sense, but neither was he a happy one who enjoyed himself and his music. In artistic and political matters alike he was an idealist, without practical objectives. It was said that he might have been chosen for the highest office, perhaps for the presidency of the Hungarian Republic after the Second World War, if he had not been doomed by then. His integrity was certainly unequalled, but I cannot think of anybody less suitable, and if his death prevented it, then at least he was spared another disappointment, of which his life had more than its fair share.

He never mentioned the music of other composers. He lived close to the aggressive Schoenberg circle but utterly ignored it. He admired Liszt, which was then an unfashionable thing to do, and played his works passionately, although he was not himself a showy virtuoso. Occasionally one was reminded that he had an astonishingly wide knowledge of music which one might otherwise have thought did not really interest him. In a letter he once quoted to me a few bars of cellos and basses which neither I nor anybody to whom I showed them could identify. They were harmonically so strange that I though he had quoted from a new work of his own. But later he confessed with some irony that they came from the first act of *Lohengrin*.

Engravers and proof-readers dreaded him. He was the most scrupulous writer himself and would not tolerate the slightest carelessness in others. If now and then he abandoned the usual musical orthography he always had a definite purpose in mind and his wishes had to be followed unconditionally and unreservedly. Only rarely did he condescend to explain his intentions.

Once he partly let the mask slip. It was at the beginning of the 1930s. The general economic crisis all over the world had hit new music hard: public subsidies were cut, orchestras had to economize and give up all experiments. With Bartók himself things had gone badly. His works were hardly ever played, he had no satisfactory position in Hungary, he had few friends and none of those were influential. A journey through Turkey, collecting folk-songs in the fastnesses of Asia Minor, was a short escape from all his disappointments. The music which he wrote in those years testifies to the artistic, social and financial crisis in his own life. It became a mirror of himself, withdrawing into a hard shell of harsh, intolerant, unbending contrapuntal despair which accepted the inevitable with utter contempt.

He then did what he had never done before: he complained. He complained that even his piano works, apart from the 'Allegro barbaro', found no favour with the public. He rightly called himself the only legitimate contemporary composer of piano music, being a pianist himself and knowing how to write not only good but real, effective piano music. I could speak only from my own pianistic experience: from J. S. Bach to the Romantics every stylistic period had its educational literature which taught the beginner about both musical style and its technical problems; after Schumann this up-to-date literature of exercises and easy pieces began to disappear and the young player still had to start and finish with Czerny, which gave him all the equipment for Mozart and Beethoven but was no help with Chopin and Brahms, let alone what followed. 'But I am always writing short, easy pieces for beginners,' replied Bartók, 'I have drawers full of them.' This was not enough, I said. What was required was a system, a method. The real difficulty of contemporary music was perhaps not technical but visual, the problem of reading. Long familiarity with diatonic music had led to superficial reading. Perhaps not always with Chopin and Schumann, but certainly with Brahms and naturally with all classical and preclassical music, one had only to glance at a phrase or harmonic progression and one could guess its continuation without precisely reading every note. But with contemporary music everything was unpredictable—as Beethoven's music must have appeared to his contemporaries—and that constituted the principal difficulty of approach. Anybody who could play Chopin's studies in thirds and sixths or the piano concertos of Brahms could cope with the technical problems of Bartók, if only he could read the music. Bartók listened attentively and said he would think it over.

The result was his *Mikrokosmos*, which I published in London in 1940. Since Clementi's *Gradus ad Parnassum*, the last part of which had been published exactly a hundred and twenty years before, nothing similar had been attempted. But Bartók, compared with Clementi and with his contemporaries, had incomparably superior mental and artistic powers. In 153 pieces, from the easiest in the range of five notes up to the most advanced grade of the 'Dances in Bulgarian Rhythm', he unfolded the whole contemporary art of music, a colourful world of little tone-poems, sad and joyful, illustrative and pensive. Never before had his power of invention and imagination been set so free. It is an astonishing work which far exceeded my expectations and made Bartók's name famous in circles which had never previously heard of him.

It is a strange coincidence that success came to Bartók just at the time when all his fears came true and the darkness of impending catastrophe spread across the world. I like to think that work on *Mikrokosmos* brought back to Bartók a fresh creative impulse which had almost been extinguished in the ten bitter preceding years. His Music for String Orchestra, Piano, Harp, Celesta and Percussion, where he again demonstrated his sheer pleasure in new sonorities, was an immediate success. But, uncompromising as ever, he would not allow it to be performed in National Socialist Germany.

Things happened with bewildering swiftness. Austria was occupied and Bartók at once broke off relations with his old and now 'aryanized' publisher. No other creative artist met the forces of evil so unyieldingly. When he concluded an agreement with his new English publisher he insisted on a clause forbidding that his works should ever be published with German titles or texts. But all this acted as a rejuvenating influence on his music. In the preceding years Bartók had been confronted with an anonymous, invisible enemy and he had withdrawn behind his contempt. Now at last he could see his adversary and he felt relieved and vigorous again. The Violin Concerto, the Divertimento for strings were gay and carefree. A new love of life sprang from his music and took hold of the listener. Never had Bartók been so successful, so lovable, as on the eve of the great upheaval.

The world outside, alas, was not in tune with this newly won inner freedom. Hungary was in the grip of Nazi sympathizers and the future was dark. Friends pressed Bartók to go to the United States. Against his better judgement he did so—and the idea failed. It was bound to fail. People in the United States have neither the time nor the patience to discover other people and their worth, and this inconspicuous, silent man could not advertise himself. As a pianist he could not easily compete with others. His playing was a precious experience for real music-lovers but it lacked the brilliance which a large public expects. And so, on the eve of the war, he returned, in the forlorn hope that Hungary might by a miracle be spared.

One year later—the war had already begun—he escaped by the skin of his teeth with his wife and his younger son, and by way of Switzerland and Genoa he found his way back to unfriendly America, which received him no more cordially than before. Hard years awaited him. My publishing house and its owner, Ralph Hawkes, have been reproached for having allowed Bartók to suffer want and distress. But those who knew him well also knew how difficult, even impossible, it was to help this proud, unbending man. When he left Hungary without a penny in his pocket a wealthy Swiss friend paid for his passage to the States. The sum was utterly insignificant to a man who had done much more for many other struggling composers. But to his despair Bartók, who needed the money, returned the exact amount a few weeks later. The war made contacts and correspondence with London difficult, cables were not accepted and letters took several months to reach their destination. The New York branch of my publishing house was instructed to give Bartók not only every assistance but also any money he might need, and Ralph Hawkes implored him to avail himself of the opportunity. But he made only the most trivial use of this offer and absolutely refused any advance or loan or gift.

There may be some who find such behaviour in extraordinary circumstances admirable. But even in such matters one can go beyond what is reasonable. It only emphasized Bartók's inability to deal with people and conditions. It was his misfortune to have been born and to live in such troubled times; for ultimately they overwhelmed him. But his new music blossomed forth as never before. Serge Koussevitzky, the wealthy and generous conductor of the Boston Symphony Orchestra, commissioned the Concerto for Orchestra, Yehudi Menuhin played the Violin Concerto and commissioned the Solo Sonata for Violin, William Primrose commissioned the Viola Concerto. With the great successes which attended these works the sun at last rose on Bartók's life—but in 1943 all hope of saving him was lost. He lived just long enough to see Hitler crushed and Hungary liberated. Would he have enjoyed the fame which had been so long in coming to him? It has been widely debated whether he would have returned to Hungary if he had still had the strength. He died in exile on the threshold of a happier time, and even his death could not dispel the shadows which had clung to everything he touched. Today, after more than twenty years, there is controversy about his estate.

Very different from Bartók was his lifelong friend and collaborator, Zoltán Kodály. They had the same aim: to make true Hungarian folk-music a valid idiom of the art. But while Bartók searched and fought, Kodály earned enormous successes. His 'Psalmus Hungaricus' of 1923 was acclaimed all over the world as the best choral work since Brahms's 'German Requiem'. With *Háry János* he gave the Hungarians their national opera. In Budapest alone it has had more than a thousand performances, while the concert suite from it remains a standard work of the international repertoire.

Kodály was more easily accessible, more human than Bartók, more sophisticated. He had his detractors—popularity always has. But it is no blind fate which confers happiness or misfortune on people. Bartók's hard intolerance attracted trouble but Kodály handled his art and the people around him with consummate skill. He was no fanatic in either an artistic or a national sense. He was endowed with a sense of humour that was never bizarre, with feeling that was never ashamed of itself, obsessed by nothing except the human and artistic conviction which he would allow nobody to touch. He knew how to treat them all: the public, the authorities, National Socialists and Communists, the war. When conditions demanded a decision he was in no doubt: Bartók emigrated, Kodály stayed behind, with a cool confidence in his own authority. He was the most prominent man in Hungary and he feared no one. Inertia or dignity? While he and his first wife, Emma, were in London after the war the extremists of the Communist Party seized power and Kodály was warned by the Hungarian Embassy in London not to return, because a man with so many friends and connections abroad must attract the suspicions of the new régime. Emma was alarmed, perhaps for the first time in her life, and wanted to stay. But Kodály did not waver for one moment. Quietly, without any pathos, he said that not only was the monumental collection of Hungarian folk-songs which he had started with Bartók forty years before awaiting him in proof stage, but, still more important, there were many people at home who needed him and his help. He could not desert them now when things were getting worse. And the Kodálys returned as they had planned.

Emma did not come back again. She died. That was the tragedy in his life; and later he wrote to me:

You can imagine what fearful loneliness she has left behind. After half a century with her I have to stumble alone to my grave. For the last four years I have left her only for odd hours and regret now every moment I have spent without her. I am amazed at the truly magic influence she had even on strangers. From the hundreds of letters I am receiving I can see that she was an inspiration wherever she went, sometimes only by a casual word. . . . I cannot think how to arrange my future life. . . . I shall need much time to become a human being again.

After having overcome all the adversities of Nazism, war and Communism he seemed to succumb now.

But the darling of the gods survived. It was Emma's last wish that Kodály should marry again, and she chose for him the young daughter of an old friend. It was more than a gesture on her part; she was a very wise woman, the wisest woman I have known. And Kodály's young second wife truly transfigured his last years with her love and devotion. The extraordinary dignity of both soon silenced the sarcastic comments of the few.

It has often been said that Kodály was not prolific or progressive enough and that he rested too soon on his early laurels. It was overlooked, or perhaps even unknown, outside his own country that for the last forty years of his life his interest and enthusiasm were devoted to musical education. He developed a method of teaching music at all levels from nursery to academy in order, as he said himself, to educate both the public and the musicians. He firmly believed that music was the essential element of a harmonious life and proved that in those schools which adopted his methods children were better disciplined and made quicker progress in other subjects. Kodály was indeed the only prominent composer of our time who really cared for musical education and worked for it. More than two thousand part-songs, from the easiest nursery rhymes to the most difficult pieces, bear witness to a life's work which penetrated deep into the consciousness of his people.

The gods were kind to him to the last and spared him the distress of a long illness. He was suddenly taken away. The day after his death I received a book from him, with his dedication written in the same firm handwriting which I had known for forty years. It was like a message from the other world.

Even for one so important his funeral was an unforgettable occasion. A crowd estimated at 80,000 followed his coffin; and the day after, when we thought we might have a few moments of quiet remembrance, thousands stood and wept at the grave. 'How merit and good fortune go hand in hand fools will never see,' wrote Goethe. . . .

5. RESURRECTION

Music between the wars was distinguished by its lack of a common style. If it can be dated with a fair degree of accuracy today the criteria are still rather negative: the absence of old-established rules, phrases and turns, rather than any common positive feature, assigns it to its proper place in the calendar of the art. Ravel, Richard Strauss, Stravinsky, Falla, Bartók, Hindemith, Schoenberg are all individually recognizable and hence datable. Where there are no common rules individuality becomes the only guide. Moreover, politics took it upon itself to govern not only public and private life but art as well. It decreed what was healthy art and what was degenerate, and in spite of the different nomenclature the ideas were astonishingly similar. What was called 'cultural bolshevism' on one side was called 'cultural capitalism' on the other. And new music was burnt at the stake. War broke out again and this time it did not come as a surprise. It seemed to be the end of everything.

But when the last bombs had fallen and the dust of ruined cities had settled new music rose like a phoenix from the ashes. It was like a miracle.

How it came about that the new teaching, now more than twenty-five years old and represented only by a mere handful of convincing works, was re-examined and resuscitated will probably never be known. Resurrection did not begin in the United States where Schoenberg himself was teaching and composing—it was rather the younger generations of Germany, France and Italy which awakened to the uncomfortable feeling that the world had left them behind. Or had the knowledge imperceptibly seeped through the cracks of consciousness in spite of war and persecution? Although material destruction in the Second World War exceeded all experience confusion was not as great as it had been after the First. There was not the same dangerous trend towards anarchy, and everything old was so remote and so disgraced that it did not irritate the present. Enough that submerged Atlantis rose to the surface again; only then did the teaching of twelve-note music spread and cease to be the exclusive practice of a black brigade.

The starting-point, however, was not the father and creator of the movement but the less successful and—one would have thought—largely forgotten Anton Webern. He alone of the whole school had resolutely turned away from the past; in him alone the new technique had also produced a new attitude. In his soft sighs there was not a breath of tradition or convention, while Schoenberg's *Moses and Aaron* was still written and felt in the shadow of *Tristan*. Both Schoenberg and Webern have orchestrated a work by J. S. Bach: Schoenberg the organ prelude and fugue in E flat major, Webern the 'Ricercare' from the 'Musical Offering'. The choice is characteristic of their different moods, and the results even more so. Schoenberg tried to produce the sound of a super-organ with a large orchestra, so much so that one might ask what purpose such orchestration could serve. Webern's score, on the other hand, looks like any other of Webern's scores. He dissolves Bach's closely-knit parts into a widespread diaphanous tissue, translating Bach into an entirely different world—Webern's world. 'Every work of Webern's is like a finely-cut diamond,' Stravinsky once said to me; not the Koh-i-noor or the Star of Africa, it is true, but a flawless splinter which, under the magnifying-glass of loving study, may even sparkle.

It has rarely happened that an artistic turning-point has been so clearly discernible. Fundamental changes usually develop step by step over a considerable period of time, and new attitudes are not normally found within one generation. But here was Webern accomplishing it alone and leaving his pacemaker far behind, not by merely implementing the new theory but by giving music a new purpose.

Such a turning-point is also a moment of truth for every honest music-lover. I have said before that it is not easy to determine exactly the point where I could no longer follow the development. I had no difficulty with the music of the masters between the wars. This was in the true sense 'la musica a' miei tempi'. I could familiarize myself with the music of Ravel almost as closely as with the music of Brahms. Access to twelve-note music was much more difficult. The vocal score of *Wozzeck*, for example, conveyed to the player little of the actual sound of the music. One had to hear it and hear it again, and I found that it left a vivid and detailed memory sufficient to reconstruct it when playing from the score. This brought Alban Berg's music within the reach of my understanding.

'Understanding' of music is a rather vague conception, just as vague as the 'meaning' of the music which is to be understood. To understand the technique, to know how it is done, though indispensable for the composer, is irrelevant for the listener. In the last resort understanding of music is no more than a feeling of satisfaction and a desire to hear the piece again. Intimate knowledge of the music itself may find more detailed justification for such satisfaction; for example, the change of key from the dark E flat major to D major when Don Ottavio and Donna Anna enter with lights in the sextet in the second act of *Don Giovanni*. This is only one of thousands of such major and minor features which strike the listener, even if he does not know exactly why. However, it is only natural that a new work is not so readily understood at a first hearing. I remember how I detested the first of Beethoven's piano sonatas, Opus 2, No. 1, after having spent my first four years at the piano with Diabelli, Clementi, Kuhlau, Haydn and Mozart.

If I could, though with some difficulty, follow Alban Berg's music without being troubled by many doubts, I could not say the same of Schönberg's. None of his earlier works—*Verklärte Nacht*, *Pelleas*, the First Chamber Symphony—seemed to compare favourably with Debussy or Richard Strauss, nor could 'Gurre-Lieder' stand up to Gustav Mahler. Nothing he wrote seemed to have the vigour of Stravinsky's *Petrushka* or *Rite* or the wit of *Pulcinella*. *Pierrot lunaire* appeared to me as an oversophisticated and pretentious attempt at reviving the long-buried 'melodrama'. But it had a peculiar fascination which did not fade with repeated hearings, and if I could not share it at least it made me appreciate the admiration the work commanded in progressive circles. I was all the more surprised to find it 'dated' when I heard it again towards the end of the war after an interval of ten years. It had lost the excitement of novelty and did not seem to have that enduring quality. I fared better with the Five Orchestral Pieces, Op. 16, though they seem to be more a 'serenade' of the old music rather than an 'aubade' of the new. However, with the Wind Quintet, Op. 26, and the Piano Pieces, Op. 33, over which I toiled for many months, I found myself quite out of touch.

No wonder that Webern's music remained outside my understanding. It made no difference that I forced myself to analyse various of his works, and particularly the Symphony, in order to learn from analysis what I could not learn from listening—and opportunities of hearing Webern's works were rare. But I could not discover the inner urge which created this music nor the desire of the listener which it should satisfy. Inner urge and satisfaction are not out-moded notions like feeling and expression. Without them every art is homeless, even senseless. Among the arts music is a 'useless' thing, which neither educates nor informs nor serves as a permanent decoration. If a man decides to spend his precious days in writing music he must be driven by an irresistible compulsion. If I am to understand his work properly, and not only in a peripheral, technical sense, my desire for it must be akin to the creative urge. And as music can have no other purpose it depends more than the other arts on this urge and this desire. This, I believe, was the origin of anonymous, spontaneous folk music, when creative urge and understanding desire were the common property of a whole nation or community. Folk music is gone, buried and forgotten, and the creative urge has become personal and individual. But it must exist as long as music is invented and required, with Webern as well as with his contemporaries and predecessors. The result, however, is overwhelmingly different from everything that happened before. Before Webern music unfolded; with him it shrinks. Before him music strove for greatness, monumentality; Gustav Mahler, from whom the whole Schoenberg school received much encouragement, could not *over*inflate music. With Webern, musical content is concentrated, its inner urge exhausted in a few bars, in a breath. After the colossal painting, the miniature.

I can feel all the ancient objections rearing their ugly heads. I have the uncomfortable suspicion that Webern's works are most important aphorisms, the meaning of which I cannot discover; that in his highly organized microcosms a universe lies hidden which I cannot approach. I might be happier if I did not try to listen to his works, because the acoustic phenomenon tends to obscure the finely chiselled structures. In his last years Webern himself did not care for performances, saying, somewhat cryptically, that the sound was ever-present. But I cannot do without the old-fashioned desire to hear music physically.

As Webern is the true patriarch of our new music I have to admit that I do not possess the key to its understanding. What am I to do? Should I join the ranks of those who write books to prove the invalidity of this new music, and quote what the Patriarch of Jerusalem said eight hundred years ago about the royal house of Anjou: '*De diabolo venerunt, ad diabolum ibunt*'?

I am convinced that Webern and his followers *had* to compose as he did and as they are doing, and that their music is inevitable. But I feel entitled to regret it, as I regret many other things that are happening today. I do not love this new music and I do not hate it. I do not believe that it is the final redemption of the art, nor its final destruction.

I know that this is a peculiarly qualified conservative or progressive view. If one considers the new to be inevitable one ought to love it, and if one does not love it one should not accept it as inevitable. From an abstract moral point of view everyone should have the courage of his convictions and make his own perceptive powers the general yardstick. But these last fifty years have ridden roughshod over all those who used every device of logical argument to try to arrest the change or give it the direction which they thought it should have. Convincing proof of inevitability is very rare. The bare fact of a change's taking place is its justification. All respectable people, the man in the street as well as the physicist, philosopher or statesman, would agree that the atom bomb should never have been invented, constructed and used. But it happened, and the bomb with its all-destructive power is being improved every day.

If I may compare the great with the small, the great wickedness with the small virtue, then I find that same fatalism in our music. I have witnessed innumerable cases where young people brought up in the strictest tradition in academies and conservatoires began to compose twelve-note or serial music as soon as they left them. Who taught them to do it? What attracted them to abandon all the comfort of old rules and proved effects? When, a few years ago, I met Bohuslav Martinu in Rome, where he had a teaching grant at the American Academy, he laughed when I asked whether he was very busy. 'This time I really have been lucky,' he said. 'Six young Americans came and asked me to teach them serial composition. When I told them that I knew nothing about it they went away and I have not seen them since. So I sit in that marvellous Villa Doria Pamphili and compose.' It is certainly not true that these young men necessarily have more talent than their elderly teachers, but they have the instinct of the present and little love of the past which makes them feel superior. As perhaps never before, music today is the epitome in sound of the glory and the misery of the time which produces it. Only in the context of the time, of its moods and its trends, can it be approached and appreciated.

6. RICHARD STRAUSS AND IGOR STRAVINSKY

··

Let us pause at 8 September 1949. Richard Strauss is dead and Igor Stravinsky is approaching the limit of experience. They were the last survivors of the great conflict, the great antagonists. I like to think of 8 September 1949 as one thinks of 28 July 1750, when J. S. Bach died and the 'old' art died with him. And yet I ought to apologize both to the memory of Richard Strauss and to Stravinsky for linking their names together. They had nothing in common, but together they symbolize the change, together they are the pivot, together they mark the storm front in the meteorology of music.

In his long life Richard Strauss was much admired and much maligned, but in the end his music has shaken off its detractors. In his obituary Ernest Newman, the doyen of English music critics, said that Strauss was the last in the royal line of great composers, the line that leads from Beethoven to Wagner and Brahms.

What was 'royal' in Richard Strauss? For me personally he came nearer the ideal type of an Olympian than any other composer I have known, as near as music may allow. Since 1922 I had met him repeatedly without making any closer contact. After 1933 I had lost touch with him. But in those turbulent times the strangest things happened. One day, early in 1942, Wilhelm Furtwängler's former secretary Berta Geissmar, who was living as a refugee in London, came to me and asked whether I would be interested in acquiring the rights in Strauss's operas.

Interested? That was hardly the word. To be Strauss's publisher was a dream too fantastic to be true—and not simply for business reasons, for the commercial prospects of Strauss's music in 1942 were rather unpromising. From my early musical days Strauss's music had had a fascination for me which was difficult to explain. Among the many wondrous things in music there is one that is particularly striking: the moment when, more immediately than in any other art, inspiration itself shines forth in all its mystical greatness. A passage such as Pamina's 'Tamino mein, o welch'

ein Glück' is such a moment, not the mere 'trouvaille' which
now and then may come to a lesser talent. With the great composers
it happens again and again: with J. S. Bach, from Gluck's to
Stravinsky's *Orpheus*, there are melodies or sometimes only some
phrases or turns which, as Vasari said of Peruzzi's 'Farnesina',
are 'not built but born'. With Strauss these moments are frequent:
in the *Ariadne* score, for instance, they glow like the carneols in
the serpentine rocks of the Lizard, in Ariadne's lament, in the
changes of mood and expression from the second dance scene with
its concluding D major dominant seventh to the glittering C sharp
major which announces the arrival of the god, in Ariadne's cry
and the dotted syncopated rhythm which, in a diminuendo sustained
through twenty bars, drops to the lower register to become the
light, undulating accompaniment to Ariadne's 'I greet thee,
messenger of all messengers'.

But I am writing neither an analysis nor an appreciation of
Strauss's works. This has been done and will be done by more
competent critics than I can claim to be. But if it has been alleged
that Strauss, with his uncontested virtuosity, was out for calculated
effects, this is but one example of a 'miscalculation' because it
escapes too many listeners. However, I did not regard it as a freak
of fortune that one day there lay on my desk the signed agreements
which put Strauss's principal works into my care. Strauss, sitting
in his villa in Garmisch, knew nothing about it.

Richard Strauss had an unusual career. In the first twenty years
of his creative life, from *Don Juan* to *Elektra*, he was a revolutionary, an avant-garde composer who rocked the edifice of music
no less than Debussy. The younger generation pinned all their
hopes on him, encouraged by all the philistine critics who found
Strauss's music abominable and destructive. Then, on the summit
after a stormy rise, he paused, became doubtful or cautious—and
the critics did not like that either. *Rosenkavalier* became the last
great operatic success in history, the last in the royal line of operas.
Ariadne in its second version briefly stole the limelight once more,
but from then on his way seemed to lead irrevocably downhill.
Four of his symphonic poems, a dozen or more songs and four
operas stayed unshakably in the repertoire. He was, in fact, more
widely performed than any other serious contemporary composer,
but the new works he wrote, nine operas and one ballet, songs and
choral works written after 1916, were composed, as it were, in the
shadow of his former glory. Only comparatively few friends believed
in him; others seemed to owe it to themselves to say something

derogatory about him and his music. It was difficult to explain. Strauss, after all, was no Leoncavallo, hitting the jackpot once and never again. It was said that Strauss lived too comfortably; that his unimpaired virtuosity and cold but expert routine still gave his orchestra an inimitable shimmer without engaging the mind.

It must necessarily happen to every composer or other artist with a large output that inspiration now and then flags and that style and routine have to camouflage the gaps. Of the 1,080 'authentic' works of J. S. Bach listed in Schmieder's thematic catalogue, more and more are being discovered to be rearrangements of other works, substituting sacred for secular texts, one instrument for another, and of half of his gigantic *œuvre* it could be said that it was written with the cold hand of a stupendous craftsman. It was no different with Handel, Mozart, Haydn, Beethoven, Schubert and Brahms and all the great composers in between. (Only the Schoenberg school would insist that every work its three leading members wrote was of equally high standard, and it is true that they wrote more deliberately than composers who could 'let themselves go' and so sometimes lost control.) However, among the uninspired or less inspired works of the famous masters of the past there are some real jewels, enjoyable, delightful music without any pretensions to profundity. Apart from being many other things music is an unparalleled pastime and a unique entertainer. Generations have enjoyed a piece like the third of Schubert's 'Moments musicaux', Op. 94.

But in the middle of the nineteenth century it became increasingly difficult to write music of such superficial charm. Serious music became pompous and grandiloquent, and such pomposity and grandiloquence became an embarrassment to all routine. This may have been the unconscious reason why light and serious music parted company. This is best exemplified in Wagner, with his big subjects, his passions, his outbursts. Music had to be big all the time. A piece like the dance of the apprentices in *Meistersinger* is a rare exception in Wagner's works after *The Flying Dutchman*. The consequence of this desire to be larger than life was that many pages of the scores of *Tristan*, the *Ring*, *Meistersinger* and *Parsifal* had to be filled with interminable sequences marking the points where the breadth of dramatic representation exceeded the breadth of musical invention. With Bach sequences are an essential part of the architecture, with Wagner they are mere fill-in material. By the end of the century Wagner's pomposity had become true opulence, opulence of sound, gesture and attitude, which can be justified only by the importance and significance of its utterances. One cannot say irrelevant things with grand gestures, in a grand manner.

This was in fact the principal reason why many people—myself among them—could not become unconditional admirers of Gustav Mahler. His invariably grand manner requires some profound meaning which is often either missing or unrecognizable, as in the first movement of his Third Symphony, or applied to an unsuitable subject, as the post-horn off-stage in the same work which tries to inflate a harmless little folk-song into a sentimental tragedy. All the more impressive are those pieces where musical significance *is* provoked and supported by a significant text: the *Song of the Earth*; the second part of the Eighth Symphony; or where playful words inspire a playful mood, as in the 'Wunderhorn' songs.

With his incomparably livelier imagination and his passion for composing, Strauss, because of the grandiloquence of his style, could not altogether escape the danger of hollowness. He came from the old school in every sense. The last 'mass' composer, he could always compose, even without an irresistible urge. He never tired of his own extraordinary craftsmanship. So it was bound to happen that now and then he said, with great aplomb, things which were not worth saying. There was no charm in that fin-de-siècle style; it could only be full of meaning or altogether empty. This cannot but diminish the value of Strauss's less inspired works as compared, for instance, with the value of Mozart's similar works which still preserve the facility, elegance and wit of his inspired masterpieces.

All the same, in happy moments Strauss succeeded better than all his contemporaries in writing 'entertainment' music of the highest standard and of great and unpretentious beauty, such as the waltzes from *Rosenkavalier* and the dance of the tailors from *Bourgeois gentilhomme*, worthy descendants of Mozart's serenades or Beethoven's Septet. But the hollowness lurking in the pompous style was a constant danger and may have carried the seeds of revolution, of the wild eruption of atonality and of the iron regimentation of the new teaching, because music was no longer capable of its old precious nonchalance. Beethoven could bid farewell to the world with a lighthearted and carefree piece (if the last movement of the String Quartet, Op. 130, really is his last finished composition). In Strauss's day this had become almost impossible. But when his inspiration measured up to his virtuosity—which happened much more often than his detractors between the wars

would admit—the result was truly 'royal'. His élan, his ability to
build up a dramatic scene from a quiet beginning to an overwhelming climax, were not matched by any composer of his time.

Like a rock Strauss stood in the midst of all the frantic efforts to
find a 'new' music. He needed no new music, he was satisfied with
his inheritance. He lived through all the great changes in life and
in art. When, at the age of twenty-four, he earned his first great
successes, Wagner's grave was still fresh, Brahms was still alive;
five months after *Rosenkavalier*, *Petrushka* was first performed.
He saw the birth, decline and resurrection of twelve-tone music.
It seemed impossible to fit him into the current of events. (In the
whole history of music I know of only one other and insignificant
example of this. Joseph Haydn had a pupil, Siegmund Neukomm,
who died in 1858 at the age of eighty. I once edited one of his
piano sonatas, not because of its intrinsic value but because of the
curious mixture it contained of Haydn, Chopin and Liszt.)

In the years 1901–3 Strauss arranged concerts of modern
music in Berlin with the new works of Bruckner, Mahler,
Pfitzner, d'Indy and many others. When I brought him the first
printed copy of the score of his *Metamorphosen* he looked at the
advertisement on the back page of the cover and said with a sigh,
'Elgar! I arranged the first performance of his *Dream of Gerontius*
in Germany . . . and Delius, I believe it was *Paris* which I conducted myself.' This is often forgotten, and one rather thinks of
him as a selfish old man who would have no truck with the new
music which had grown up around him.

To every German composer who started his career in the
shadow of Wagner and of his towering musical achievement—as a
very young man Strauss worked in Bayreuth as an assistant and
narrowly escaped marrying one of Cosima's daughters—Wagner
was at once an inspiration and an obstacle more formidable than
Wagnerites in other countries could imagine. Strauss himself once
said to me, 'You could not go beyond Wagner; you could only go
another way.' And at the end of his life, feeling the loneliness of
a changed world, he added with some bitterness, 'With Wagner,
music has reached its summit and I am only a straggler.'

But is he a straggler who concludes an age? Bach, too, had no
historic mission. His 'Art of Fugue' was a testament, not a promise.

Such thoughts went through my mind when, on 31 December
1945, after an adventurous journey from London through France,
I walked gingerly down the steep, icy road from the railway station

in Baden near Zurich to see Strauss again at the hotel where, in happier days, he and his wife had been welcome guests. They were not so welcome now; they had no money, no car, no driver. In the cold house in Garmisch, Frau Pauline had been unable to recover from pneumonia, and the American commander in southern Bavaria had arranged their journey to Switzerland, where they were welcomed with a similar lack of enthusiasm. Many rumours went round, and some Swiss papers were outraged at the thought that Switzerland should shelter a man so much maligned. All I knew was that the stories of a large fortune hidden abroad were untrue. Strauss, in fact, did not possess one penny. He had brought some manuscripts with him, which the owner of the hotel kept in his safe as a surety. He copied some of them carefully, dating and marking the copies in order to have some pocket money. What was I to hear? Complaints, accusations, assurances?

Nothing of the sort. Strauss met me in the corridor, a little bent but still very tall, his face a little more wrinkled than I remembered it but otherwise hardly changed. I had to tell him in detail how it had happened that his major works had found their way to an English publisher, and he made no objection. 'But,' he asked very seriously, 'do you really think that I am still a business proposition?'

Richard Strauss and money had long been a favourite subject of gossip among both experts and laymen. It was said that his commercial acumen far exceeded his musical genius. As his publisher I know more about it.

Strauss had no business sense at all. His contracts were drafted by his lawyers and he trusted their advice implicitly. In investing his money he relied on the counsel of experts, which was not always good. His houses in Garmisch and Vienna were not speculative investments; he built them for himself and never parted with them. But, in circumstances which he had helped to create, his music earned big money for concert-promoters, opera-houses, conductors, producers and singers. His were box-office successes, and Strauss, who was no hypocrite, felt entitled to his fair share, said so and demanded it.

Since *Salome* he had been an expensive composer who, following Wagner's example, sold his publishing rights for large sums and retained the performing and mechanical rights for himself, though not without allowing his publisher the usual share. His demands were high but not disproportionate. When, after the First World War, his publisher could no longer afford the high price for the publishing rights Strauss published his operas at his own expense and left the distribution to the publisher, remaining faithful to him although he was bound by no exclusive contract. He never traded with his music. Only twice in his whole life did he accept commissions in the proper sense—once to write a hymn for the 1936 Olympic Games, which he thought he could not very well turn down ('Fancy me, writing a hymn for sport, which I detest!' he wrote); the other for the celebration of the 2,600th anniversary of the Japanese Empire in 1939, because he had nothing better to do and found some excitement in trying his hand again at a symphonic poem. He did not bargain. 'If it is too much for you, don't do it and we shall remain good friends,' he used to say.

When, in 1947, he needed money more urgently than ever before he declined without hesitation an offer of £20,000 for the film rights of *Salome* and *Rosenkavalier* because Sir Alexander Korda would not give him a guarantee that both works would be filmed without changes or cuts. He was invariably correct and reliable in all his dealings and had absolute confidence in his partners. It would never have crossed his mind to check accounts or to have them checked by accountants. Twice he lost his fortune: the first time in the First World War, when friends had advised him to invest his money in Britain and it was impounded as enemy property; the second in the German catastrophe of 1945. He occasionally mentioned it, but the destruction of German opera-houses and concert-halls grieved him more. However, he could now and then make facetious remarks about 'the paying public', while Schoenberg rather held the view that the public should be fined and punished for not listening to his music.

Professed or presumed idealists were also irritated by Strauss's appearance and way of life. Though very progressive in other respects, they preferred the old-fashioned notion that an artist should be obsessed with his art in a manner visible to everybody, slovenly in dress, accepting worldly needs as a necessary evil, a romantic figure with long hair and dirty fingernails and a mind of childlike innocence.

In photographs of the 1880s Strauss did look a little like this ideal image of the artist. But his hair soon thinned, and he married a lady who was a stern disciplinarian and surrounded the genius with normality. As he himself insisted, that was one of the reasons why he chose her. He saw himself in danger of becoming a dissolute and ineffective dreamer, and knew that Pauline de Ahna, the daughter of a Bavarian general, would help him to avoid such a disaster. She was a singer of distinction who sang Elisabeth in

Bayreuth's *Tannhäuser* and created the leading soprano part in Strauss's first opera, *Guntram*. For the first ten years of her married life she sang the songs which Strauss wrote for her and travelled with him all over the old and the new world. Then she gave up singing to devote herself to her main task: the establishment and maintainence of a perfect equilibrium between a genius and the world.

This required much self-denial and sacrifice and untiring vigilance, but she succeeded in making him an ideal husband and father and was to him an ideal wife. She was a capricious woman and there was occasional friction. Strauss himself has drawn her portrait in his autobiographical 'bourgeois comedy with symphonic interludes' *Intermezzo* (though 'bourgeois' is not a satisfactory equivalent for the German '*bürgerlich*', which has no social overtone but simply means ordinary as opposed to pretentious people). They loved each other wholly and unreservedly, and there are no stories of love affairs or adventures in either of their lives. They could not live without each other. When Strauss died, life lost all its purpose for Frau Pauline. Nine months later she followed him into the grave. I cannot help thinking of Clara Wieck, who attempted a similar task with Robert Schumann but was overwhelmed by him and could not prevent the ultimate tragedy. This could not happen to Pauline Strauss with her strength of character and determination, sometimes gentle and sometimes ruthless but ever-present and ever-ready.

Strauss himself appreciated the healthy balance between his art and the world around him. He could speak of his wife and son with the same enthusiasm as he spoke of Mozart and Beethoven. He looked like a financier or industrialist; he was never conspicuously dressed but always carefully groomed; he lived comfortably and enjoyed the comfort; he kept a pedantic order in his manuscripts, sketch-books, letters and diaries—and in playing skat, a German card game which he loved passionately.

This made him an object of suspicion to the superficial observer. The real bourgeois liked to think of the composer of *Salome* as a lascivious half-savage in an attic filled with junk and wild dreams—but Strauss composed *Salome* in the very orderly ironing-room of a rented villa in the Bavarian mountains. If he once wrote that when composing hand and head had to be as cool as marble, the philistines read into it an excuse for, or a defence of, good living and skat. It has often been told how Strauss composed at certain hours of the day, conducted rehearsals and performances, had his game of skat

and could continue composing the next day exactly where he had
left off.

No daemon was to be discovered in all this apparent routine.
Where was, in fact, the daemon which created the cyclopic *Elektra*
music or the Emperor scene in *Die Frau ohne Schatten*, the genius
of the *Rosenkavalier* trio or Helena's monologue or the *Arabella*
duet? Many people could only think of him as the characteristic
representative of an age which, under the German Kaiser, corre-
sponded with the Edwardian age in England, an age of imperturb-
able self-satisfaction and self-indulgence, unwilling to worry about
the problems of an uncertain but inexorably approaching future.
The struggling younger generation was bound to feel bitter about it.

But the man who looked a bourgeois in that 'Wilhelminian'
sense had the finest hands imaginable, firm, long and thin with
firm, long and thin fingers, sensitive hands such as the Lord has
never bestowed on any philistine. And he was an untiring worker.
To his last days he knew no idleness. He not only left an enormous
œuvre: he was an equally prolific letter-writer, never using a
secretary but writing his letters—thousands of them—in his thin
gothic handwriting and making excerpts of the more important
ones in his diaries. These he kept year by year, a whole library of
them, where he entered appointments, family events, performances, thoughts that crossed his mind. Even as a reader he was not
idle. In his very large and discriminating library in Garmisch there
are hundreds of volumes of poetry, history and philosophy with
innumerable notes, and with words and sentences underlined.
And he played skat wherever he went, with bankers and indus-
trialists, singers and conductors and, in Garmisch or Oberam-
mergau, with peasants and factory-workers. There are two distinct
types of busy people—those who are breathlessly so, never having
time for anything, and those who calmly go about their various
activities and seem to have time for everything. Strauss belonged
to the latter class. He had all the time in the world and was never
flustered, never harassed.

Strauss was an expert collector of pictures and furniture. In
London he examined the Van de Veldes in the Wallace Collection
very carefully and then said, 'I think mine are better.' He assembled
his treasures around him and lived with them in a natural and
unforced way. His home was homely and not an art gallery. There
was the same solidity which distinguished his whole life. In this
solid order, under Frau Pauline's watchful eyes, creative spirit too
had its orderly place.

His diligence and his thirty years as conductor, pianist and accompanist had given him an astounding knowledge of music of every type, operatic, symphonic, instrumental and vocal. Once, in a little Italian restaurant in London's Soho with Clemens Krauss, the conductor, he laughed until the tears ran down his face when he remembered all the Meyerbeer operas he had had to conduct in Berlin, because the Kaiser had a passion for Meyerbeer. The Kaiser, who also had a passion for military marches, ordered his *Generalmusikdirektor* to write some new ones and when Strauss replied that he did not know how to do it the Guards' band was lined up in the courtyard of the Schloss and Strauss had to listen for a whole morning to march after march. 'How many beats of the triangle do you think there are in *Siegfried*?' he asked me once. I did not know, but guessed there might be many in the forging songs. He laughed. 'No, there is one single one in the whole score, on the last page of the first act.' Or he said, 'German composers are often criticized for the *squareness* of their melodies. But Mozart wrote some irregular ones and they are among his best. The slow movement of the Clarinet Quintet begins with a melodic paragraph of nine bars.'

In spite of such detailed knowledge Strauss never conducted without the score in front of him. He seldom glanced at it but conscientiously turned the pages. He once told me why he did this. As a young man he, like anyone else, thought it would impress the public if he conducted whole operas without a score. This he did until, when he was conducting *Don Giovanni* in Weimar, the following happened: everything went well up to the last finale; Elvira ran out, shrieked at the sight of the Commendatore, Don Giovanni sent Leporello to the door, he staggered back on to the stage—and, in a moment of splendid confusion, the Commendatore followed him in, fifty-four bars too soon. Strauss knew every note of the score but not the rehearsal numbers, and the musicians in the pit could not see what was happening on the stage. 'D-minor chord!' Strauss shouted to the orchestra but they did not understand what he meant. Don Giovanni and Leporello looked helplessly at the conductor and stopped singing and the orchestra, sensing that something was wrong, stopped playing. The curtain fell. 'Imagine it! And the Grand Duke was there! Such a thing happens only once in a lifetime and since then I have never conducted without the score in front of me.'

Richard Strauss was no less enigmatic as a conductor than in many other respects. In his later years he conducted with almost imperceptible gestures and people might have thought that he was taking it rather easily and relying on the orchestra. His performances had a naturalness that was not easy to explain—the listeners simply had the feeling that Strauss's interpretation was authoritative and right. His beat was like the pendulum of a metronome, regular and merciless. From the first note the tempo of every piece was firmly and unmistakably laid down. 'One can conduct the prelude to *Tristan*,' he used to say, 'only if one has the tempo of the last bar of the opera exactly in one's ear.' After a rehearsal I heard him say to the conductor, 'You cannot conduct with the baton alone.' Indeed, when conducting his eyes wandered constantly through the orchestra, from one player to the other, and they all felt his magnetic influence. There was nothing loose or casual in his performances. At a *Fidelio* rehearsal at the State Opera in Vienna he told the orchestra and the singers, 'There are things *you* have to do for Beethoven: sustain every note as you find it printed in your part, make it neither longer nor shorter; and do not drop the end of a phrase as you often do when speaking, but sing or play it clearly to the end. As for the rest, you only have to look at me.' Strauss was a famous conductor. But here, too, the daemon was concealed below an outward surface of composure and self-control.

During his long life Strauss had to share the misfortunes of Central Europe, and of Germany in particular. Prominent and unpolitical as he was, he was bound to incur somebody's displeasure every time he was expected to adopt a definite attitude. He was unpolitical almost to the point of absurdity. Politics did not interest him. Irrespective of what they were and what purpose they had, he considered them to be an evil which distracted men from better things in life such as music. Undoubtedly and not surprisingly he regarded German music as the best. To him Bach, Gluck, Mozart, Beethoven, Weber, and Wagner were the greatest composers, but whether the Germans were the best people never crossed his mind. In a letter which was to become notorious, Strauss wrote to Stefan Zweig: 'Do you think that Mozart consciously wrote 'Aryan' music? Do you believe that I was ever guided by the thought that I am German (perhaps, who knows?)? For me there are only two categories of men: those who have talent and those who have none.' Strauss never wrote a 'patriotic' work. When the 1914 war broke out he was the only prominent German who refused to sign the anti-British manifesto, and was openly called a traitor. He made no attempt to defend himself and retired to his villa in the Bavarian mountains to orchestrate some of his early songs—and to compose *Die Frau ohne Schatten*, erecting round himself a world of magic and symbolism which did not admit any thought of the unhappy reality of war.

Nor did Strauss become involved in the troubles which followed. He felt them, like the war itself, as a personal injustice; he felt himself innocent of any complicity in bringing about the inflation and shortages which affected him personally and, worse still, affected musical life. He had served grand dukes, kings and kaisers and saw them disappear with complete indifference. For him music had to survive, no matter who its patrons were.

But then things became more difficult and decisions more momentous. Almost without realizing it, Strauss found himself in the midst of human, moral and political problems. It was said afterwards that he should have emigrated. He and his wife loved their Jewish daughter-in-law and their grandchildren, who were exposed to many humiliations. He would have suffered little discomfort in emigration; he could have been among the heroes of his time. But emigration requires a conviction which he did not possess. He did not emigrate. On the contrary, he became the first president of the new Reichsmusikkammer. All musicians outside Germany and many people inside were profoundly shocked at what appeared an act of sheer opportunism. He conducted the notorious Berlin concert in place of Bruno Walter, who was no longer allowed to appear in public.

Strauss never admitted to having done anything wrong in either case. After the war he still insisted that he had never been concerned with the Nazi régime but only with the Berlin Philharmonic Orchestra, with which he had been connected for more than thirty years and which he had been conducting when Bruno Walter was still a schoolboy. The orchestra had been in difficulties; he had wanted to help them, and had given his fee of DM 1,500 to their pension fund, thus drawing no benefit from it. Should he have helped to prove that the Nazis could kill music in Germany? Music, after all, was more important than Hitler or Bruno Walter . . . It was useless to argue with him.

And the presidency of the Reichsmusikkammer? Was he not the greatest living German composer and did he not have the right and the duty to have a say in the organization of music in Germany? To Stefan Zweig, in the letter quoted above, he wrote, 'I would have accepted this aggravating job from any government but neither the Kaiser nor Herr Rathenau have ever offered it to me. . . . How the scribblers interpret it in the Press does not concern me. I want to do some good and prevent excesses. . . .'

The Nazi authorities soon had to recognize that Strauss was not their man. And they could have no hope of persuading or seducing him as they did with Furtwängler. After Hofmannsthal's death Strauss had found a new Jewish librettist in Stefan Zweig, who wrote for him the libretto of *Die schweigsame Frau* in 1932, before Hitler came to power. On 1 April 1933 the decree boycotting the Jews came into force and four days later Strauss wrote to Zweig, 'As I did eight days after the outbreak of the famous world war I am at my desk working. Am in the middle of the first act [of Zweig's libretto].'

Zweig was an Austrian living in Salzburg and was not immediately affected by the new measures taken in Germany. But rumours started in May 1934 that Strauss's new opera would be banned because of Zweig. Zweig read about them when in London and hastened to inform Strauss; the latter immediately went to see Goebbels, from whom he received some reassurance. 'We shall have no difficulties with our Morosus,' he wrote to Zweig and pressed him to think already of a new libretto. 'Perhaps I can make some suggestions,' Zweig replied, 'even if I do not carry them out myself.' Strauss did not take the hint. A meeting arranged in Salzburg in July did not materialize. After the assassination of the Austrian Chancellor Dollfuss, Strauss was not allowed to conduct at Salzburg. In the end they did meet, but we do not know what they discussed.

In August Zweig outlined a possible subject for a new opera, and added, 'I shall have no objection if you hand this draft over to somebody else in order to save yourself any political trouble.' Strauss replied on 24 August, 'Of course, I could not consider any other poet . . . but tactically it may be advisable not to tell anybody if we write one or more works together. If I am asked I will say that I am not working at all and that I have no libretto. In a few years, when we have finished, the world will be different.' Zweig recommended the work of a Swiss poet. 'If you will allow me,' wrote Strauss, 'I will stick to Stefan Zweig.' He became more pressing. 'The score of the third act will be finished in a few weeks,' he wrote in October, 'and then I shall be out of work.' And again: 'If I have the good fortune to receive from you one or more libretti we will agree not to tell anybody. The score when finished will be locked up and will be opened only when we both feel the time is ripe for a performance. Will you then take the risk of writing something new for me—perhaps for my estate?' Zweig felt that he had to make his point clear beyond doubt: it would be undignified and unworthy of them both to continue a clandestine co-operation. There could be no further discussion. But Zweig would be happy to help and advise anybody writing a libretto for Strauss if such help or advice was welcome. 'You letter has made me very sad,' replied Strauss. 'If you desert me it would leave me an ailing old man without purpose.' And two months later, when Zweig reaffirmed his determination not to write another libretto for Strauss: 'I understand your depression. But you cannot be more depressed than I am.' And Strauss was still president of the Reichs-musikkammer.

The day of the first performance of *Die schweigsame Frau* drew nearer and Strauss went to Dresden. Zweig, of course, did not come. There was, after the war, a version current that Zweig had prohibited the performance but that Strauss had gone ahead without taking notice of Zweig's wishes. This was not true. Zweig had all along done everything to make himself inconspicuous and to remove difficulties as far as he could. On 13 June Strauss wrote to Zweig, 'My librettist is Zweig—he needs no collaborators—you could have convinced yourself personally after yesterday's rehearsal of the first act. Your libretto is simply first class. . . .'

The Royal—or, as it became after the First World War, the State—Opera House in Dresden had had the distinction of first performing Richard Strauss's operas. It began in 1901 with *Feuersnot*; *Salome*, *Elektra* and *Rosenkavalier* followed. Then Strauss's close friend, the conductor Ernst von Schuch, died and it took a few years for the old confidence to be re-established between Strauss and the new men in charge, Alfred Reucker, the Intendant, and Fritz Busch, the Generalmusikdirektor. *Intermezzo* and *Die ägyptische Helena* were again first performed in Dresden in 1924 and 1928 respectively. There was no question that the next opera, *Arabella*, was also to have its first performance in Dresden. Strauss dedicated it to his friends Alfred Reucker and Fritz Busch. But when it came to the performance, on 1 July 1933, Hitler had already seized power and both Reucker and Busch had left Dresden and Germany. Strauss wanted to withhold the work but was forced to fulfil the contractual obligation into which he had entered long before the change had taken place. But the dedication had to stand. Now, with *Die schweigsame Frau*, Dresden was to prove even more troublesome.

The new Intendant thought that he owed it to his convictions and to the authorities to suppress Zweig's name on bills, posters and programmes. Two days before the performance, perhaps with some vague suspicion in mind, Strauss demanded to see the proofs, and he flew into a rage when he found that Zweig's name had been omitted. 'You can do that, but without me. I shall leave tomorrow morning.' So Zweig's name was duly restored.

But worse was to come. We do not know Zweig's answer to Strauss's letter of 13 June, but Strauss's reply has become notorious. 'Your letter of the 15th drives me to despair!' he exclaims. 'For me "the people" exist only at the moment when they become an audience. Whether they consist of Chinese, Bavarians, New Zealanders or Berliners makes no difference to me.' And he concludes, 'The performance here will be excellent. Everybody is full of enthusiasm. And I should do without you? Never, never!' This letter was intercepted by the Gestapo and never reached Zweig. The performance took place on 24 June 1935. No Hitler, no Goebbels, none of the 'guests of honour' arrived. After the second performance the opera had to be taken out of the repertoire and was not heard again for more than ten years.

On 10 July Strauss wrote a memorandum for himself and for posterity in which he recounts the events.

> On 6 July Herr Ministerialrat Keudell appeared here with a demand for my resignation as president of the Reichsmusik-kammer, for health reasons. I at once resigned. He repeatedly showed me the copy of a private letter to my friend and collaborator Stefan Zweig which apparently had been opened by the police although my name as sender was written on the back of the envelope. I did not know that I was under the surveillance of the Gestapo. . . . When I conducted Bruno Walter's concert I was suspected of being a servile, selfish anti-semite, while on the contrary (and to my own detriment) I have been telling all the influential people here that the Streicher–Goebbels Jew-baiting was a disgrace to German honour, the lowest form of warfare waged by untalented, lazy mediocrity on superior intelligence and greater gifts. I openly say that I have received from Jews so much encouragement, so much friendship, assistance and inspiration that it would be criminal not to recognize it gratefully.

This was the end of Strauss's contacts with Nazis and Nazi institutions. He lost what privileges he had and retired to Garmisch, where he composed unwillingly the libretti by Joseph Gregor— the ideas were Zweig's—*Friedenstag* and *Capriccio*, and Hofmannsthal's *Die Liebe der Danae*, and orchestrated some earlier songs. Not he but Frau Pauline told me a characteristic story. When during the war an official came to the villa to requisition rooms for refugees and reminded the protesting composer that there was a war on, he received the reply, 'As far as I am concerned you need not have started this war.' His friends in Munich, Clemens Krauss, the conductor, and Rudolph Hartmann, the producer, arranged exemplary performances of his works, but otherwise he disappeared from the public eye.

Stefan Zweig emigrated to South America where he took his life.

After the war much was made of a photograph of Strauss, with a dedication, found in the office of the Munich Gauleiter, Frank. The explanation was simple and less publicized. Strauss had to protect his daughter-in-law and his grandsons and to do so made sure of the goodwill of this powerful man, whom he had hardly known personally.

At a time when heroes were few and scoundrels in abundance, all this was contrary to the code of either. Few musicians who were not forced to do so had left their countries. Toscanini in Italy, Paul Hindemith in Germany, were the shining examples of musicians manning the barricades. Strauss was not made for this. Everything connected with politics was abhorrent to him. He never made his peace with the régime, never accepted a title as Furtwängler did, never entered into any discussion. This brought him into conflict with his friends and those in power alike and made him an object of suspicion to both. But, next to his own kith and kin, it was music which ruled his life. And music is a despotic and ruthless ruler. He needed all his worldly skill to keep his head above water.

So he sat in Garmisch while the world around him collapsed. Among the Americans who occupied Bavaria there were many musicians who visited Strauss and the villa, both admirers and critics. Some were even surprised to see Strauss alive.

In the autumn of 1945 Strauss decided to go to Switzerland. All he sought there was as quiet an evening of his life as the unhappy times would allow. He was not like Furtwängler, who still sought publicity and, after the incident in Winterthur, sent from his place of exile in Clarens protest after protest, received every reporter and told everybody the story of his personal misfortunes and innocence, which was as eagerly contradicted as it was told. I had to sit with him far into the early hours of a February day, listening to his tale of woe, at the end of which he handed me a memorandum asking me to submit it to the British Foreign Office.

It produced no result, and Furtwängler, a victim of his own weakness and vanity rather than really ill-intentioned, had to wait. Strauss was neither weak nor vain. He received no reporters, made no statements and nothing could shake his conviction that he had nothing to justify, nothing to explain. Silently he suffered all the abuse that surrounded him in those first years after the war.

But it seemed a gloomy end to a life which, at one time, had achieved everything a human life is capable of achieving. However severely he might have been judged one could not but feel the tragedy of his old age. His music seemed out of favour, his manuscripts were pawned to pay the hotel bills, the future of his children and grandchildren was dark, German opera-houses and concert-halls were destroyed. Strauss thought up a theory to explain the fateful course of events.

> Every nation has a historic mission, and once this mission is fulfilled it disappears. The ancient Greeks had their sculpture, the Romans their jurisprudence, and once they had reached the summit there was no more for them to do but to succumb to so-called barbarians, nations with new ideals and a new mission. The mission of the German nation was music and it was fulfilled with Richard Wagner. After him they were doomed. What the Kaiser did in 1914 and Hitler in 1939 was the action of desperate, doomed men. And that the Germans followed them with such diabolical enthusiasm was a sign of the doom of the whole nation. The Germans will never rise again.

I always returned deeply depressed from my frequent visits to Strauss. Something had to be done to rescue him from this end-of-the-world mood, which even his avid reading of Goethe could not dispel. I talked it over with our mutual friend Willi Schuh in Zurich. The confusion on the Continent was indescribable. If something was to be arranged, London was the only place where life was tolerably normal. With Sir Thomas Beecham, a fervent admirer of Strauss's music, I discussed the possibilities of a Strauss Festival in London in 1946 or 1947. It had to be more than one casual performance if Strauss was to undertake the journey. And he needed money too. Sir Thomas lent his help and the British authorities were exceedingly forthcoming, granting the necessary visa and lifting the embargo on payments to enemy aliens.

So, on 4 October 1947, at two o'clock in the afternoon, Strauss, my wife and I sat in a DC3 aircraft of Swissair at Geneva airport, waiting for the moment when we should fly into the cloudless blue sky of a warm autumn day. It was only then that we realized our heavy responsibility. At eighty-three Strauss was making his first air journey. How would it all go? The unreliable London weather, the concerts, people, the Press! But Strauss was happy as I had not seen him for a long time. The flight was for him a sensation which he enjoyed like a schoolboy. Those were still the days of small, slow, unpressurized aircraft, floating with the clouds at 3,000 feet, and every little cumulus bumped the machine like a boulder on a bad road. My wife carried a whole chemist's shop with her, pills and drops for heart trouble and air sickness. But Strauss needed none of them. He looked down through his lorgnon and said, laughing, 'From here the whole world looks like a patched-up coat.'

Although I had avoided all publicity the news had spread. At Northolt airport, and even more in the lounge of the Savoy Hotel, we had to fight our way through throngs of reporters and photographers. In the next few days masses of letters arrived, the most touching coming from a lady in Wales, who sent a postal order for ten shillings, saying that she had read about Strauss's difficulties and felt that she should make a contribution to a man whose music had given her so much pleasure. She did not confuse him with his namesake, like the reporter who wanted to know when he had written 'The Blue Danube'.

Although we kept interviewers away as much as possible, the most important ones had to be admitted. 'What would you say,' asked a clever one, 'about the different uses of woodwind in French and German scores?' Strauss looked somewhat surprised. 'I don't know what you mean,' he replied, 'but do you know the difference in the use of horns between other German scores and mine?' And when the interviewer could not find an answer, Strauss said with a smile, 'I will tell you. I write for four horns and the others for a horn quartet.' I wonder whether the interviewer understood that. Another, a lady with a notebook and a battery of sharpened pencils, asked at the end of her interview the inevitable question: 'What are your plans for the future?' 'Oh,' replied Strauss with a roguish smile, 'to die.'

The Strauss Festival was an unqualified success. The first concert at Drury Lane was conducted by Sir Thomas. When Strauss stepped into his box at 8.15 p.m. the audience rose from their seats and greeted him like a king. The second concert, again at Drury Lane, was no less of a sensation. Then came the third, to be conducted by Strauss himself at the Albert Hall.

Strauss was somewhat anxious about it because of his health. He had chosen the difficult Sinfonia Domestica, which the orchestra did not know, *Don Juan* and the Burlesque for piano and orchestra, the latter in order to give the pianist Alfred Blumen an opportunity to earn a few pounds. Strauss refused to conduct sitting down—'If I cannot stand then I shall have to give up conducting.' It was quite amazing to see him teach the orchestra the whole programme in three rehearsals of two hours each, most of the time being devoted to the Sinfonia Domestica. The moment when Strauss walked through the orchestra and on to the rostrum, and 7,000 people in the gigantic overcrowded hall rose from their seats, remains unforgettable. Strauss conducted, as always, with spare but firm gestures. The tempi were a shade broader than one remembered hearing from him in previous years but there was all the tension and control of the old days. The audience was duly enraptured and the applause lasted until long after the orchestra had left.

There followed a studio performance of *Elektra* for the BBC, conducted by Sir Thomas. When Strauss arrived there were shouts of 'Speech! Speech!' Strauss, who did not speak English, bowed and said, *'Guten Abend, meine Herren!'* Finally there was a concert conducted by Sir Adrian Boult, again in the Albert Hall, Strauss himself taking over to conduct *Till Eulenspiegel.* Before he left the artists' room he said, 'Well, the old horse leaves the stable again.' There were again scenes of wild enthusiasm.

The remaining days he devoted to the National and Tate Galleries, the Wallace Collection and the British Museum, and on 1 November Frau Pauline could embrace her Richard in Montreux again. With relief and compassion I saw the two old people talk, with tears in their eyes, of the days of their separation.

Strauss's appearance in London had created a true sensation. The Press, English as well as foreign, had been very good, better than he had had for many years. There was no word about Nazism, no allusion to any of the stories which had been current after the war. Strauss was suddenly back in the centre of musical life, and people began to look with friendlier understanding upon the works which had previously found so little favour with the critics and the public. Not only did *Arabella* become as successful as *Rosenkavalier*, *Friedenstag* run for forty performances in Brussels and *Die schweigsame Frau* for over fifty in Berlin, but the works which he had written towards the end of the war and shortly afterwards— *Metamorphosen*, the Oboe Concerto, works which he had described himself as 'workshop compositions'—were played all over the world and the beauties of *Daphne* and *Capriccio* were discovered. Strauss should have had a few more years to see his fame rise again alongside the new palaces of the arts which were now replacing the old and shattered ones.

But the happy mood of the London visit did not last very long. Though Strauss's own financial troubles were somewhat alleviated, worries about the future of his family stayed with him. He was bothered with denazification procedures; became suspicious and oversensitive. His health broke down and he felt forlorn and lonely. 'It would be good if you could come over for a few hours. Am quite alone!' he wrote from Montreux in November 1948. Still he worked: a 'Duet Concertino' for the Swiss–Italian radio, and five orchestral songs, of which he could finish only four. They were to be his farewell to music and life, a farewell of gentle reminiscence and quiet resignation without any bitterness. After a last operation on 31 December 1948 he dictated to the nurse at the Clinique Cécil in Lausanne a letter to me. 'What a New Year's Eve! . . . my life is gone and I am asking myself why I have been recalled to this earth where, apart from my dear family and a few good friends, everything has become disgusting or indifferent. . . . I wish you and your dear wife a better New Year than is awaiting me in this torture-chamber, Yours desperately . . .' Underneath was his signature, hardly readable, written in a trembling hand.

Strauss recovered once more and, in the spring, was able to return with his wife to Garmisch, celebrate his eighty-fifth birthday—and die. I often read one of the many letters and notes which he wrote to me in those three years of trouble and sorrow, and it is a great comfort to me that his work has never been more appreciated than it is now. On 22 May 1950 the Four Last Songs were first performed by Wilhelm Furtwängler (now rehabilitated) and Kirsten Flagstad. As the last bar of the last song died away the audience, deeply moved, remained silent for a long time. Strauss had often been reproached for seeking sensation: here was a quiet death and unobtrusive transfiguration.

Taken all in all, music is a selfish art; it has neither wisdom nor goodness. Against all the criticism that has been heaped on Strauss's head I know from close acquaintance that music was to him, as it is to the composer in the *Ariadne* prelude, a holy art. He knew nothing more holy in this world.

*

It almost looks like a mistake of nature that two men as different in every respect as Richard Strauss and Igor Stravinsky should have had the same purpose in life. In external appearance and manner the contrast could hardly have been greater: the towering height of Strauss, and Stravinsky's slim frame; Strauss's calm and composure, and Stravinsky's quick and sparkling wit. Their lives were equally contrasting.

While Strauss clung to his orderly existence through wars and revolutions, refusing to allow them to disturb it, Stravinsky on the other hand found himself deprived of comfortable circumstances at the very beginning of his career, with nothing but the general success of *Firebird* and the hotly contested sensations of *Petrushka* and the *Rite of Spring* behind him, homeless throughout his creative life, unaccustomed and as naturally averse to suffering but compelled to earn a living for himself and his family. Such a fate might well have overwhelmed Strauss, but Stravinsky accepted it without flinching.

He did what every sensible *émigré* has to do when the bridges behind him are burnt: he determined to forget his past. It is said that in Tunisia there are still some Arab families who keep the keys of their Spanish houses as a symbol of the undying hope that they may one day return. Stravinsky kept no such key. Prokofiev did, returned and died an unhappy man, but Stravinsky turned away from the past and resolutely faced the future. When, fifty years later, old recollections returned and he was about to see Russia again, he said with a touch of sarcasm, 'I want to see whether the girls on Nevsky Prospect are still selling flowers.' He expected no great emotional impact from the visit; he went to Russia not as a prodigal son returning to his father's house but as a stranger to a strange land. 'The salt is better in Russia,' he said on his return; and, 'Khruschev told me that every family in Kazakhstan has a refrigerator.' There was no hint of nostalgia.

Stravinsky is now habitually reproached for his many changes of style, his borrowings and appropriations of music from very different periods and artistic climates—Pergolesi and Tchaikovsky, Gesualdo and Donizetti, Bach and Grieg. Put together like this, it does indeed sound a curious mixture of values and moods. But his art must be seen in the context of his life. Wherever he turned he was a stranger who could come and go as he pleased, owing nothing to any place or to any convention. Those who grow up and remain within the same particular surroundings experience the world from one particular viewpoint. They are—in ideal cases, unconsciously—

English or American, French, German or Russian, which implies a selection and limitation of experience and outlook, a distinction between the things one can share and those one can only understand. It is indeed not easy to determine the point at which a shelter becomes a prison. Stravinsky lost the one and escaped from the other with only his temperament and a most penetrating intellect to guide him.

Of course, much in Stravinsky's daily life is unalterably Russian: his attachment to his kith and kin, his generosity and hospitality, all the little instinctive things which intellect cannot control. But when others were chained to tradition, Stravinsky was completely free. It would be futile to speculate what might have become of him if there had been no world war in 1914 and no Bolshevik revolution in 1917 and he could have lived comfortable and care-free in an unchanged St Petersburg or in the country at Ustilug. There must have been much restlessness and impatience in him when everything still seemed secure. The *Rite of Spring*, after all, was written in the years 1911 and 1912, and Stravinsky's teacher, Rimsky-Korsakov, would have been just as scandalized had he lived to hear it as Haydn was at Beethoven's early wild movements in the minor key. But despite all his manifest disrespect for what he had been taught, *Firebird*, *Petrushka* and the *Rite* were still 'Russian'.

With knowledge of the man, it is fascinating to follow the disappearance of the familiar, inherited Russian element from his music and to see how the world at large takes possession of him. It did not happen all at once, and probably not without a struggle. The Russian flavour is hardly detectable in the *Nightingale*, which is a contemporary of the *Rite*, but in the smaller works and in *Renard*, which are the first fruits of emigration, it is unmistakably present. Then the *Histoire du soldat* of 1918 sheds all thoughts of the past. After a few minor relapses there follows *Pulcinella* in 1919, on the way to musical cosmopolitanism, and nothing Russian can be discovered in 1920 and 1921. Then, surprisingly, came two more major flashbacks to the past, *Mavra* (1922) and *Les Noces* (1923). They were the last. From then onwards Stravinsky was a freebooter who owed allegiance to nothing and nobody. For a few years he was stateless, then he concluded a marriage of convenience with France, and when the new storm gathered he packed his bags and became an American citizen. At the screening which preceded his naturalization the examiner asked him naïvely, 'What do you think of Lenin?' To his utter consternation Stravinsky replied, 'I admire him.' Then, to soften the blow, he added, 'I admire all true professionals.'

Stravinsky's changes of style are not as complete as most critics consider them. His utterly original and iconoclastic self is the same in the 'barbaric' *Rite*, in the neo-classical *Oedipus*, in the serial *Threni*. The attentive listener will discover in *Firebird* a distant suggestion of *Agon*, written forty-five years later, and in *Oedipus* many a hint of the *Rake's Progress*, which was said to be another volte-face in Stravinsky's tortuous *œuvre*. I wonder whether the authors of the innumerable books, treatises and articles on Stravinsky's music have perhaps paid too little attention to his personality, which remains the same in all its disguises.

Stravinsky was not the only pacemaker of musical internationalism but he was certainly its dominant figure, and nobody was better equipped for it. Schoenberg and his school, who arrived at the same goal by another road, were hardly known when Stravinsky shook the sumptuous edifice of 'national' music which had been erected during the preceding fifty years. His was a modernity of deeper significance than all the new formal theories, which at the time seemed not to interest him. After the italianate eighteenth century, the nineteenth had discovered musical nationalism. Not methods but temperament separated Italians and French, Germans and Russians, Czechs and Poles and Hungarians. Even after the First World War the musical world paraded in colourful national costumes. Ravel was as French as Richard Strauss was German, Falla Spanish and Kodály Hungarian. There had to come one man like Stravinsky, who in his own life anticipated the homelessness of future mankind, to replace the polyglot variety by a musical language which found its vocabulary in any part of the globe and any period of history.

Now, fifty years later, all the dreaded uniformity of the world has come true: the burning sun of the south and the cold showers of the north find people dressed after the same fashion, living in houses built to the same design, enjoying the same amenities. Will this egalitarian varnish eat into the very texture of life, into thinking and feeling? The Brussels *Exposition Universelle* of 1958 was a truly crushing experience. Here Europeans, Arabs, Japanese and Negroes exhibited models of factories, schools, hospitals, turbines and tractors which all looked the same. A little golden pagoda stood forlorn in the midst of all this uniformity. Nobody seemed to be keen on showing who he was, but only who he would like to be and would be one day. In the end, perhaps, cuisine will be the last survival of the old variety, and in Italy one will still eat *lasagne al forno*, in France *escargots à la bourguignonne*, in Valencia *paella* and in Vienna *Apfelstrudel*—perhaps. There are some who would doubt even this, and Stravinsky himself seems to prefer the international steak to Russian *blinis*.

It is with a slight shudder that one recognizes the prophetic element in Stravinsky's mission. In his life and work the fate of mankind seems to glow as in a burning glass. Stravinsky never founded or belonged to a school. But there always gathered around him a circle of artists, writers and philosophers who felt the malaise of a vanishing epoch and saw in him the symbol of a new spiritual existence: Picasso and Giacometti, Cocteau and André Gide, T. S. Eliot and Stephen Spender, Aldous Huxley and Isaiah Berlin— countless names, which are among the greatest of our time. This circle, embracing every field of thought and human creation, never degenerated into a clique or coterie such as formed around Schoenberg. It was no permanent association, no exclusive club, but from the little man at its centre there emanated a tremendous force of indefinable inspiration.

There is no room for romanticism or sentimentality in this new world which Stravinsky accepted. In Russia he explained to a baffled audience of young composers, 'The heart in music is an invention of the eighteenth century.' How could they understand that a life such as Stravinsky leads today and mankind will lead tomorrow can break a heart but never comfort it? It is not the heart which is increasingly becoming the ruler, the tyrant of this world: it is the intellect. Many experts, not only among conservatives but among the advocates of the latest trends in music, disapprove of Stravinsky's mixing with the young and discovering in his old age what he could have discovered forty years ago. But it is not true that Stravinsky simply does not know how to grow old with dignity. Never in his whole life was he a late-comer. Having measured the whole length and depth of musical experience and turned it into his own inimitable image, the intellectual play with note and interval relationships and contrapuntal complexities had to enter the field of vision of necessity. However, doctrine and intellect are not as despotic with him as they are with the less independent young. The short interludes in 'Movements' of 1959 are almost little romantic pictures in sound; in his 'Variations' of 1964 there are some phrases which one seems to have heard in *Apollon* or *Persephone* or in the Symphony in C. The individuality of the man, which one seeks in vain in the works of others, is ever-present, and the shadows of former days still float above the hard lunar landscape of his late works.

A man who accepts homelessness with such determination as Stravinsky must lose all reverence for any tradition. Indeed Stravinsky's irreverence is breathtaking. He despises Richard Strauss and hates Wagner. He displays a certain professional politeness towards J. S. Bach, but I am not sure whether he tolerates Mozart. He certainly has no time for Beethoven. He thinks highly of the amateur Gesualdo, takes off his hat to Tchaikovsky and admires Webern. Nor does he dilute such verdicts with a conciliatory gesture to the effect that these are his personal views and that they need not spoil anybody's enjoyment of Mozart or Beethoven.

But his irreverence is not of the cheap variety, vociferous when dealing with others but rather anxious when dealing with itself. One day Stravinsky demanded that his *Sacre du printemps*, known and famous for fifty years under this title, be officially renamed *The Rite of Spring*, the English title only to be printed on the scores and parts and mentioned in programmes. During the Second World War he had reorchestrated the last movement for small orchestra as 'Danse sacrale' and wanted this version to supersede the original. He finally changed the spelling of his name as a concession to English pronunciation.

With all this, Stravinsky is a man of inexhaustible fascination. The way he mixes in conversation and letters three or four languages, and pronounces utterly original and individual views about everything, countries, people, weather, food, music, painting, is a pleasure of which one never tires. When this little, frail man as he is now steps before the orchestra and raises his fists—those disproportionately large hands which Picasso so incomparably portrayed —a demon leaps out of the humble frame. In his early years Stravinsky was not a good conductor, and experts may say that he still is not. But this is not a matter of technique. It is that demon who forces his will upon the orchestra and drives the audience into a frenzy. I have experienced it often and in many places and each time it was like a natural phenomenon.

Stravinsky's mode of life perhaps corresponds better than Richard Strauss's well-ordered private life with its correctness and dependability to the idea of an artist's earthly pilgrimage. But even more than Strauss he is after money, and this may not fit into the ideal picture. When a few years ago he was offered a Dutch medal for an *acte de présence* at the Holland Festival, he declined: 'I am collecting money, but not medals.' His music has indeed earned much money for him and for innumerable others and he has every conceivable right to it. But he has no inclination for bourgeois comfort or an orderly way of life. He rises late in the morning, has an irregularly late lunch and goes late to bed. He does not work at particular times but when in the mood, irregularly and moodily. He is an excellent draughtsman—Ramuz called him a calligrapher —and the shape of treble clefs in particular fascinates him. He draws them with care and delight. In spite of his years he travels indefatigably and without careful plans. It is as if jet planes had been invented specially for him. In all his apparent disorder there is a certain pedantry: he packs his luggage himself and among the many pieces there is always a small, flat case with the manuscript on which he is working and papers of all sorts, contracts, letters, everything very tidy and handy. He is neither absent-minded nor forgetful. If now and then he appears confused the confusion is simulated for some reason or other. As the romantic artist with long hair, fluttering tie and empty stomach no longer exists, Stravinsky may be the perfect type of the modern artist: wealthy, pedantically confused, restless in the luxurious manner of the time.

He sometimes sets his publisher a hard task, as the story of the first performance of *The Rake's Progress* shows.

Work on the opera went on through the years 1949 and 1950. In December 1950 I received the score of the first two acts; the third was not yet completed. It had been agreed with Stravinsky that the first performance should be given in the English original. W. H. Auden's verses were too good not to be heard at least on this occasion. Unfortunately, the vast English-speaking world was poorly provided with opera-houses and altogether insufficiently opera-minded to do justice to the work. The Metropolitan Opera House in New York was not much interested and lost a great opportunity. There remained only the Royal Opera House in London, which, with strictly controlled enthusiasm, agreed to present the work at the Edinburgh Festival in August 1951 and to continue performances in London in the autumn and winter. The contract had already been signed in the spring of 1950. Financial prospects were not very rosy. The German opera-houses were either destroyed or in the process of being rebuilt; only the Scala in Milan had risen from the rubble more splendid than ever. Its management would have liked to have the world première and would have made considerable sacrifices if the performance could have been in Italian. Eventually they secured the first performance on the Continent of Europe for the month of December 1951.

So everything seemed to have been arranged as satisfactorily as conditions permitted. Then, early in February 1951, I unexpectedly

received a cable from Stravinsky: HAVE PROMISED FIRST PERFOR-
MANCE TO VENICE STOP IF YOU DON'T AGREE I CANNOT FINISH THE
WORK. What had happened? It did not take long to learn from
Italian friends that the Italian Radio, sponsors of the annual music
festival at the Venice Biennale, had offered Stravinsky a substantial sum for the right of the first performance with Stravinsky
himself conducting. Times were still difficult and Stravinsky needed
the money. I could not argue with him but had to try to free him
and myself from our obligations.

Covent Garden was easy enough. Without hesitation the
gentlemen were offended and did not insist on their rights—the
Rake has still never been performed at the Royal Opera House.
But the Scala did not give up. They had the right of first performance on the Continent and were determined to take the matter to
court. The superintendent, Dr Antonio Ghiringhelli, threatened
to appeal to the public, to have costumes, decors and music impounded in Venice and to prevent the performance by every
means. Before long I received a pile of Italian newspapers with
long and most uncomplimentary articles about Stravinsky and his
publisher. In the Italian Parliament a question was put to the
Minister of Finance asking how it was that there were not enough
dollars in the treasury to import badly needed flour but enough to
pay for the first performance of an opera. A major scandal seemed
to be imminent, and I took the next plane to Milan.

Would it not be possible, I asked, to combine Scala, Radio and
Venice? 'Never,' said Dr Ghiringhelli. 'Never,' said Ferdinando
Ballo, the organizer of the Venice festival. I took the train to
Rome. San Luca greeted me from its hill above Bologna—a few
years before the war I had almost been arrested there when I
strayed with a camera into a 'military zone'—Santa Maria del
Fiore in Florence floated past and the cathedral of Orvieto was just
visible above its steep cliff. It was early March and in the Tiber
valley the almond trees were in full blossom and teams of white,
long-horned oxen were ploughing the fields. Somewhere in the
open country the train stopped and in the sudden stillness the larks
could be heard singing in the blue sky. The country is unsuitable
for awkward problems. One should enjoy it and forget everything else.

But—'Never,' said Giulio Razzi, the Director General of
Italian Radio. Just then a vendetta was raging between the Scala
and the Radio. Italian law gave the Radio the right to broadcast
every public manifestation without the consent of the organizers.
This had led to an affray, as the Scala resisted and police had to be

called for the protection of the radio engineers. Since then the Scala had been bent on revenge.

I looked up all my friends. 'Never,' said Mario Corti, once one of the best violinists, and now, in his old age, director of the 'Argentina'. 'Never,' said Guido Maria Gatti, editor of *Rivista musicale*. I went to see the bearded under-secretary at the Ministry of Education, de Pirro, but 'Never,' he said compassionately.

When I returned empty-handed to London I had, in spite of my anger, to admire these stubborn Italians. They fought tooth and nail for an artistic event which could bring them no material advantage. At the Scala every evening was sold out, the hotels in Venice in September were full, particularly with Americans spending their precious dollars who were not coming to hear a new opera. And still everybody seemed to be obsessed with the first performance of the *Rake*, as if the future of the whole nation depended on it. Only Covent Garden had disdainfully thrown it away. What a contrast!

Three times in the following weeks I made my way to Milan and Rome. Considering its purpose, the journey was always disproportionately enjoyable. In those days planes did not cross the Alps but flew to Nice, where one had an hour's rest in the sunshine at the water's edge and then followed the coast at only a few hundred feet as far as Genoa where the plane turned inland. Once I took the train from Zurich, and at Airolo the meadows were covered with white crocuses and garlands of red primula stretched along the rocks. It was beautiful beyond description and produced a seemingly unjustified optimism. When another attempt at mediation had failed and I sat with Ferdinando Ballo at Biffis in Milan we laid a bet for a plate of *gamberetti* and a bottle of *soave*. 'You will in the end collaborate with the Scala,' I said.

Stravinsky knew nothing of all these difficulties. He believed that everything was settled, sent me the third and last act and the production of scores and parts went ahead. But May arrived and nothing was decided. Nobody studied the opera. As an amicable understanding was impossible it had to be enforced. Once again I flew to Rome. The headquarters of the Italian Radio was then in Via delle Botteghe Oscure, a few steps from the Piazza Venezia and the Capitol. I explained to an assembly of officials led by Giulio Razzi that I could not break signed and sealed contracts. If the Radio, the Biennale and the Scala could not come to an understanding I would have to fulfil my obligations to the Scala and would supply no material to Venice. Would the Radio and Venice really want to sue Stravinsky? Were we all not bent on helping him? But time was running out and a decision had to be taken there and then. The gentlemen were really worried and asked for time to consider the situation which, they said, was new to them. I replied that I would return to Milan by train the next day at twelve noon, and if I had no positive decision by then the matter would be closed and events would take their course.

Despite it all it was a beautiful evening on Monte Celio, and I sat there with the view of the Eternal City until night fell. The next morning at ten o'clock a messenger from the Radio brought a letter: the Radio was willing to collaborate with the Scala, which was to be responsible for the performance in Venice and supply the cast, orchestra, costumes and decor, the Biennale to make available the chorus, the theatre and all the administrative services. Ferdinando Ballo had been ordered to travel at once to Milan and to settle all the details with the Scala and myself. '*V'è un miracolo!*' exclaimed Emilia Zanetti, the charming public-relations officer of the Biennale, who had been my secret ally in these last decisive discussions and had come to Rome to help.

The next morning Ballo and I met Luigi Oldani, the secretary of the Scala. The two behaved like obstinate schoolboys who have to shake hands after a fight. 'You will have to persuade Ghiringhelli,' Oldani said eventually. I shall never forget the visit to Ghiringhelli's house and the half-dozen black-and-white-spotted Great Danes as big as calves hurling themselves down the stairs and straight at me. Ghiringhelli saved me only just in time, and in his theatrical manner promised his collaboration. In the afternoon we drafted a formal agreement, into which Ghiringhelli inserted more and more clauses to guarantee the artistic supremacy of the Scala. It was late in the evening when, quite exhausted, we put our signatures to the document. '*Gamberetti con soave?*' I asked Ballo. 'We are not there yet,' he said.

Indeed we were not there yet. I could now inform Stravinsky that the performance was scheduled for 14 September at the Teatro Fenice in Venice, and he received the news as if he had never expected otherwise. But summer was at hand and nobody was engaged. First of all a conductor was required to study the work with cast and orchestra and to conduct the second and third performances and the performances later in the season at the Scala. 'Talk to Cantelli yourself,' said Ghiringhelli, who was afraid of the *maestro* and of Toscanini's shadow behind him. I did, but poor Cantelli nearly had a nervous breakdown at the mere thought of learning the score by heart in three months. Following his great teacher and patron, he would not think of conducting from the score. In the end I had to implore him to forget all about it. At the beginning of July only Elisabeth Schwarzkopf in Vienna and Jenny Tourel in New York were definitely engaged, but nobody seemed to worry.

At the end of July we climbed our mountain in the Valais, 6,000 feet high, without road or railway, but with a telephone. Not until the middle of August did the long-expected panic break out. Oldani rang me from Milan to say that he had succeeded in engaging a conductor, Ferdinand Leitner, the Generalmusikdirektor from Stuttgart who happened to be conducting a few summer concerts at the Maxentius basilica in Rome. But the chosen producer, Visconti, was in Australia. Could I suggest someone else? Carl Ebert was still at Glyndebourne. I telephoned him. He was not very enthusiastic because I had recommended him in the first place and the Scala had refused, but eventually he accepted for Stravinsky's sake. A few days later Oldani was on the telephone again: he could not find a bass-baritone for the part of Nick Shadow. Again by telephone I persuaded Otakar Kraus to accept and to learn the part in three weeks.

When we arrived in Venice on 7 September large posters greeted us: *La Biennale di Venezia ed il Teatro alla Scala presentano la prima mondiale . . .* But we had hardly reached our hotel room when Dr Ghiringhelli appeared in a towering rage: if the posters were not removed immediately and replaced by new ones putting the Scala into first place he would withdraw his personnel and leave at once. So there was another half-hour of wild shouting and excitement in the offices of the Biennale in the Palazzo Giustinian, but Emilia Zanetti intervened and the next morning the new posters proclaimed: *Il Teatro alla Scala e la Biennale di Venezia presentano . . .* Some sharp-eyed Italian may have noticed the change. The foreigners for whose benefit the whole show was staged certainly never became aware of it.

It was indeed a miracle that on the day of the dress rehearsal an orchestra sat in the pit, the curtain rose and the singers—with the notable exceptions of Schwarzkopf and Tourel, who knew not only their own parts but the whole opera—had a vague idea of what they were expected to sing and to do. Costumes and decor made for the Scala fitted only approximately and everything seemed improvised on the spot.

It was the longest dress rehearsal I can remember, starting at

five o'clock in the afternoon and finishing long after midnight.
Nothing worked. Stravinsky conducted with his head buried in
the score as if he had never seen it before. He could not know what
was happening on the stage. Once Elisabeth Schwarzkopf stepped
forward and interrupted the maestro: 'This is too fast, at this
tempo one cannot reach the other end of the stage!' In the wings
brave Jenny Tourel gave a last lesson to the tenor, Carl Ebert
shouted from the dark stalls to the stage 'Imbecili!' when the
chorus, singing in a sort of English, did not know what to do. The
interludes were too short for the old-fashioned equipment of the
Fenice, and each time the scene changed and the curtain went up
one could see stagehands running about between slanting props, but
Stravinsky stubbornly refused to allow short intermissions. A
veritable babel of languages made communication almost impossible. Exhausted, we staggered back to the hotel with Stravinsky.
Might it not have been better if Venice and the Scala had not
agreed to co-operate?

The next morning there was a sirocco. Sweltering heat enveloped
the lagoon like a hot, wet cloth. Before lunch I found Stravinsky
in his room wearing only his pyjama trousers, a towel round his
neck and a large bottle of mineral water on the table, the score in
front of him. He had hardly slept and was utterly dejected. He had
asked for another piano rehearsal but the singers had refused.
'Comment expliquer, cher ami?' he cried. 'The recitatives must be
sung in tempo!' I tried to comfort him. A bad dress rehearsal was
the best omen for a good performance.

The evening was a social event of the first order. All the famous
film stars were present—the film festival coincided with the music
festival—furs, jewellery and dresses were fabulous. From Campo
S. Moisè to the steps of the Fenice Venetians lined the narrow
streets and enjoyed the spectacle. The performance of Stravinsky's
first and only full-length opera was of secondary importance. In
the beautiful auditorium of the Fenice the heat was murderous.
We sat in the back of a box, took off our ties and dinner-jackets
and waited anxiously. After the confusion of the dress rehearsal
everybody was calm and composed. Carl Ebert had forced another
drill with the stagehands, the singers seemed by a miracle to know
their parts and Stravinsky himself was all confidence and authority.
The public was not greatly interested in what happened between the
intervals and expressed its appreciation with condescending applause.
But the critics who had come from all corners of the earth had
a great evening. At half-past two in the morning I sat with Ferdinando

Ballo in the Taverna della Fenice and had my *gamberetti con soave.*

The next day, at noon, there was a great reception at the Palazzo Loredan. Stravinsky was led by a procession of resplendently dressed dignitaries and guards into the great hall of the 'Municipio' and the Mayor of Venice made a long speech: all great men of history had come to the fairy-city in the sea, Julius Caesar, Attila, Charlemagne—and now Stravinsky. It was all very moving. When the same picturesque cortège led Stravinsky back to the entrance, he whispered to me in passing, 'Have you got the cheque?' The suspicious Italians had put it into the contract that the fee should be payable only the day after the performance. Yes, I had received the cheque.

There is probably no other place on earth where the sacred and the profane can live together as they do in Venice. In the Museo Correr there is, among many beautiful and indifferent things, one which is usually overlooked: Francesco Morosini's prayer-book. It is also a pistol-case.

Is *The Rake's Progress* a good opera? The experts have never been able to muster much enthusiasm for it, and there is a lingering suspicion that Stravinsky did not mean it seriously but was merely toying with a parody on opera at its worst—the opera of Bellini and Donizetti. And since parodies have to be short in order to be effective they did not find the full-length *Rake* amusing. Once more, and for the last time, Stravinsky had traversed the wide realm of music, from Monteverdi to Handel, from Gluck to Donizetti, picking up bits here and there. In his cavatinas and cabalettas, strettas, duets and trios the past sparkles like cats' eyes in the dark. And all this made an opera as only Stravinsky could create it, weird and gripping: the dance in the brothel, the ghostly parade of the servants carrying the possessions of Baba the Turk, the organ-grinder's melody which accompanies the stones-into-bread machine, the scene in the cemetery. The *Rake* has the best *buffo* scene in recent operatic literature in the auction, and one of the most beautiful melodies Stravinsky has ever written in the lullaby with which Ann sings her Tom into death. Never before and never since has Stravinsky shown such a wide range of expression, the serious and the comic, the bizarre and the gruesome, nor such sincerity of feeling. He gave his own past a magnificent farewell—and turned away.

Stravinsky has written many works on commission and for important fees. But he has never made artistic—or financial—

concessions. Once he was himself doubtful, and I had to warn a lady who had commissioned a piano concerto that she could not expect a concerto in the usual manner. But she insisted, and received a very short, very difficult piece which gave her little opportunity to show her pianistic virtuosity. 'He used to write such nice music,' she said when she saw the score.

In his old age Stravinsky discovered Webern. But what should, what could the style of his old age be? Verdi could draw upon the experience of his long life. Richard Strauss could return to a musical homeland which he had never quite abandoned. Stravinsky can do neither. There can be no sublimation of the *Rite*, there is no single, overall outcome of his life's work. He always locked the doors behind him and never had any desire to settle down in one particular province of music.

For a weaker man of his age this could have become a tragedy. But Stravinsky continually draws new strength and *joie de vivre* from it. He is still, in his habits, the Russian gentleman of former times, happy like a child if something pleases him and angry like a child if it does not, religious with a touch of superstition, lively in spite of his frailty, and often surprisingly humble. In Hamburg he complained, about the production of his *Flood*, 'I have created a Lucifer—and what do I see? A red cat.' But he did not insist on any change, as Richard Strauss would have done.

Stravinsky does not collect old paintings or old furniture. His wife Vera, herself an artist of great gifts, once said, 'We do not like Rome where everything is old and venerable. We like New York.'

The *enfant terrible* of yesterday is today the subject of an admiration no other living composer has earned. There is a feeling that he is the last of the great, the last link with the greatest epoch in music—with which, however, he never wanted to be associated. 'All my life I have thought of myself as the youngest one, and now, suddenly, I read and hear about myself as the oldest one,' he wrote not long ago. Indeed, he always seemed younger than his contemporaries, with whom he had nothing in common but co-existence. He too experimented, but the result was achievement and not mere experiment. And even now when he uses a technique which he has not invented but often modified it testifies to his inimitable, unrepeatable personality: his *Requiem-Canticles* of 1966 have the same direct appeal as his *Oedipus Rex* of 1927 or his *Rite of Spring* of 1913 or, indeed, any of the great works of the 'Golden Age' before him.

After Stravinsky it will be as it was after Michelangelo. . . .

7. NEW DEVELOPMENTS

··

The accomplished artist must combine two faculties: imagination and craft. The artisan without art is, in his modest way, a respectable contributor to man's man-made environment. The artist without artisanship contributes nothing, creates nothing that could be appreciated by others. 'He has taste,' said Haydn of Mozart, 'and great technical knowledge.' Knowledge, the servant of imagination and inventiveness. Everything depends on the balance between the two, on the moment when the divine and the human join together to create a work of art, be it music, poetry or painting. The fate of every art is governed by this balance: the art flourishes when the balance is perfect, declines when it is disturbed.

This, precisely, is the central problem of new music. It is sometimes said that, in music more than in the other arts, periods of severe discipline alternate with periods of great freedom. But since really 'old' music has vanished, since we know only the music of the past five centuries and truly understand only that of the last three, all we can really say with conviction is that, before our very eyes, music has freed itself from many restrictive rules, has lived through an era of considerable freedom and, more recently, has returned to stricter rules. Whether this is a regularly repeated rhythm it is difficult to tell, but there is no doubt that during the era of freedom which we know best music has, as far as our knowledge of it goes, acquired properties which it never possessed before. The fact that after such a period of freedom composers are again seeking the greater security of explicit rules must be taken as a sign of our times. It was precisely this that Schoenberg prophesied.

After the Second World War, when all cultural, political and authoritarian control was broken, when the new teaching had begun to spread beyond the Vienna School and Webern's example was generally accessible, the former uncompromising orthodoxy was relaxed and a new generation felt encouraged to seek renewal and reformation, in order not to abrogate the new laws but to refine and develop them. Generally speaking, as I have observed before, the complete twelve-note row provided the composer with four basic forms: the row itself, its inversion, its mirror and the inversion of the mirror. If, for instance, that row is divided into three groups or series of four notes each, the composer gains twelve new basic forms in addition to the original four, to which all the rules and possibilities apply. This is the simplest formula for turning twelve-note music into serial music and twelve-note composition into serial composition. Composers did not stop at such primitive discoveries and found that the serial technique of row, inversion, mirror and inversion of the mirror could be extended to rhythm and tone colours, dynamics and tempo, to everything which may be called a musical element, and this increased the possibilities of combination and permutation almost as widely as the seven or eight chromatic octaves of diatonic music. Almost—for there were many possibilities in extended serial music, but little freedom. In principle this development has some similarity with the change from pre-classical monothematic to classical polythematic music. Then creative imagination strained at the leash of overpowering crafts-manship. Is it this creative imagination which compels an extension of the rules today?

The result was, and still is, an unending series of experiments. It is worth noting that the centre has definitely moved away from the old haunts of new music. If any proof were required that the choice of Vienna had been a mere coincidence, there it was. The genius of change left Austria without a backward glance and settled in France—in Paris, where, with Olivier Messiaen, a new intellec-tual impetus gathered momentum. We shall repeatedly have to quote Pierre Boulez, Messiaen's pupil and the best brain in new music. Reviewing the events of the last fifteen years he speaks of 'terrible and regular epidemics', of 'ciphered rows', of 'tone colours', 'co-ordinated tempi', 'stereophonics', 'actions', 'chances' and 'informalities'. In fact, as an outsider and a non-composer one is confounded by all the complications which today surround any attempt at writing a piece of serious music. From an ever-growing and an ever more bewildering literature I can only quote the most important composers—theorists who actually do as they say or say as they do: Boulez himself, Ernst Křenek and Karlheinz Stockhausen.

Stockhausen pleads for an 'indeterminate' music. He gives the performers a kind of basic rule of the game and then leaves it to them to find and to play one or more of the hundred million possible variants of a piece like 'Refrain'. On the other hand, one reads in the preface to Ernst Křenek's 'Questio temporis': 'Every-thing one hears is determined by exact measurements of entrances and durations of the acoustic elements based on the units which result from the intervals of the basic note row and its derivatives obtained by rotation of the notes. . . . Where the density of the texture increases beyond a certain level (this aspect, too, is determined serially), statistical scattering takes the place of exact measurement.' And Boulez once wrote in respect of music, 'Time, like pitch, possesses the three dimensions: horizontal, vertical and diagonal.' But this only proves that confusion of thought cannot always hide behind dark meanings and tortuous phrases. For time *has* no dimension, it *is* a dimension; therefore music, which is a function of time, has no other dimension but duration. Everything else, including the diagonal, is direction. Yet, while noting this, so to speak, in the margin, I do not wish to get involved in any polemics. This is not meant to be a technical guide to, or through, new music. I only want to show how painful even the approach to music has become.

'Structure' is the imperative of new music. 'When one meditates on the new structure of mathematics, of theoretical physics . . . one can realize exactly what an immense road musicians still have to travel before arriving at a general synthesis' (*Boulez*). Perhaps we can catch a glimpse here of the process of creating music today. There has always been a mysterious connection between mathematics and music which has intrigued mathematicians but rarely bothered musicians. But now music seems to be irritated by it. And at once Boulez varies Debussy's famous phrase: what music must touch is not the bare flesh of emotion but the bare flesh of evidence. Are we not here on the threshold of a new, neopythagorean harmony of the spheres? Of a music which consciously and avidly seeks contact with exact sciences and wishes to share with them the quality of 'evidence'? Evidence is almost the opposite of imagination, which in turn is the source of all the arts. At the end of a long and abstruse treatise Boulez finds himself using the 'fatal' word 'inspiration', replacing it at once with the more comfortable 'imagination', as if he had picked up a hot brick. But where evidence is sought imagination has no place. To surmount the obstacles of evidence is, or was until recently, the very purpose of the arts. The mathematician and philosopher Leibniz formulated the mystery of music, at a time of severe regimentation: '*Musica est exercitium arithmeticae occultum nescientis se numerare animi*'— 'music is a mysterious arithmetical exercise of the mind which is unaware that it deals with figures'. What matters is not arithmetic, not evidence, but mysterious, unconscious application.

Our generation has experienced so much new evidence that everything mysterious or unconscious or instinctive has become an object of suspicion. And music strives to create 'structures' which could vie with the newly found structures of mathematics, physics, chemistry and biology. What a strange obsession for a musician! It means that 'how' attracts all the talent, all the diligence, all the speculation, while 'what' seems to lose all its meaning. In all the literature written for the ordinary listener and music-lover rather than the budding or mature composer there is ample explanation of *how* the composer does or should put notes together, but no word about *what* he wishes to convey to the listener. That every interval is strictly measured? Or that every note is improvised from a given pattern? Structures? Is all the meaning, all the purpose of this new music exhausted on technique? The unbiased listener to the old, conventional kind, so far as his existence is still justified or admitted at all, will have to concede that the audible result of this music in no way bears witness to the amount of thought and theory which go into the making of a new and usually short work. From the new structures of mathematics, physics and chemistry have sprung the atom bomb, the space rocket, antibiotics, radar and innumerable other things which mark the evidence of all the theoretical assumptions and calculations. But what evidence is brought forth by those complicated structures of new music? A magma, as a French critic once said to me, which obscures all the niceties of painfully calculated intervals and differentiated rhythms. It is certainly true that a piece like Boulez's 'Le Soleil des eaux' first strikes the listener with a new and very clever sound but this sound does not change as the work progresses and the overall acoustic impression is that of a static lifelessness.

The conventional listener will have to admit also that this new music of our time has lost much of the ferocity with which it stormed the fortresses of diatonic music after the First World War. But he cannot escape the menacing question: where does the boundary lie between music and noise? The organization or structure of noise cannot be the decisive criterion, for every engine produces a mechanically organized noise. Is it intention rather than fact which differentiates between the two? The engine serves a practical purpose and in doing so makes an incidental and un-desirable noise. Does this or a similar noise become music if the practical purpose is removed? Is it music-making in any accepted sense to play Stockhausen's 'Cyclus' from a score on a great battery of percussion instruments? Stockhausen himself provides the answer: 'Whether organized sound is called music does not interest me.' But the matter is too dangerous to be dealt with so summarily. In one of his statements the following obscure words occur: 'The first question is to *avoid* the separation of sound and noise. . . . The zero value of the noise scale is then the sound.' I will not attempt to discover the exact meaning of this observation, but the conclusion is inescapable: the acoustic result of the 'structure' is irrelevant.

John Cage, who has a few followers inside and outside the United States (though one could scarcely call him, as his admirers do, a leading intellectual power in the world today), seems more concerned with the purpose and meaning of music than his more articulate contemporaries. 'Our lives are not based on melody or harmony or polyphony. . . . We can enjoy entering into chaos.' And he then demonstrates this in his own works, ranging from 'silence', with neither music nor noise, to shattering noises with no rhyme or reason.

All these various tendencies show the same perplexity as to what exactly is intended. This is obviously why all creative effort is bent on 'how' to the detriment of 'what'. In vain Boulez quotes (from sources which are not necessarily valid) evidence that there is no contradiction between form and content. Music is and remains an acoustic phenomenon, just as painting and sculpture are visual ones. One must first see a picture and hear a piece of music before one can think about them. To read about them—and a score is no more than a description—is not enough. In times of great formal freedom form is no longer a vehicle for the content; in times of severe formal regulation form and content become closely linked. J. S. Bach, too, could compose 'fantasias' where form and content are further removed from each other than in his fugues, although his 'fantasy' was more rigorously controlled than either Mozart's or Beethoven's. But only by listening can the congruity or discrepancy between form and content be judged. If the acoustic phenomenon obscures the form and is uncertain of its content the listener is left with little to go by.

But perhaps this new music is not meant to be heard? It is here that Webern—rather than the two romantics, Schoenberg and Berg—proves to be the true inspiration of new music. His disregard of the actual sound of his music, his merciless elimination of all emotion and every hint of a 'meaning' from it, are the soil in which our new music grows. Some may say it is an arid soil and desert vegetation that grows in it, but it certainly is something

Schoenberg and Berg never intended and never achieved: a new attitude to music, to the arts, to the world and to humanity. Whatever reservations one may have, this change in attitude must be seen in the larger context of the time in which we live.

Boulez, and with him all the composers of new music, deny that they are 'boundlessly' abstract. But one need only look at a random selection of titles to recognize how a form or structure imperceptible to the ear has absorbed the content: 'Segmenti' (Kazimierz Serocki), 'Polymorphia' (Krystof Penderecki), 'Spectra' (Gunther Schuller), 'Circles' (Luciano Berio), 'Figures, Doubles, Prismes' (Boulez), 'Available Forms' (Earle Brown), 'Extreme' (Boguslav Schaffer)—and occasional obvious absurdities such as 'Variations without a Theme' (Tadeusz Baird). There is perhaps a very fine difference between abstract and absolute music. In 1878 Wagner wrote of Bach's 'Wohltemperiertes Klavier', 'This is pure music. Everything *we* do is applied music.' He was thinking, no doubt, of his own music dramas as much as of Liszt's programme music or of Schumann's 'Haunted Place'. 'Absolute' music has no clearly defined or definable meaning either. As long as music was essentially vocal the problem did not arise, because music borrowed or appropriated the meaning of the words even if it did not seem to have any close and inner contact with them. But instrumental music certainly posed the problem of an independent meaning; and this problem was solved with great ease. In the seventeenth century, when instrumental music developed, it set out to be first and foremost beautiful, agreeable. It gave up much of its former cleverness so that beauty should not be impaired. And later, in the course of the eighteenth century, it discovered its faculty for expressing moods, for being hilarious or sad. Occasionally this interfered with its beauty, but it provided a 'meaning' without being forced to spell out the reasons. Neither moods nor ornaments need justification so long as they are welcome. One would not call either Corelli or Haydn 'abstract'. 'Prelude' or 'sonata' are absolute musical forms. But the titles of new music I have quoted above are abstract subjects, 'segments' are geometrical, 'spectra' physical notions, just as Liszt's 'Tasso' is a literary one. If absolute music is the music which seeks and finds its subject in itself and applied music the music which receives its inspiration from other, non-musical sources and not only from literature, then this new music is not absolute but applied, and, as the subjects to which it is applied belong to the most abstract exercises of the human mind, new music becomes, despite all protestations, abstract.

Many observers may find a spiritual kinship between abstract painting and sculpture on the one hand and abstract music on the other. But, apart from John Cage's slightly scurrilous ideas, nothing in new music has that deliberate object of avoiding all rules which distinguishes abstract painting and sculpture. If a comparison between music and painting is at all admissible a work of new music might be compared with the green turf of the Ghent altarpiece which, on closer examination, proves to be a carpet of minutely drawn flowers and blades of grass. Similarly in new music the sound covers every detail of the construction and only close scrutiny reveals the innumerable details.

It is perhaps the insufficiency of the purely musical, acoustic result which compels the composer of new music again and again to explain his methods and his technique. Never before has the public been pestered with so many complicated, impatient and sometimes aggressive treatises of a theoretical and technical nature. They seem to be begging—or warning—people not to be misled by mere sound but to look for the consummate art and effort behind that sound, which assign the necessary and correct place to every note and every dot. Beethoven's music too has a basic theory which is beyond the great majority of listeners, and irrelevant to the enjoyment of his works. With new music this is not enough. The listener should also know how it is composed. It may be said that this is a higher level of appreciation altogether. But the artist is exceptional: the ordinary mortal does not need to know how a divine spark can be turned into an intelligible message.

Sometimes I think that the same happens to new music as to certain technical innovations. The first locomotives or motor-cars were ugly, cumbersome things. Their pride was not in their appearance but in their technical attributes, their pistons, cylinders, sparking-plugs. Some even spoke of new aesthetics. Only when the purely technical sensation had abated could a new sense of form or shape hide all the gadgets beneath a shining exterior. And the more they were hidden the more efficient the machines became. Many mistakes had to be made before a satisfactory solution was found— even coal tenders, for example, were painted with flowers. But in the end the right answer was found.

In a similar way the composers of new music may today be so obsessed with their own techniques that they never stop talking and writing about them. But the day may come when they will have more confidence in their works and leave technicalities alone, just as Mozart or Beethoven did. Such explanations will then be found only where they belong, in textbooks for students of composition.

This much, however, the layman can learn from all these writings: music is no longer for simple people—neither simple composers nor simple listeners. The instinct which once could find in the dark what knowledge could not see in broad daylight has been extinguished.

The increasing difficulty of composing music, the requirement of higher intelligence and deeper thought—and, therefore, greater experience—has removed from music two things which in more carefree times belonged to it as to no other art: early maturity and large output.

Gone, at least for the time being, are the days when a very young man could write masterpieces like those of Pergolesi, Mozart, Schubert, Mendelssohn, Chopin and even Richard Strauss (who was only eighteen when he wrote the Serenade for Wind Instruments, Op. 7). There are certainly people who prefer full maturity to precocity. But such early maturity has a particular charm, which nobody has better described than Carl Maria von Weber, writing of Mozart's *Entführung aus dem Serail.*

> I venture to state my belief that in the *Entführung* Mozart's artistic experience has reached its perfection and it was the experience of the world around him which thereafter guided his pen. The world was entitled to expect from him operas such as *Figaro* and *Don Giovanni* but he could not write another *Entführung*, which was for him what adolescence is for every man, the happiness which can never be recaptured again. For by improving on shortcomings, irretrievable charms are lost.

In those carefree days youth and music naturally belonged together and we have still not quite abandoned this idea. Who, even today, would think of music as a grey-bearded monster? But music has become altogether too difficult, too stern, too complicated. Its heights cannot be stormed by audacity and fiery impulse alone. A heavy burden of knowledge and thought has to be carried painfully uphill, and this cannot be acquired in a few years or by instinct. In some respects it is strange that younger men, who a century ago would have been considered much *too* young, have a larger share in the affairs of the world today than they have had since the Middle Ages, when life was simpler and its span much shorter. But to music, or the arts in general, this does not apply. Real youth lacks the perseverance which New Music requires.

This also explains why, by comparison, the output of composers of new music is small. A large output came as naturally to music as it came to painting. '*Sempre disegna!*' Raphael insisted with his pupils; and he did it himself, for designing was a difficult art, eye and hand had to achieve virtuosity through constant training, and such virtuosity had to be so perfect that it was not only a faithful servant of inspiration but could, if necessary, produce remarkable works without it. It is no easier to catch and shape a flashing musical 'thought', and training produced the facility which in turn resulted in a prodigious output. As far back as we can see, composers were prolific to an extent which is almost incomprehensible in our time; not only J. S. Bach or Handel, but also Orlando Lasso and even Donizetti.

But the composer of New Music cannot be compared with his predecessors. Schoenberg once said to me that if he had not composed as many works as Mozart he had certainly written as many notes. This remark was as true as it was ominous. In one phrase, it told the whole sad tale of the new creative process. None the less Richard Strauss in his eighty-five years wrote more than three hundred works, some of them very large indeed. Schoenberg, after seventy-seven years, left scarcely eighty, of which only *Gurre-Lieder* compares in size with Strauss's operas. To younger people this will still appears as a large *œuvre*. Virtuosity has become useless, dispensable. It is only by the sweat of the brow that a work of strictly controlled structure enters this world. Hard-headed conservatives accuse the composers of new music of being swindlers to a man. But the true swindler is a man who tries to possess himself easily, quickly and illegally of things for which the good citizen has to work hard and long. How could any man who writes music with sweat and blood be a swindler? The carelessness with which Rossini could toss off a whole opera in a fortnight is now roundly condemned. Today it takes weeks and months to write a few bars. That the works cannot be long follows from their contrapuntal nature. But they cannot be numerous either, and the fruits of all this cerebration and calculation remain small. The composers of New Music are not flooding the world with their works as their forebears did.

There is a strange quality about a work of art at its height of perfection. Not only does the faultlessly shaped content grip the observer; in such works there glows the joy of creation, which touches even the onlooker or listener as mysteriously as the finger of the Lord touches Adam on the Sistine ceiling. But no creative joy shines through the overburdened works of New Music. Only the dull flame of an inner urge flickers there.

It is a surprising and a contradiction that an element of improvisation can creep into the anxiously controlled music of today. As far as the heavy chains of calculation and consideration allow, this improvisation tries to escape control. This does not only happen with Stockhausen. Others such as Lutoslawski indicate, for instance, long, rising chains of trills without writing down definite notes, and others again, such as Gilbert Amy, ask that certain bars or groups of bars should be repeated, or inserted in other places, as the performer pleases. One might have thought that such arbitrary behaviour had ended with the *basso continuo*. From Beethoven's Fifth Piano Concerto onwards composers even hesitated to leave the cadenzas to the performers. Rossini, and Verdi even more so, complained about singers who would not respect the printed text of their parts. Now, in the midst of carefully elaborated structures, the performer is called upon to make his own contribution.

It is also noteworthy that the leading representative of the younger generation of composers, Boulez himself, is often in doubt about the finality of a work and produces new versions after having arrived with great labour at what seemed irrevocably and necessarily the one and only solution to his chosen problem.

This tendency towards change and instability soon combined with the new ways of producing sounds electronically which have a colour or indeed a nature different from the sounds which the human breath, the finger on a string or a tuned pipe produce. There is nothing fundamentally new in the quest for new sounds and sonorities. At any earlier time, when new sounds were wanted new instruments were constructed. In the beginning was the composer—and the instrument-maker followed him. One only has to think of the introduction of violins at the end of the sixteenth century and their striking advance in the seventeenth. The younger generation then demanded a more violent sound, while their elders lamented the shrill noise after the dark whisperings of lutes and theorboes. These new instruments were an inspiration to the musical art, and two generations later, when they had spread from the Cremonese workshops throughout the western world, they became the ideal of beauty of sound. They created a literature of great richness: and they dominated the orchestra.

The orchestra grew louder and louder, and its colour changed. First were added clarinets, which contributed to the rounding-off of its sonority. They, again, were new instruments, and Mozart was the first to appreciate their qualities. His orchestra seems to have been in perfect balance. He obviously had all the instruments he needed and the instruments had all the required capabilities. But with Beethoven this balance is already disturbed. In his big symphonies, in the *Missa Solemnis*, his orchestra does not measure up to his grand design and later improvers such as Gustav Mahler and Felix von Weingartner tried to remedy these defects with the perfected instruments of their time. The generation after Beethoven had what it wanted—fully chromatic trumpets and horns, and Wagner tubas filling the gap in the middle baritone register; Berlioz (and Wagner himself) showed how to handle an orchestra which had grown in every section and was capable of effects never heard before, from the delicate sound of divided violins in the *Lohengrin* Prelude to the thunder of the 'Ride of the Valkyries' and the eighteen-strong brass section of Strauss's *Heldenleben*. Mozart had sent Tamino and Pamina through their fire-and-water ordeal to the same melody of the magic flute (and a soft accompaniment of trombones and kettledrums which just hinted at the danger of their journey). But in Wagner's orchestra the flames of the 'Fire Music' blaze and through it flows the mighty Rhine. It is perhaps unnecessary to remember that at the same time the piano had developed from a chirping rustle to a real thunder machine.

But satisfaction is only momentary. A new mood asked for more new sounds and sought for these sounds not among the old-fashioned instrument-makers but in the wide field of electronics. In those early days the most successful pioneer in new, 'dehumanized' sounds was Maurice Martenot, but it was not until after the Second World War that research and experiment began on a larger scale. In the United States of America electric organs with manuals and pedals but no pipes or bellows had been built before the war, and these new 'theatre organs' could replace whole jazz bands. However this was not the right way to imitate sounds which could be produced by conventional instruments. In America, as well as in Europe, new sounds were produced in costly laboratories by costly devices.

In January 1950 I visited Paul Collaer, head of music of the Flemish section of the Belgian radio and a steadfast champion of new music. 'You have arrived at the right moment,' he said. 'I have just received a parcel of tapes from Paris, the latest thing in music, "*musique concrète*". Let us hear it!' We listened, half amused and half astonished, as it groaned and moaned, shrieked and whimpered. The author was Pierre Schaeffer and the tape had some indecent title which I do not remember. When it was all over Collaer said, quite seriously, 'This is really new. For the first time we have pornographic music.'

Often enough technical innovations make this kind of aimless start before they discover their more reasonable application. '*Musique concrète*' was soon forgotten and electronic music found a more serious purpose. For the World Exhibition in Brussels Edgar Varèse, one of the oldest experimenters, invented a kind of electronic symphony, a vast piece which, as he said himself, was by no means as improvised as it sounded.

To create music from entirely dematerialized, 'de-humanized' sounds, a 'music of the spheres' as it were, is a great temptation for both the technician and the musician. Perhaps the organ had the reputation of being God's instrument because it was the nearest approach to the mystery of sound. But it still needed the expertise of a skilful player, and this human element was to be eliminated as well. This at least is more sensible than the misuse of traditional instruments for purposes and effects for which they are not made. For the performance of new music a large orchestra is often assembled, but each musician has only occasionally to play this or that note, usually in some extraordinary and unexpected manner. It is an absurd thought that the violin in the hand of the orchestra leader, dangling idly for most of the time between his fingers, now violently plucked and then disrespectfully slapped on the back, could be a Stradivarius. Such large orchestras are designed for large outbursts or for homogeneous sonorities; but none of this is sought in new music. Therefore, such 'obsolete' congregations of instrumentalists are an unjustifiable waste and their replacement by an electronic apparatus which can be served by one or two technicians is held to be more practical and more satisfactory than all the unbecoming tricks with which traditional instruments are being misused.

However, there is something uncanny about all this new machinery, about 'synthesizers' designed to make music. One cannot help feeling uneasy when one reads the list of 'instruments' required for Boulez's 'Poésie pour pouvoir', such as sinus-wave generators, rectangle generator, low-tone generator, tone generator for electronic pick-up, wobble adaptor, tone modulator, decay controller, variable oscillator, echo chamber, eight-track magnetophone and half a dozen other contraptions. Will there ever be a time when educated musicians know these devices as well as they now know an oboe? We have spoken about music and technical progress in another context, in connection with the preservation and transportation of the acoustic phenomenon which has affected the art itself. Here is yet another instance where the musical art is in an obvious danger of being overwhelmed by technique.

A host of new problems arises from this new method of music-making. The most obvious is a legal one. As long as a work is not written down it cannot be protected. Tapes or discs are not fixtures in the legal sense. The law, which cannot follow such developments quickly enough, still requires a written record of the work which must be so objective that any infringement can be recognized with certainty. I have called the score a recipe for the re-creation of a musical work. As long as rhythm, intervals and chords are not too involved my inner ear can hear the music when I am reading a written score which endows it not only with a graphic but also with a specifically musical quality. However, there was a time when notes were represented by letters; and solmisation, such as the 'Tonic-Solfa' notation, is still in use. If you give the singer—and it is necessarily a method for singers only—the first note, he can sing the whole piece from the letters, dots and dashes, intervals as well as rhythms. There is still a visual or graphic description of the music. The graphs of electronic music on the other hand—dots, circles, dashes, arrows, waving lines—disclose no quality or property of the sound. The performer can do no more than follow the instructions when attending to the apparatus and be surprised by the result. This does not require a musician so much as a technician, and the performer in the true sense is eliminated.

This ought to be the greatest moment in the whole history of music, a change which overshadows all other changes. It should accomplish what mechanical reproduction of music cannot quite achieve, requiring as it does at least one first performer. With electronically produced music, the art should finally master a basic problem which was of little importance from early times until the nineteenth century but has increasingly worried composers ever since: the elimination of the interpreter and of interpretation. Would not Gustav Mahler have cried 'Eureka!' if he could have composed his symphonies into a machine for a technician to have reeled them off with infallibly the same details, the same tempo and the same expression?

But this ideal concept is baulked by visible and invisible obstacles. The visible obstacles are of a technical nature. I am told that electronic equipment is not standardized and that the technician who is

called upon to reproduce a piece of electronic music from the graph
has to adapt or arrange or paraphrase it according to the machinery
at his disposal. Such adaptations may require a musical technician
who is distinguished from the traditional interpreter not so much
by trying to be faithful to the original but by the disqualifying
knowledge that he is unable to reproduce it at all.

The invisible obstacles are more deep-seated; here, in fact, is the
whole problematical relationship between man and machine in
microcosm. Machines are invented and operated in order to be
useful. Until computers were invented, machines in general were
designed to replace human physical exertion. Now computers are
capable of replacing mental effort as well. This is a serious step,
beyond the original conception of a 'machine'. Man used to be
proud of his mental capabilities, the talented enjoyed their mental
efforts, only to the idle and indolent was it a burden. There is a
curious love–hate relationship between man and machine: love
because of the comfort it offers, hate because of a feeling of redundancy which creates far-reaching social and psychological problems.
But the machine in electronic music, the 'synthethizer' or whatever it may be called, has no practical purpose, no apparent usefulness. The physical exertion it saves is irrelevant. A good composer
loves not only inventing but also writing down his music. The
machine takes over invention itself and leaves to the 'composer'
only the act of selection from a number of possibilities. Here, to a
truly ominous extent, the machine replaces the mind. Is the
human mind to be dismissed from music? Or can it be so brought
together with a machine that the two form an acceptable union
on a higher plane?

The results so far do not seem to justify such high hopes. The
pedigree of electronic instruments may not be inferior to that of
traditional ones, but the difference is that in former times new
sounds were invented for a clear and definite purpose, while
electronic sounds caught music unawares; only after the event have
attempts been made to find a use for them. Purely electronic music
does not convey the impression of an art which knows what it
wants. If at one time the idea was conceived (and is still canvassed)
that people could assemble in a concert-hall and listen to the
howling, whispering and coughing noises of an anonymous con-
traption—which is too expensive to find its way into private
homes—this only shows how greatly the distance between man and
machine can be underestimated.

Igor Stravinsky, always curious about and receptive to every innovation, rejects electronic music. 'It is boring,' he once said. 'Harmonics on the double-bass are more interesting than all electronic sounds.' He admires Boulez, but after hearing 'Poésie pour pouvoir' at Donaueschingen he shrugged his shoulders and said, '*Il s'est perdu.*'

Electronic music *per se* has not found its proper purpose. But there can be no reasonable objection to combining it with traditional instruments in order to achieve a new sonority and colour. The 'ondes Martenot' in Messiaen's *Turangalila* are no less legitimate than the trombones in *Don Giovanni*.

'We need a new definition of music,' said one of the theorists. If only there was an old one! Over the centuries many vague things have been written about music but no one has ever arrived at a definition. How could it be attempted today, when even its fundamental properties have become uncertain and art and artisanship have become almost indistinguishable? Are we not too easily inclined to take for art something achieved with great cleverness and hard labour but without the divine spark which alone lifts human achievement beyond routine explanation?

If an art such as music (and the visual arts) undergoes a profound change, we are easily inclined to philosophize and to look, as Ernest Ansermet has done, for the way back to God, who has created everything and has left it to its fate. No doubt God exists in music too—in every kind of music, sacred or profane, serious or popular. Music is not only physical but also metaphysical and the younger generation may feel more acutely the superhuman elements of creation. However, there is little comfort to be gained from seeking God in music when the human intellect has taken possession of it so violently. What use can it be to try and find what Ansermet called the '*ressemblance de Dieu*' in music when it has become almost impossible to find it in a universe which we have certainly not created ourselves? Whatever we touch, wherever we turn, we meet only the image of man.

Romanticism, which still lingers with us, thought of music as a magical spirit which enters human life like a fairy unaware of the sorrow of experience, free from the burden of learning, the child of primeval nature, an echo of a long-lost past.

But new music is no errant child of a carefree muse. It does not float into life, but is born with great labour. We must free ourselves from all these complicated and profound theories and take a hard look at the works of new music themselves in order to measure the change which has taken place before our eyes.

When discussing Schoenberg's music I mentioned the old notions which have to be abandoned when we deal with pure twelve-note music. Still more of these old notions have to be forgotten when listening to music which goes beyond Schoenberg.

New music, in its many varieties, is not beautiful. It does not want to be beautiful. Beauty in any accepted sense is outside its nature, and therefore outside its capabilities. This is not criticism or reproach but a simple statement of fact. The physicist Heisenberg, who many years ago received a Nobel Prize for his pioneering work in nuclear physics, once said that a perfect mathematical formula was beautiful in an aesthetic sense. In the same way a piece of ingenious serial construction may be equally beautiful as long as it is not corrupted by transposition into actual sound, for the sound which obscures the built-in ingenuities instead of revealing them is never beautiful, even in the most far-fetched sense. Webern himself may have had this in mind when, in later years, he became quite indifferent to the performance of his works.

However, beauty as such has no standard or permanence. The attitude towards it is one of the visible signs of the mood of an age. In 1535 Duke Henry of Saxony had the decorations on his artillery pieces designed by Lucas Cranach, the best artist he could find. Two hundred and fifty years later, on 5 October 1786, Goethe noted in his Italian diary, 'The era of beauty is over. Our time knows only hard necessity.' Yet in 1786 Goethe, like any wealthy man of his time, wore an embroidered waistcoat and lace cuffs and shoes with silver buckles, and may have carried a walking-stick with a handle of Dresden porcelain, none of which was necessary; in 1786 all quality furniture was carefully carved and inlaid, the façades and ceilings of houses were covered with stucco ornaments, hundreds of everyday articles which now fetch high prices in the antique trade were made by artisans who were more than half artists; in 1786 Mozart's *Figaro* was first performed. But Goethe, looking at the palaces in Venice, felt the decline from real beauty to mere prettiness. The sense of beauty, once so strong and sure, began to decline.

Three-quarters of a century later it was in full retreat. Palaces were built in the style of mediaeval castles, town houses in the manner of Palladio. Victorian and Edwardian crafts have recently found their collectors and admirers, but they are second-hand products of a time which had to borrow from the past. Many new things came into use which did not fit into the old aesthetic ideal—

not only railways, telephones and gas lights. We have only to look at the fashions of the Second Empire to recognize the 'crisis of beauty' which, after the First World War, all but exterminated the craftsman. Our technological era has lost the nostalgia which disturbed the last decades of the nineteenth century; we have resolutely turned away from the old ideals. What would Goethe say if he could see the new blocks of steel and glass where people today live in infinitely greater comfort and healthier conditions than their forefathers did under their stuccoed ceilings and with their carved chairs and elaborate doors?

We should not regret the departure of beauty from our life and our art. It never was a sign of better people—but was it perhaps the privilege of better times? 'Few periods are receptive to the pure beauty of form,' wrote one of the great historians of the nineteenth century. 'Only the happiest times can produce it.' There can be no serious argument about the happiness of our time, a time of unfulfilled expectations, irresistible though somewhat aimless temptations and uncertain anxieties. This may sound a little melodramatic: but why are we sending artificial satellites into space, why are men to travel perilously to the moon and beyond? For military purposes? For quicker communication so that we of this hemisphere can see and hear at any moment what they are doing in the Antipodes? Or out of sheer curiosity and boredom with our own shrunken planet? And why are we building and perfecting atom bombs at fantastic cost, while piously professing that we would never use them? There is some sinister humour in the ceaseless exhortations to help the starving half of mankind while we spend fabulous amounts of money on seemingly useless projects. But more and more scientists and technicians are wanted, more brains to replace brains. This is a strange world of exploding population and diminishing '*Lebensraum*', of man possessing everything except himself. It is not that happy time when man could measure his world and take a reassuring reading of his own position. For the arts it is an unfriendly climate, and beauty cannot thrive where there is no time to enjoy it. Should the arts be blamed? Should music?

Indeed music, which is the true expression of our age, must distrust the dream-world of quieter times and must of necessity become scientific—or pseudo-scientific—and intellectual, a delusive image of pure spirituality, purer even than mathematics, which at least is wedded to a purpose. But intellect is unalterably human. If it takes possession of the most divine, most heavenly art everything

226 MUSIC AND THE MIND

divine and heavenly must disappear. This complicated, calculated music of our time knows no emotion, it cannot weep and—worse still—it cannot laugh. In its structures there is no breath of life, only the grimace of human intellect. Rossini's 'Fac me cruce custodiri' was too beautiful and too thoughtless to be pious. New sacred music—which exists—is too unbeautiful and too intellectual to approach the mystery of belief. Here the predominance of 'how' over 'what' explains itself. For 'what' has no intellectual quality, and therefore disappears or breaks down under the weight of the intellectual 'how'.

Is this not a truly dramatic change? In two centuries music learnt to penetrate deep into the human soul, and within a few decades it has lost all interest in it and therefore all the power it once had. For the younger generation intellectual play has an inexhaustible fascination. Passion can be assuaged but thinking cannot rest. This new music knows no satisfaction, no finality, no accomplishment. It must try and try again, only to arrive at the same uncertain result, whether it be laid down in detail or half improvised. Not only is the similarity between the works of different composers striking, but the works of the same composer resemble one another much more closely than did the works of Beethoven from the same period of his life. If Schoenberg's music lost, involuntarily, tempo, dynamics and rhythm while still clinging to expression, the step beyond, indicated by Webern and accomplished by his successors, has lost expression too. Complete objectivity is the aim, and this finds only one single object of veneration in the whole of creation: the thinking, human intellect. Here is the imbalance within the art and we shall have to face its consequences.

I cannot help looking with some compassion at the composers of this highly intellectual new music. Our day and age allows little enjoyment of life. How could music and its composers enjoy it? So much is withheld from them that was once so generously bestowed on the creative genius—the delight in creating, the satisfaction of achievement. Intellect knows no individuality. Where intellect reigns, everything personal and individual vanishes from the art of music, disappears in this much vaunted objectivity. One may call that impersonal uniformity the style of new music, but this style is no longer the former community of phrases and turns but the uniformity of the spirit. The effort of finding an adequate musical formula for that spirit is great, greater than at any time we know, perhaps for many too great.

8. TRADITIONALISTS

It is, of course, not true that all music written today is dode-caphonic, serial, electronic or otherwise new, committed to a future still unknown even to the prophets. The composers of the years between the wars who did not subscribe to any particular 'school' have had their successors, although their number has diminished and their music seems more traditional to us than Ravel's or Stravinsky's sounded thirty or forty years ago, when the Viennese School was isolated from the main stream.

It would be difficult to think of any names of traditional com-posers in Germany, France or Italy who have come to the fore since the Second World War, although Hans Werner Henze has shown some tendency to return to more traditional ways of com-posing and he, at least, has enjoyed a measure of success. The leading American composers whose reputation and works have reached beyond the United States, Aaron Copland and Samuel Barber, belong to the generation which, in its decisive years, was not confronted with any decision. In particular Copland, the pupil of Nadia Boulanger in Paris, deliberately avoided any involvement in Schoenberg's teaching.

Among those who were still young at the end of the Second World War Benjamin Britten stands head and shoulders above the rest. One would like to believe that, in the face of all the innovators, he would vindicate all that is 'traditional' and dear in music—inspiration, expression, melody. His music is what music has been in the last two hundred years, save only for the fashionable garment of clashing dissonances. This does not please the avant-gardistes; nor does it please them that Britten, of all the composers of his age-group, is the only one whose successes with the public compare with those of the Golden Age; the only one who can instil a large audience of listeners, erudite and simple alike, with enthusiasm; the only one whose music has penetrated to the consciousness of the people. These are facts which the biased and unbiased can check and verify. Never before (with the possible exception of Dunstable, though not Purcell) has England produced a composer of similar stature, although William Walton and Michael Tippett have established the reputation of English music more surely even than Elgar and Vaughan Williams.

Such quick and general success as Britten's music has achieved is all the more conspicuous at a time when musical successes are far rarer than they were even a generation ago; and this has aroused opposition and suspicion. It was, and perhaps still is, said in certain circles that the ruthless propaganda of his publisher led to a gross over-estimation of Britten's music. But propaganda can give no more than initial impetus. It can exaggerate a first success, but it cannot maintain it. Britten has contributed at least a dozen symphonic works to the concert repertoire which are still being given hundreds of performances annually around the world, after more than twenty years. This is a long time. Works of such staying-power cannot be cheap entertainment, of which one soon tires; nor can they be fakes, which are soon discovered. No sales promotion can achieve this. And since Britten ignores the problems and currents of 'new' music, it is not surprising that his more ambitious rivals feel bitter about his successes. 'Epigones,' writes Boulez, with an unmistakable pointer at Britten, 'are, as far as I am concerned, definitely written off.' But not so the public. Britten's music has once again achieved something which great masters before him fulfilled, and which today is the source of great argument and of obscure programme notes—namely, to move, to excite, to uplift and, above all, to give pleasure.

It follows almost naturally from the character of Britten's music that his way of writing is reminiscent of former and happier times when inspiration was the sole creative stimulus. In his earlier years Britten's application was truly phenomenal. One has only to look at the dates of the first performances of his operas in order to appreciate this. *Peter Grimes* was first performed on 7 June 1945, *The Rape of Lucretia* on 12 July 1946, *Albert Herring* on 20 June 1947, *The Beggars' Opera* on 24 May 1948. There were some major works written in between, such as the second string quartet, 'Variations and Fugue on a Theme of Henry Purcell' ('The Young Person's Guide to the Orchestra') and 'Saint Nicholas'. Although the purely manual work of writing a score for twelve or thirteen players is less than that involved in a full orchestral score it is still prodigious to conceive and complete a full-length opera in eight or nine months. My publishing house—and I myself—were often suspected of driving Britten into such hectic activity. But Britten was driven by an overwhelming urge, and it was, if anything, an embarrassment for his publisher that time and again a new opera was performed before its predecessor had had a chance to make its way in the world.

There is something Mozartian in Britten's method of working, in its speed and in his unwillingness or inability to alter what he has finished. Of fifty-four works in twenty years only four were later revised, and even these revisions are somewhat superficial although two of his operas, *Billy Budd* and *Gloriana*, might have benefited from the kind of rethinking that Beethoven devoted to *Leonora*. Nor would Britten condone those cuts or alterations that are almost invariably inflicted upon operas at the hands of conductors and producers.

A discussion about *Billy Budd* with Victor de Sabata at the Hyde Park Hotel in London stands out in my memory. De Sabata was then the chief conductor of La Scala, which had secured the right of first performance of the opera on the Continent. After studying the score he wanted to be free to make such cuts and changes as he thought would benefit the work. I could not authorize this, but suggested a discussion with Britten, and the three of us met at lunch. De Sabata began in his most Italian manner. Making use of great gestures to fill the gaps in his English vocabulary he declared that for him *Billy Budd* was the most important dramatic work since *Tristan* (which was an unwise thing to say because Britten hates all Wagner). Unperturbed by Britten's apparent discomfort, de Sabata continued to explain the difference between the English and the Italian public, the latter being much more experienced and much quicker, and tending to become impatient when told the same thing twice. All of which Britten disliked no less than the comparison with *Tristan*.

As de Sabata did not seem to be coming to the point I reminded him that he wanted to make certain suggestions. 'Oh yes,' he said and opened the vocal score, 'this aria comes too late.' 'You mean,' I asked, 'that it should come earlier on?' 'No, no,' de Sabata replied, 'it must be left out.' That was enough for Britten, and he departed somewhat abruptly. I had to release the Scala from its contract, and it substituted *Gloriana* for *Billy Budd*. But *Gloriana*, then no more than an idea in Britten's mind, also failed eventually to find favour with de Sabata, and was never performed in Milan.

Later Britten became more self-critical, writing more slowly and examining what he had written more closely. *A Midsummer Night's Dream* and the *War Requiem* were more thoroughly revised between the first performance and the printed score than any other earlier work.

Although Britten is no innovator he has perhaps perfected one existing form: the 'chamber opera', the opera which is full-scale on stage but small-scale in the pit. The idea did not arise from purely artistic considerations. The Sadlers Wells Opera, during and immediately after the Second World War the only opera-house in London (or in the entire British Isles), had given the sensationally successful first performance of *Peter Grimes*, but the attitude of the administrators was not what one would have expected. Before the performance they were rather sceptical. When I asked for thirty complimentary tickets for the foreign Press they refused. 'We have had English operas here before,' they said, 'and this time it will be as it has always been: four performances, that will be all.' I had to buy the tickets. The subsequent success, an artistic and box-office success such as the Sadlers Wells Opera had never had before, strangely enough failed to change their unfriendly attitude, and this led to disagreements with the enthusiastic central figures of the first performance: Peter Pears, the first Grimes; Joan Cross, the first Ellen Orford; and Eric Crozier, the producer.

The outcome of this was the foundation of the English Opera Group, where necessity and virtue became almost indistinguishable. Some of Britten's friends, and Britten himself, believed that chamber opera was the whole future of opera, a belief apparently supported by the fact that in Germany, the fairyland of opera, most of the old opera-houses lay in ruins and were not expected to be rebuilt to their former size. It was, alas, an optimistic view. No opera-house could carry on without its traditional repertoire of 'grand' opera, without Verdi, Puccini, Wagner and Richard Strauss, and the newly rebuilt German opera-houses were without exception larger than the old ones; a fact which was prompted by economic considerations no less than by those of repertoire. Chamber opera has in consequence remained somewhat exotic, outside the main stream of operatic life. There is also a purely artistic reason: opera is an '*arte rappresentativa*', a necessarily large canvas which cannot very well be painted in water-colours. However, Britten has contributed the most accomplished works to this *genre* and if they have not enriched the general operatic literature to the extent that their musical excellence would merit this is due to a misjudgement of the conditions in which opera-houses work and exist.

There is one more point in Britten's activity which is reminiscent of the practice of former times: he seeks and needs live contact with his public, as pianist and as conductor. There is nothing theoretical or secluded in his art or in his approach to it. Everything is alive and present—as it used to be before intellect erected a high wall between itself and the dreamworld of the arts. Yet in his private life Britten is happy only in the small circle of his chosen friends.

One would like to be fortified in one's belief that the enormous world-wide success of Britten's 'traditional' music conclusively proves that the new tendencies which rob music of its time-honoured purpose are no more than a passing storm. The fact remains none the less that Britten is the only truly successful paladin of tradition. None of the other traditionalists of his age-group or of the younger generation have achieved anything comparable. He certainly has imitators, as Ravel, Stravinsky and Bartók had, but that imitation which distinguishes the true epigone is appreciated by neither the experts nor the public. It seems that mere talent can find little of that satisfaction in the traditional way of writing music that it certainly could when what today is traditional was new. Every epoch had its minor masters and the minor masters had their merits: Telemann next to Johann Sebastian Bach, Christian Bach next to Mozart. But today, when 'tradition' is in obvious difficulties, nothing less than true genius is required to find what gold is left in the abandoned mines.

Britten is indeed a very solitary figure in contemporary music, and it would be difficult to find another period of European music when the public success of one man stood out so conspicuously as his does today. As the publisher of the greater part of his works to date I am speaking with facts and figures in my mind and not from a vague assessment. Such solitude and lack of convincing succession should make the most determined conservatives think. Is this that rare link which discovers new ways without losing the old ones? Britten's music lives not in the centre but at the very periphery of the music with which my generation has grown up. It is melodic yet dissonant, tonal yet with innumerable trespasses on traditional harmony. It has all the twilight qualities of the sunset music of the masters between the wars. But its spirit is the spirit of music at its most moving and endearing. It has a more hazardous existence than its general acclaim would suggest. Its success is the success enjoyed by music in former times: feeling and melody and—sometimes—sheer entertainment of a high order, all the things of which new music wishes not to be reminded. But it is a sign of how extreme and exposed his music is that, even with his vivid invention, mere routine seldom produces a satisfactory result. In short, it can degrade into a mere mannerism what formerly was the general style of the art of music.

This is no less apparent in the later works of Shostakovitch, who, though a few years older than Britten, is his only rival in the domain of traditional music. Listening to his Cello Concerto, to his Eleventh and Twelfth Symphonies, one gets the impression of a certain perplexity which seems to indicate the end of the road.

How was it so once upon a time? Classical Greek art accumulated a treasure of artistic experience which for nearly seven hundred years provided the Western world with works of art. Twenty generations had to do no more than repeat, rethink and re-create. But even after so long a period of security the day had to come when the procession of expressionless saints on the walls of S. Apollinare Nuovo in Ravenna was more satisfactory than all the beauty, all the naturalness and all the accomplishment of the great masters of the past. And so one wonders whether with Benjamin Britten this 'old' music is celebrating its farewell: beautiful, moving and melancholy.

9. THE PUBLIC AND NEW MUSIC

....

As a rule the public feels instinctively the topical nature of any art, and loves it. The artist formulates what is vaguely in people's minds and they are grateful for being offered this expression of what they cannot express themselves. Where then is the public of new music? In those highly intellectual circles where it is bred and appreciated, it is said that in this age of mass civilization true art must be reserved for an élite, and that the thinking man or woman must choose between Boulez and Menotti (though I suspect they meant Britten), between the all-too-difficult and the all-too-easy, the forward-looking or the left-behind, the *avant-garde* or the straggler. Such radicalism is no less dangerous in artistic matters than in politics. When Mozart was writing *Die Entführung*, his father reminded him, 'I advise you to think not only of the musical but also of the unmusical public—you know there are a hundred ignorant people for every ten true connoisseurs, therefore do not forget the popular.' And his son replied, 'You need not worry about the so-called popular, for in my opera there is music for people of every type.'

In mass civilization (or should we say mass education?) too, ignorant people are divided from connoisseurs. The proportion of ten to one may not have changed since Mozart, but both classes have greatly increased in numbers and the more numerous connoisseurs have a claim to new music, just as new music has a claim to them.

These claims are unsatisfied today. It must be said quite brutally that the new serial, electronic, improvised, determinate or indeterminate music has no public—or at least no public which could keep both that music and its composers alive. There is a fundamental difference between the new visual arts and new music. Economically and artistically it is sufficient for a new painting or sculpture if a single enthusiast or eccentric millionaire or even speculator is found to pay a high price for a few blobs on a canvas or an unidentifiable lump of stone. But music needs tens or hundreds of thousands to understand and appreciate and pay for it. As a publisher I cannot be misled by the fact that now and then a

hall is filled with curious people and perfunctory applause. Sales
and performance figures speak a language which cannot be silenced
by even the most vociferous propaganda.

This is very strange. I must insist again and again that this new
music is what it must be, the legitimate child and the true expression
of our time. Therefore there ought to be a deep understanding
between composers and public and the urge which compels the
composer to compose should encourage the listener to listen. This
is what has happened to music from its earliest days. More decidedly
and more violently than with any other art the public turned away
from old music to new. This is why music has not accumulated
and why 'old' music has been lost. Past music was never felt to be
an adequate expression of the present; it was not worth preserving
for the future, it was discarded and forgotten. There was never
any permanent value or wisdom in any musical work, however celebrated in its time, that was found to be acceptable to a new generation.

One has to realize the magnitude of the change which has
taken place in the last half-century and to see it in its context of the
importance that music generally has acquired in our time. A hundred and fifty years ago an opera season at Shrovetide without one
or more new operas was unthinkable. Haydn had to write innumerable new symphonies, masses, operas and chamber pieces for his
employers, who fêted their guests with new music. He would not
have had the lucrative offers he did from London if it had not been
for the new symphonies he had to bring with him. There was an
insatiable thirst for new music and *more* new music, not only
among a small number of patrons but from an ever-growing public.

It is never easy to discover the first signs of a malaise. Was it the
rediscovery of Mozart in the early years of the last century, when
music had already changed profoundly? Or the even more startling
rediscovery of J. S. Bach, whose music was really 'old'? There had
never been any need for rediscoveries, and there was no obvious
need then except perhaps a vague premonition. Italian opera was
at the summit of its success, Beethoven was new, Mendelssohn
idolized, Liszt, Paganini, Chopin—music had never been so
colourful and exciting. Indeed, music had an exciting quality.
From a performance of Auber's *Muette de Portici* the audience
went straight to the barricades and started the revolution. And
the public could become very angry with music which did not
please them. It was almost like a personal offence.

This involvement of the public was still strong with Wagner
and Brahms. 'Why this may-beetle hurry?' wrote Brahms to his

publisher when he was pressed for new works. There were battles over Stravinsky's *Rite of Spring*, Schoenberg's *Pierrot lunaire* and even after the First World War over *Wozzeck*. But the more immodest and revolutionary the music became, the more modest became the outbursts of pleasure or displeasure. One might have expected that, on the watershed of the old and the new, passions would clash more violently than at a time when only comparative opinions and no principles were at stake. Instead passion spent itself until no passion was left. If the new music cannot be received with frantic applause it should at least meet with violent opposition; it should stir people one way or another. But when, on rare occasions, a work of new music is performed, the audience usually listens with dull indifference, dismisses the performers with a polite gesture and walks away unmoved. It is indifference that kills.

This is a state of overwhelming absurdity, unprecedented in the whole history of music. It cannot be argued that this new music is not the right or adequate expression of the mood and temper of our time, that Tchaikovsky, because of his persistent success with the general public, is more up to date. Nor could one easily reconcile oneself to the idea that our new music is ahead of the time, a 'music of the future' which may need another fifty years to be understood. While Nietzsche's conception of the backwardness of music has not applied for the past three hundred years, Wagner's 'music of the future' was equally misconceived. He would indeed be greatly surprised if he could see how music has travelled after him. Ideas may be ahead of their time. Democritus's idea of the atom anticipated its scientific proof by more than two thousand years. But art, every art, is chained to the time which produces it, or can precede it only by the one step which distinguishes the individual genius from the collective genius of mankind. There never has been and never will be an art which can free itself from the present. There has never been an example of an art which was not recognized in its own time but only discovered and appreciated by posterity. In fact, I doubt whether such an art would have any chance of survival. New music has been with us now for half a century. If its pioneers had successfully turned over the soil it would today be a stronger and healthier plant.

Both the nature of new music and the apathy of the public account for the scarcity of performances. The larger public on which music invariably depends has never come to grips with it and never become familiar with its works.

New music is difficult—difficult to grasp and difficult to perform. But difficulty alone could not explain the gulf between it and the public. It has always been difficult, but in every period of the art the efficiency of the performer has increased with the demands made upon him. But formerly it was the amateur who mattered, the amateur who learned to play Beethoven's 'Kreutzer Sonata' and Chopin's Scherzi, Schumann's 'Symphonic Studies' and Brahms's Violin Concerto, Liszt's 'Années de pèlerinage' and Debussy's 'Cathédrale engloutie' and all the transcriptions of operas and symphonic works, the disappearance of which I have deplored. In contrast there is no room for the amateur in new music. It is strictly confined to the one and only combination of instruments, voices or electronic devices for which it has been conceived, for the actual sound has become an essential element and must not be changed. Transcription would be technically impossible. In an extreme case such as Iannis Xenakis's *Metastasis*, written for sixty-one performers playing sixty-one different and equally important parts, there can be no question of transferring it to any other medium than a gramophone record or a magnetic tape. So the re-creation of new music is left to the professional. Music has, in fact, become highly professional, exclusively professional. The one art where the amateur played a vital part now excludes and eliminates him.

It is strange and striking to see how different things coincide to produce a cumulative result, so much so that cause and effect can no longer be determined. As music became more and more difficult and professional, broadcasting and recording became more efficient, to absolve the amateur from any active participation in music-making. At a time when music might have required a more dedicated effort from the amateur his ambition was blunted or paralysed by the fact of listening to music while leaving all the making of it to the professional performer.

Reading music is largely irrelevant; making music is, for the public, out of date. Listening is the last tenuous link between music and the multitude who fill opera-houses and concert-halls and switch on their radios or turntables. Music has become a subject for exhibition, like painting and sculpture. But is new music exhibited often or persistently enough to become familiar, like a statue in a public park or a picture in a public gallery?

It is almost common-place to say that our musical life in every part of the western world is a museum of antiquities. We live on the musical diet of our predecessors, on pre-classical, classical, romantic, neo-romantic and neo-classical music. In the long history of the art it has never happened that contemporary music was all but absent from the main stream of musical activity. This is all the more remarkable at a time when music is ubiquitous and has become an integral part of our daily life.

In the field of opera there is an atmosphere of crisis. Not so much an economic crisis, because at present the mounting deficit of opera-houses is still met out of public money, as a duty to culture in general. The crisis is rather an artistic one. Since Richard Strauss's *Rosenkavalier*—that is, since 26 January 1911—only one opera, Berg's *Wozzeck*, has established itself in the regular international repertoire. Before giving some statistics I must emphasize that the 'old' repertoire has been much reduced or impoverished since the beginning of this century. I remember all the operas which, before the First World War, were regularly played: Bellini's *Norma* and *Sonnambula*; Donizetti's *Don Pasquale, Elisir d'amore, Lucia di Lammermoor, Lucrezia Borgia* and *La Fille du régiment*; Boïeldieu's *La Dame blanche* and *Jean de Paris*; Auber's *Fra Diavolo* and *La Muette de Portici*; Adam's *Postillon de Lonjumeau* and *Si j'étais roi*; Meyerbeer's *Les Huguenots, Le Prophète* and *L'Africaine*; Flotow's *Martha*; even Maillard's *Les Dragons de Villars* and Wagner's *Rienzi*. Most have disappeared, and probably deservedly so, but they have not been replaced. To this list Wagner himself has been added more recently; if not *Tristan, Meistersinger, The Ring* and *Parsifal*, then certainly *The Flying Dutchman, Tannhäuser* and *Lohengrin*. All these operas were, after all, the most successful masterpieces of their time and the comparatively few survivors of an enormous output. It would be wrong to say that their disappearance is due to the lack of the virtuoso singers who once were available in abundance. Such singers, no doubt, would be available today if they were wanted. But in order to repopulate the deserted land of opera it is not these old masterworks which are revived but operas long since dead and buried: Rossini's *Otello* or *La gazza ladra* or *La pietra del paragone*, Bellini's *I Capuletti ed i Montecchi* or *Il pirata*, Donizetti's *Anna Bolena*, none of which can have another lease of life and disappear after a few performances.

How much the operatic repertoire has aged appears from statistics published by the Zurich Opera House on the occasion of its 125th anniversary in 1959. The average age of operas performed in the first season, 1834–5, was twenty-four years. In 1891–2 it was

fifty-six years and in the jubilee season 1958–9 it had already risen
to ninety-one years. Now, ten years later, it must exceed the
century. One easily forgets that *Rigoletto* was first performed in
1851 and that even *Tristan*, which still sounds comparatively
modern, is over a hundred years old.

It is widely believed that Germany, which has more opera-
houses playing opera all the year round than the rest of the world
put together, is ahead of other countries in the choice of its repertoire and in the catholic taste of its public. But the statistics published by the Deutscher Bühnenverein, which includes all the
theatres in Germany, Austria and German-speaking Switzerland,
for the ten years 1955–65 presents the same picture. These statistics
include both operettas and ballets. Leaving out operettas (headed
by Johann Strauss with 15,555 performances in ten years) the first
fifteen opera and ballet composers and the number of performances
are:

Verdi	20,631
Mozart	18,064
Puccini	12,794
Lortzing	8,719
Wagner	7,763
Richard Strauss	5,343
Donizetti	4,118
Rossini	4,082
Tchaikovsky	3,672
Bizet	3,555
Weber	3,463
Smetana	2,715
Stravinsky	2,665
Nicolai	2,422
Prokofiev	2,226

As can be seen, there are only three composers among those
fifteen who could be called contemporary. Their performances
provide almost exactly 10% of the total performances. If one were
to count Richard Strauss among the 'old' composers the percentage
would be only $4\frac{1}{2}$, and if one takes the performing-time into consideration it would be no more than 2%, the Stravinsky and
Prokofiev performances being mainly ballets not exceeding thirty
minutes each, while all the operas listed are full-length works of
not less than two hours' duration.

Where, then, does 'modern' opera come into the picture? In

those ten years, 41 operas, both German and foreign, had their first performances in the territory of the Association, the foreign works having in a number of cases had their world premières elsewhere. This total would not be too bad for ten years, but these 41 together achieved only 1,619 performances or, on an average, only 39 each, compared with 4,263 performances of the *Magic Flute*, 3,813 of *Figaro*, 3,447 of *Madam Butterfly*, 3,275 of *Carmen*, and 454 even of Strauss's *Elektra*. As far as 'new' music goes, *Wozzeck*, now over forty years old, is the only representative of the new generation, with 324 performances.

How do these figures compare with the spoken drama? The most frequently played author is Shakespeare with 24,902 performances. But among the first fifteen authors are six contemporaries, and among the first fifty are no less than twenty-seven modern playwrights. Modern drama is an essential part of the repertoire; theatres could not continue without it. Yet in the opera-house contemporary works are non-existent and altogether dispensable. I once went to the Scala in Milan for a performance of Ghedini's *Bacchanti*. Above the box office there was the usual notice *Esaurito*, 'sold out', but the theatre was almost empty. 'Oh, the subscribers just don't come,' said the 'sovrintendente' to me with a shrug of his shoulders. In the theatre subscribers easily get bored with too many 'classics'. In the opera-house they want to hear nothing else. Neither in Germany nor anywhere in the world could opera be kept alive without Verdi and Mozart, Puccini and Rossini.

Now we have a new music which insists on being objective, on expressing nothing. It still has a predilection for literary texts and vocalists. But it does not set these texts to music, it uses them as pretexts. This is not the attitude that can create an opera or any musico-dramatic work. It would have been grotesque to see Webern working on an opera. The younger ones, Messiaen, Boulez and Stockhausen, do not even consider it. They have probably buried opera as an art form altogether. When one of them, Luigi Nono, tries to force his structures onto the musical stage the failure is inevitable. Even the comparatively successful younger opera-composers, Britten and Henze, have been unable to provide the repertoire with new works which the public would regularly want to hear and opera administrators therefore have to revive regularly. One must therefore ask how long an art form can survive on a choice of a shrinking stock of old works without receiving any new blood or new spirit apart from those extravaganzas of producers and designers which in themselves sound a warning-bell. The question is all the more painful if one considers the enormous treasury of music deposited in opera. Could anyone honestly believe that new life can be injected into it from still remoter times, that Monteverdi can do for opera what contemporary composers are unable to do?

Concert life has not reached such a critical stage; or at least the crisis is not so obvious. There is a much larger pool of works to choose from, covering a period of nearly four hundred years of European music, roughly from Palestrina to Stravinsky. For some time after, when successful new operas had become very scarce, the concert repertoire still received considerable infusions of new standard works. Broadcasting, too, plays a somewhat irregular part in concert life, being independent of public taste. Reaching as it does a much wider public than all the concert-halls put together it should be the most effective and most audacious champion of new music.

Let me take as an example the British Broadcasting Corporation's Third Programme (now Radio Three) in one week chosen at random. This is a programme for connoisseurs. It can only be heard by about 5,000,000 out of a total of 15,000,000 licence-holders, and broadcasts a very high proportion of serious music between 7 a.m. and 11 p.m. In the week from 18 to 24 December 1965 the number of works broadcast was 213; works of every type, instrumental and chamber music, orchestral and choral. Of these 144, or nearly 68%, were written before 1900; 46, or 21%, between 1900 and 1939; and 23, or 11%, after 1939. Of these 23 works only two, a late work by Dallapiccola and an organ piece by Messiaen, could be termed new music. The rest were five works by Britten, three by Poulenc, Stravinsky's Symphony in C, the Oboe Concerto by Richard Strauss and so on.

Such statistics are not as informative as one would like them to be, as the works broadcast are of very different duration—for example, Brahms's German Requiem beside Messiaen's organ piece. If statistics are to give a proper picture they should take into consideration the times allotted to old and new music respectively. I have therefore taken another week, considering not titles but only duration.

In the week from 2 to 8 September 1967 this same programme broadcast 5,398 minutes, or 89 hours and 58 minutes, of serious music of all types. Music by composers who had been dead for fifty years or more ('non-copyright' music) took up 3,571 minutes or $60\frac{1}{2}\%$ of the total, and of this 2,711 minutes were taken up by music written before 1867, or a hundred years or more ago. Then 987 minutes, or $18\frac{1}{2}\%$, were devoted to music written since 1917 but which could not be termed 'new' music (Ravel, Debussy, Prokofiev, Britten, de Falla, Shostakovitch). As for new music, five composers (a late Stravinsky, Messiaen, Schoenberg, Berg and Stockhausen) occupied 232 minutes, or $4\frac{1}{2}\%$ of the total broadcasting time.* Both Stockhausen with 90 minutes and Messiaen with 78 had an exceptionally good week, but I would be inclined to regard this as a good average of broadcasting programmes showing how very small is the share of new music in the available time.

To prepare similar statistics for public concerts is more difficult. Commercial considerations, the need to sell as many tickets as possible and to put available performers to the best use, no doubt interferes with artistic considerations much more heavily than on the radio. I can give only examples, again chosen at random.

In the month of December 1964 there were in London 43 public concerts, song and piano recitals, chamber, orchestral and choral concerts. Of the 162 works performed, 111 (69%) were written before 1864; 39 (23%) between 1864 and 1939; and only 12 (8%) after 1939. But of these 12 works, 7 were performed at a special Arts Council concert of new music before an audience of about 300 and only 5 works could be heard at regular concerts.

Taking another example, the three halls in London's Festival Hall complex during the week of 2 to 8 April 1967, the picture is as follows.

In the large Festival Hall 28 works were performed, 22 of which were written before 1900 and only 6 in this century. There was no work of new music among them. Contemporary music was represented by two works by Britten and one each by Respighi, Stravinsky, Szymanowsky and Prokofiev.

In the same week 26 works were performed in the smaller Queen Elizabeth Hall, of which 20 were written before 1900; but among the 6 twentieth-century works there was one work by Webern, the rest being by Pfitzner, Kodály, Britten, Bartók and Malcolm Arnold.

In the still smaller Purcell Room 21 works were played in the same week, 13 of which, ranging from Dowland to Berlioz, were

---

* I have omitted broadcasts of contemporary but not *avant-garde* music by young British composers of little consequence, which the BBC has a duty to perform once and probably never again.

written before 1900. Among the remaining 8 one work by Matyas Seiber represented new music, the rest being by Debussy, Honegger, Hindemith, Poulenc, Tippett, and so on.

There were, however, three concerts of contemporary music at the British Commonwealth Institute, with works by John Cage, Earle Brown and others, but these were concerts for the 'élite' and not for the general public.

The picture would be only marginally different in any other country. The London concert-going public is not inordinately conservative. On the contrary, I have often found it more open-minded than the German public, if perhaps not as patient.

It is not a convincing argument that new music needs time. More than forty years have gone by since the Twelve-Note Manifesto, a time which, even with less widespread mass civilization and slower means of communication and dissemination, should have been sufficient to open the doors to new music. With our modern facilities every decade should count as much as centuries before. The 'élite' proclaims (and I personally agree) that Boulez's 'Marteau sans maître' is one of the most characteristic and, in its own right, most accomplished works of new music. Should it not be as well known as Beethoven's 'Eroica' was in 1820? Or Chopin's piano music in 1840? Or Wagner's *Ring* in 1900? Of course, it is a difficult and highly professional work and the amateur has no hope of ever trying to perform it himself or of identifying himself with it, as he could with Beethoven, Chopin or Wagner. But he should hear it again and again, he should *want* to hear a work which, though not expressing anything specifically musical, eloquently and convincingly expresses the mood and spirit of our time, which should be the mood and the spirit of the listener as much as that of the composer. But this is not the case. Performances are lamentably few and far between, and the desire of the listener is, to say the least, not very strong. And remarkably few records of the work have been bought by music-lovers. Only a few works written in the last fifty years have found general public acceptance on a scale comparable to that enjoyed by an enormous number of works of the preceding two hundred. We can take any twenty-five-year period between 1700 and 1900 and we will have both hands full of works which the average music-lover today knows intimately and loves dearly. Try the same after 1900 and you will see for yourself how the number of such works has diminished.

So new music, the music of our time, recedes from the centre of our cultural life and the ever-growing public for serious music enjoys instead the happy products of a happier time. Decades of instruction and insult have passed without any visible effect, without establishing any contact between the public and the music of its time. It is a state of things which has no parallel in the whole history of music. The reasons must lie deeper than in mere conservatism, for conservatism has always existed and has always been overcome.

10. POPULAR MUSIC

There is one type of contemporary music which has a vast public. Popular music today is much more popular than ever before—and more contemporary. The change it has undergone is no less than the change that has taken place in serious music. The road from Brahms to Boulez is no shorter than that from Johann Strauss to the Beatles.

As popular music is not affected by theoretical and programmatic considerations it has had a greater resistance or staying power than its more ambitious serious counterpart. While, before the turn of the century, Debussy and Richard Strauss were filling the musical skies with thunderclouds, the whole world danced the waltzes and polkas of the Viennese operetta and sang the songs of Piedigrotta: 'Funiculì', 'Mattinata', 'O sole mio'. It must have been a wonderful world of illusion, even tending to forget the acid beneath the frivolity of Offenbach's cancans and couplets. The illusion of popular music before the First World War was quite serious. It took entertainment seriously and was determined not to be unsettled by the disturbing events all around it. One thinks with a kind of embittered nostalgia of this unreal reality of sweet tunes, of this world of lax though not dissolute ladies and gentlemen who had no other purpose in life than to flirt and to sing, to give and attend parties, to pretend to be heartbroken at the end of the second act, knowing full well that at the end of the third everybody would be happy again. Vienna supplied most of the musical entertainment of the world, although in Vienna the warning of imminent trouble must have been even clearer than elsewhere. But if any uncertain fears penetrated into the sanctum of the Karlstheater of the Theater an der Wien, where so many world successes first saw the light of day, they only heightened the passion for the illusion of *The Merry Widow, The Count of Luxemburg* or *A Waltz Dream.* People spoke of the heroes of this heroic time as children speak of fairy-tale princes and princesses, and princely names they were.

I am no cultural snob. Although I am at home in serious music I have a deep respect for music as a harbinger of joy. Let no one rob it of this precious gift! In the Viennese operetta, with its stupid libretti and its even more stupid words, it rose to its full stature with no other purpose but to please. It had no rival in this field. Neither the visual arts nor poetry, not even the most riotous comedy, had anything similar to offer. While the other arts were already troubled by an uncertain premonition of great upheavals this carefree music still lavished its blessings on millions of people all over the world. Perhaps no monuments will be erected to the memory of Franz Lehár, Oscar Straus or Leo Fall because their art did not aim at eternity (which aim is a mistaken attribute of immortality). But it would be grossly ungrateful and ungenerous to exclude them from Apollo's grove.

But fate had to take its course: the beautiful illusion succumbed to the war, though Lehár still wrote operettas afterwards and Emmerich Kálmán and Ralph Benatzky joined him. In *Land of Smiles, Circus Princess* and *White Horse Inn* the old illusion took a grandiose farewell. But Piedigrotta no longer had its festival of popular songs. In Italy they sang 'Giovinezza'. In the midst of all the confusion of new frontiers, new currencies and common inflation the source of enjoyment was all but buried and all the lightness of heart was gone. In an uncomfortable Europe there was no corner left where it could still thrive.

But on the other side of the ocean, in that huge and prosperous land which had hardly been affected by the war, a new popular music was discovered.

In matters musical, the United States of America had only the reputation of paying the highest fees to foreign artists; not so much to composers but to conductors, singers and instrumentalists. Gatti-Casazza, the last worthy successor of that famous Barbaja, and the older generation of millionaires risen from newspaper-vendors had made the Metropolitan Opera world famous. For a few weeks each year all the celebrated singers and conductors congregated in New York and presented grand opera on the grandest scale to the richest audience in the world, rather as elephant trainers present their elephants. Attempts had been made to make America the permanent home of great musicians. All races, talents and temperaments had settled in the New World, and the climate of liberty had achieved great things. There was no reason why music should not feel at home in a world ruled by money. But it did not. Neither Dvořák nor Mahler stayed. There seemed to be something in the atmosphere which was favourable to the material and the profane but inimical to music.

But now came the historic hour of American music. New Orleans, previously a rather obscure place in Louisiana which even legend could not beautify, took the place of Vienna, where the impoverished gods of luxury, culture and art were mourning the departure of their old glory. Jazz, the light music of poverty, followed the gay music of opulence.

Music of poverty can be neither gay in the proper sense nor beautiful. It is savagely hilarious or melancholy. Jazz and the Blues came with heavy syncopation, 'breaks', 'swings', 'smears' and 'dirty notes', like swarms of birds of prey or locusts, to devour all the charming European tunes. This was not the music of the European settlers, like Stephen Foster's songs, but a mixture of African freedom and American slavery, music of the poorest of the poor in the richest country—music soon destined to make its best exponents very rich indeed.

This touched a facet of the European mind which the convulsions of serious music had not reached. If it is true that music springs from the innermost feelings then it remains a strange phenomenon that it could unite people of such different origin as the Europeans on both sides of the Atlantic and the American Negroes. But music is essentially anonymous. The lost paradise mourned by the Blues and the present misery against which the wild outbursts of Jazz seemed to revolt were very different from any similar European experience, but the expression was welcome to Negroes and whites alike.

Serious music, which in better times had displayed a certain condescension towards light music, felt more affected by this new musical entertainment, with its serious—not to say sinister background. The justification of atonal music was far less obvious than the atonality of jazz, and there were not a few serious composers who discovered more in it than mere entertainment. Indeed, jazz was formally invited to take a seat alongside serious music. Stravinsky himself was one of the first to try his hand at Dixieland sounds. There was a man named Zez Confrey (oh, these strange, monosyllabic Christian names which came with all the new technical terms, just as Italian had once provided the vocabulary of serious music! Ernest Newman took exception to such abbreviations and once suggested in one of his witty columns in the *Sunday Times* that familiarity ought to be extended to the great masters of the past by calling them in future Joe Haydn, Lou Beethoven and Heck Berlioz). Zez Confrey wrote piano music in the 'novelty' style, at least one item of which, 'Kitten on the Keys', became world famous, and eager prophets saluted the new Chopin.

But the kitten never grew up to become a respectable cat.

Stravinsky did not repeat his early essays and the efforts of many minor composers to discover the deeper meaning and the higher purpose in jazz did not succeed. The stream of new entertainment music was too shallow to carry heavier traffic and the product of misery defied all attempts at refinement such as had raised Passepied, Gavotte, Minuet and Waltz to their high status in music. George Gershwin with a piano concerto, a most impressive but—for the ordinary repertoire—unsuitable opera, a 'Rhapsody in Blue', went as far as was possible. He, at any rate, was the most gifted and successful in the realm of this half-instinctive, half-improvised music. For a time 'symphonic jazz-bands' toured the world. Paul Whiteman and Jack Hylton became very famous indeed, and the public, irritated by evil-sounding serious music, flocked to their performances in their thousands. That sound which in serious music shocked the listener was quite natural in this new entertainment music, which, without much speculation and without any far-fetched theories seemed to have achieved everything that serious music was trying so hard to achieve. Duke Ellington was as 'modern' as Stravinsky, Bartók or Webern but he had a large and enthusiastic public. But apart from syncopated rhythms, jazz proved unfruitful ground for serious music, which had learned more from Stravinsky's *Rite of Spring* than from the whole jazz movement.

After the Second World War a new change in light music became apparent. It had lost much of its 'Africanism' and had found a purer Americanism which also delighted in Latin American tunes and rhythms. Jazz, prematurely aged, became 'classical', in the sense that the Capitol in Washington is classical as compared with the United Nations building, and people began to talk about it with great reverence as a heroic deed at a heroic time. New Orleans dynasties were counted as one counts the dynasties of Egyptian kings of old. New popular music could not measure up to such nobility. But American supremacy, now without any serious rival, was finally confirmed. From America came the songs, the musicals, the new sound of dance-bands and crooners of both sexes, everything which was musical entertainment and diversion. Music in the fifteenth century came from Burgundy and the Lowlands; the mother tongue of music in the seventeenth and eighteenth centuries was Italian. The new entertainment music was American, and hardly ever before had music been so dominated by one well-defined type. Projected by broadcasting and gramophone records, it achieved a popularity which far outstripped that of French and Viennese light music in their heyday.

It may remain impossible ever to define exactly the qualities which produce such universal enthusiasm. But whatever these qualities may be, they must be important and not simply superficial. In some respects American 'light' or popular music is the opposite of its European predecessors. It is not illusionist in any way; it does not attempt to deceive itself or its listeners but is entirely 'realistic'. If sentimental, it does not take itself seriously. The leading lady in *South Pacific*, when about to lose her lover, does not make a scene as the leading ladies of the Viennese operettas did in similar circumstances but simply washes her hair: 'I'm gonna wash that man right outa my hair'. And if this music sings of a 'baby', it does not go beyond a finger-snapping parody of a love song. This is a new attitude which aims at and finds the very kernel of the modern human mind.

The predominance of American popular music made the path of 'serious' American composers outside the United States somewhat hard to tread. It took some considerable persuasion to make conductors in the Old World examine the scores of Aaron Copland or Samuel Barber, of Vergil Thompson or Roger Sessions, who were the first of a steadily growing number to deserve attention and to achieve recognition. But it was—and to some extent still is—an uphill struggle against a widespread prejudice that the competence of American composers begins and ends with popular music, with the songs of Irving Berlin and the novelty numbers of Leroy Anderson.

In the fifties yet another type of popular music travelled across the Atlantic like rain clouds before a westerly wind, more sinister, more ominous, more elemental than its predecessors: Rock 'n' Roll. Its howling, frightening abandon was as far removed from any accepted meaning of music as Stockhausen's noises, but it was perhaps more courageous and uninhibited. It had a shattering effect on the young and sent them into paroxysms of destruction. There were broken dance-halls and broken heads and police had to intervene, not only in New York or San Francisco but in London, Rome, Paris and Berlin. Was this still an echo of the primitive mysterious power of music?

Rock 'n' Roll passed and 'beat' music took its place. The Beatles with their 'Mersey sound' began to usurp the American 'pop' scene. 'Beat' music excited teenagers no less and was no less excessive than its predecessor. It cannot be glibly called 'light' or 'entertainment' music, for it is not simply popular. It is pop music with a sinister undertone; it does not aim to please or to entertain but to excite, to stir up. It is a temptation and a lure into an inexplicable freedom, into an imaginary wilderness untouched by rule or order such as cannot be found in cities or countryside, life or work.

Young and old presumably always had their problems in understanding each other. But it was something respectable which divided them—outlook, temperament, things which the wisdom of the old could understand. Now it is mainly music which keeps the generations more widely apart than they were before.

With 'beat' music, as invented and practised by groups of long-haired youngsters with hoarse voices, droning guitars and clattering percussion, the older generation can have but little sympathy. It is the music of the teenagers, the angry young men and women, an angry music for an angry mood. In former times this age-group received no special consideration or treatment. Apart from a few rare misfits we had to go to school or to work. We read edifying books and suitable specimens of the arts—theatre, music, pictures—were carefully selected for us by our elders. If my recollection is correct it was by no means an unhappy time. But today the teenagers have gained a status in life which runs like a crack through the whole fabric of our social order. True, they too have to learn and go to work, but they grow tall like towers and are, alas, so precocious that the constraint of order and regularity, natural to us, becomes an unbearable burden to them. They are rebellious, revolutionary and angry and insist on showing their rebellion and their anger in the slovenly or extravagant way they dress. If they only knew more clearly against what or whom they are rebelling and what they want to revolutionize! They cannot explain it; and we can only assume that they are doubtful of a future which tampers with the universe, delegates the powers of human inventiveness and planning to electronic devices, promises aimless leisure. All this would be enchanting for dreamers but for the disheartening fact that this noisy, bustling, shrinking world of machines and fantastic enterprises will admit no dreams. It is there that music comes to their rescue. In music they need not spell out their rebellion and their anger. They can abandon themselves to howling and raving without being obliged to say why. Our popular music is not gay, not carefree, not entertaining. It has a serious, perhaps even dangerous purpose: to free the young from constraint, from themselves.

Who would have thought that in the midst of advanced civilization music still has such satanic power? It is all the more astonishing and frightening that it happens at a time when 'serious' music aims at the very opposite effect and is calculated to express nothing, to excite nobody, to avoid any emotion, to be nothing but intellectual. Are these two types of music not children of the same goddess?

I cannot help feeling that serious and popular music react on each other. The more serious serious music becomes, the lower popular music sinks, first in accepting and then in exaggerating the role in which serious music has failed: to excite its listeners, to transport them away from the drabness of everyday routine.

It must be remembered that the antagonism between serious and popular music is of fairly recent origin. They have separated almost before our eyes, and the destinies of the art have been deeply affected by this separation, although the historians have paid little attention to it.

In Mozart's time there was no great difference between entertainment and serious music, and Mozart himself did not find it beneath his dignity to write variations on popular songs such as 'Ah, vous dirai-je, maman', 'La belle Françoise' or 'Lison dormait dans un bocage' by one Dezède, or 'Hélas, j'ai perdu mon amant' by Albanèse, or 'Ein Weib ist das herrlichste Ding auf der Welt' by Benedict Schack. One of the most successful and lasting 'hits' was a minuet from a rather difficult violin sonata written in 1751 by André-Joseph Exaudet, which was soon provided with words and was still sung as a 'bergerette'—'Cet étang qui s'étend dans la plaine'—at the beginning of this century. But most came from operas, both comic and serious. Mozart, among others, wrote variations on tunes from operas by Grétry, Gluck and Salieri, a fashion which lasted far into the nineteenth century when Liszt wrote his monumental fantasias on tunes by Rossini, Bellini, Meyerbeer, Wagner and Verdi; and in 1786 Mozart reported from Prague that the urchins in the streets were whistling 'Non più andrai'. Forty years later street musicians played 'Durch die Wälder, durch die Auen' from Weber's *Freischütz*, and I can still hear the plaintive 'Mira, o Norma' which an organ-grinder used to play at the street corner opposite the house where I lived as a boy. And a funny little man in a black coat, with a large black tie and broad-rimmed hat, nicknamed 'Fra Diavolo', used to walk from table to table in the better restaurants in Prague singing to the accompaniment of a mandolin the ballad from that opera. There was no clearly defined dividing line between serious and popular music.

But as early as the 1820s the first signs of a rift had appeared, and there were soon complaints that the musical world was being inundated with cheap waltzes and marches. A certain resentment which had been unknown before seemed to grow up among serious composers. The two types of music began to drift apart, and with them the public divided.

In 1856 entertainment music must have been ripe for reform. On the occasion of his famous competition Offenbach promised to revitalize the *'art primitif et gai'*. And he did. In such musically fertile times popular music too was capable of its own perfection. The new Parisian 'opéra-bouffe' of Offenbach himself, Lecocq, Audran and Hervé, the Viennese operetta of Johann Strauss, Suppé and Millöcker, the 'operas' of Gilbert and Sullivan, far surpassed the comedies, vaudevilles and musical farces which had sullied the name of musical entertainment. In those days serious and popular music supplemented each other and the respective composers felt some mutual respect. Offenbach longed to write a real opera but died before he could finish it. And when, in an interval of *Der Zigeunerbaron*, the Emperor Franz Josef told Johann Strauss that he liked the 'opera', Strauss wrote delightedly, 'Opera, he said, *opera*!' Indeed *Die Fledermaus* was admitted to the Vienna Court Opera with full honours.

But it was the last. The level of the *'art primitif et gai'* declined once more, while revolution and anarchy threatened serious music. Paris faded, Messager's operettas did not achieve the fame of their predecessors and it was left to Vienna to become the capital of musical entertainment, with Lehár, Oscar Straus and Leo Fall. Brahms and Johann Strauss had been friends, but between Richard Strauss and Lehár no friendship seemed possible. People began to talk about the 'classical' operetta, the 'classical' waltz. The popular music of the preceding generation acquired a touch of the aristocratic in the face of a further decline. This time there was nobody to revitalize light music. After the First World War a Berlin-type of operetta appeared with Jean Gilbert and others which, by comparison even with the last of the Viennese genre, was brash and vulgar. Reconciliation through jazz failed and the two types of music became still more estranged. Now they are as far apart as day and night. There is certainly a marked difference in artistic level and intention between a Brahms symphony and a Strauss waltz, but Boulez and the Beatles represent different worlds which can have no conceivable contact with one another. Nor have the composers of new popular music any desire to share the less lucrative but more respectable laurels of the serious art. Respectability has vanished altogether from the vocabulary of popular music and today it is stripped to its most elemental function. Nor do the pop fans wish to understand the lovers and connoisseurs of serious music.

The two types of music have now arrived at their extremes: new serious music is complicated, new popular music is primitive to the point of absurdity; the one is totally ineffective, the other effective beyond measure. A few thousand people in the whole world may listen to the strange, unemotional sounds of new serious music, but many millions are enraptured by the harsh and sinister voices of new popular music. There is only one feature that both have in common: popular music, like serious music, has become highly professional, excluding the amateur almost as rigorously. If the amateur is incapable of coping with the complexities of new serious music it is likewise beyond his power to generate the frenzy at which new popular music aims. Yet here is contemporary, new music, music without a precedent, which commands all the passion music could ever command. All the new means of communication, of preservation and transportation are at its disposal. Pop music, in fact, is the music which is ubiquitous at all times of day or night. If we try to assess the comparative quantities of popular and serious music in circulation today, and think of the equivalent situation two hundred years ago, we realize at once the savage change which has occurred. Who or what is to blame—if any blame attaches? The time and its temper? Serious music? The public?

11. IS MUSIC STILL A GREAT ART?

I have tried to draw a picture of music today: of the intellectual, expressionless, unemotional serious music and the wild, ranting popular variety. Nobody would be so frivolous as to attribute the one to a mere whim and the other to reprehensible speculation. In both there is the same compulsion which has made the visual arts what they are today, and no disapproval can alter it. Even if a symphony in pure C major could be written today the public, indifferent to all types of new music, would reject it. I share the optimism of the young that our new music is the best music that can be produced in our time. There is no double-meaning or sarcasm in this statement. It is my honest belief.

We are all more or less convinced that mankind in general is steadily becoming more and more efficient, if not necessarily better. Particularly since the Second World War efficiency has made great strides, and even in the Far East the age-old stagnation has been broken once and for all. The thinking man may be tormented by the suspicion that too much knowledge inhibits wisdom. But knowledge grows and accumulates inexorably, and never with greater fervour than in our time.

Not so the arts, which long ago grew up to maturity and ever since then have changed but not developed. It may be said that maturity in the arts is purely external—mastery of the means, better chisels to work the stone, better colours to paint with, a wider vocabulary and better syntax to express thoughts more clearly and in greater detail. Once all this is achieved there are no more worlds for the arts to conquer. Biology binds the present to the past, history strives to cancel the past. It would be idle to compare Henry Moore with Praxiteles, whose artistic experience is as unwelcome today as any artistic experience of our time will be to future generations. In extreme periods the arts behave as if they had no traditions at all.

Just as there is no process of development but only a process of change, so there is no steady rate of advance either. Our comforts have increased enormously in this twentieth century. Innumerable things, both large and small, in our daily life are better, in the true sense of the word, than they ever were before. But the brain which understands quantum mechanics is in no way better than the brain which conceived the *Metaphysics*. Both progress in our material life and change in the arts need inspiration; and inspiration, which is derived from a variety of circumstances, is not always the same, not always equally strong, not always aimed at the same objects or at the same manner of expression. And as the arts, more than any other human manifestation, are the work of pure inspiration, their quality and standards vary from age to age. I have hinted at one reason for rising or falling artistic standards: the balance between inspiration and skill. There are others, too.

In the other arts those fluctuations in standard are instantly recognizable. One has only to think of Elizabethan England and Philip's Spain, of France under Louis XIV, of German literature in the late eighteenth and early nineteenth centuries, and compare them with other periods, to find that it is not the fortuitous appearance of one single genius which decides the level of an art. At certain times a collective flowering of talent and ingenuity produces a general climate wherein the arts thrive. At other times talent seems diffuse, so that even the best cannot scale the highest peaks. This is no regular or predictable rhythm. Beneath the surface of easy explanations, there are deep and unexplored causes which raise the fateful question: how and when does genius arise? Is it eternal and omnipresent, waiting for the propitious moment to summon it forth, or is it created by favourable circumstances and destroyed by adverse conditions?

The example of the other arts cannot easily be applied to music. I must again revert to the strange phenomenon that for thousands of years we know little more about it than that it did exist and enjoyed great respect and affection. But we do not know the works of antiquity, or if we think we know them we cannot appreciate them. What kind of music was taught in that music school which is so minutely depicted on an Attic phial of the fourth century BC? There can be no reasonable doubt that music, despite its divine origin and the reverence which credited it with supernatural powers, did not produce works which could compete in intention or achievement with the apparently immortal works of poetry and the visual arts.

European man already had a rich artistic heritage when music first began to emerge from that anonymity which is invariably a sure sign of imperfection. Not until the twelfth and thirteenth centuries did the first uncertain outlines of individual personalities become recognizable: the School of Nôtre Dame in Paris, Leoninus and Perotinus the Great. From then on there developed a craftsmanship which tends to make all music uniform.

In spite of the prestige which the music of the fifteenth and early sixteenth centuries has acquired in our historically minded time, it was a craft, the special craft of Lowlanders, not so very far removed from the special craft of making swords and daggers in Damascus or Toledo. This music, consisting of short, uniform, cleverly composed pieces, was a small art but a great skill. It is worth remembering that the famous Binchois and still more famous Dufay were contemporaries of Brunellesco and Donatello; and that Josquin lived at the same time as Leonardo and Raphael. This shows the difference in size and scope between the two arts. No historian can persuade us that any work of these greatest composers of their time compares with the cupola of Santa Maria del Fiore or Gattamelata's equestrian statue. Jacob Burckhardt has called the figures in Leonardo's 'Last Supper' the first-born sons of perfect art. Who could pay such a tribute to any of the music sung in Santa Maria delle Grazie while Leonardo was painting his mural next door? At that period—a time of widespread spiritual and artistic excitement—music was a favourite pastime, one of the sophisticated amenities of the day. Vasari recounts how Leonardo himself began to study music, and then took to the lute, to the accompaniment of which he could improvise beautiful songs; or how Giorgione enjoyed the pleasures of music, singing and playing so beautifully that men of substance invited him to take part in their music festivals. This is not the way of immortality.

Not until the middle of the sixteenth century was the first faint breath of change felt in the art of music. Was it Arcadelt's 'Ave Maria', which, three hundred years later, Liszt heard in Rome with such emotion? It is a simple piece, indeed one of the simplest of the time, which in its thirty-three bars (in modern notation) repeats five times a melodic phrase that has already something of the purely melodic invention of later times. Or was Palestrina the Beato Angelico of music, drawing the sweet face of a melody into the rigid folds of counterpoint? At the end of the century there began the greatest evolution in the history of music of which we have knowledge. We can read how, in the seventeenth century, all the old artificiality was abandoned piece by piece, how individuality superseded stereotyped convention, the soloist emerged from the chorus, and instrumental music freed itself from texts and words. This is no longer the music of craftsmen from the Lowlands. It becomes Italian, it begins in that same Florence where, two hundred and fifty years earlier, the brightest light of the Christian era had risen. This may be mere coincidence but one would hesitate to call it chance that it happened in Italy. For the spirit which created this new music was mysteriously akin to the spirit of Italian Renaissance.

This great spectacle of a newly blossoming art has such striking similarities with the development of the visual arts and poetry and learning that a comparison reveals what we may call the 'mechanics' of the rise and fall of a spiritual movement.

In the thirteenth century there is hardly any indication of a widespread genius for the visual arts in any of the Italian cities and provinces. The most accomplished works of Romanesque art, the Cathedral and Baptistry in Pisa, are probably the work of northern artists, Gulielmus of Innsbruck and Rainaldus Bonannus, artist-craftsmen of whom little more is known than their un-Italian names. Gothic art, a century later, also came from the north too, mostly from France, but one of the few Italian artists, Arnolfo di Cambio, gave it its first Italian flavour. With him, for no discernible reason, native talent begins to stir. Cimabue is still in the shadows, but beneath the rigid surface of his great Madonna in the Uffizi Gallery there are the first stirrings of a new and mysterious life. She no longer gazes into space as her Byzantine or Gothic predecessors did, but looks at you as if she wanted to say something to you but could not find the words. Giotto stands on the very threshold of this new life: here a figure lifts an arm, there it turns its head; here is an expression of amazement, there a gesture of dismay. Did it happen because the old authors were being read again? Because the *Commedia Divina* was being passed from hand to hand? One would like to believe that the old tomes in the Laurenziana, with their now illegible marginal notes, which were once the treasured property of Cosimo the Elder, are the source of that flash of lightning which split the darkness of conventional thinking. Yet the change remains unexplained.

It remains as unexplained as the change in music nearly three hundred years later, when Monteverdi discovered the individual human soul and stepped out of the uniformity of mannered craftsmanship into nature and naturalness.

Conditions of life were not altogether favourable to either movement. In the fourteenth and fifteenth centuries the visual arts—and poetry and learning—grew up in the midst of wars and revolutions, acts of violence and tyranny. General physical insecurity surrounded the greatest upsurge of the European creative mind. But nothing, not even the recurrent outbreaks of the Black Death, could halt it. The arts in general, and none more so than painting, sculpture and architecture, are often accused of paying lip service to money. Poverty, it is true, has no inclination for embellishing life with unnecessary things, and architecture in particular needs munificent customers. In fact there was money everywhere where the arts flourished.

Sometimes this connection between art and money is quite obvious: in Pisa, for instance, the arts kept strict pace with the political and economic fortunes of the republic, and the defeat of Meloria marks the end of Pisan art proper. In Venice this was not so. When the arts there reached their peak the glory of the city and the fortunes of its great merchants were on the wane. After all, there were other countries and other places where there were money and good living: Paris, Vienna, Madrid or Augsburg, but these stimulants did not awaken the arts. What became a truly popular movement in Italy remained the private parish of a few artists and patrons north of the Alps. Perhaps the same urge which kindled enthusiasm for the arts in Italy produced the religious reformation in the North. Money may therefore be the necessary catalyst which brings enthusiasm and the arts together. The otherwise faintly disreputable soldiers of fortune in Italy, the *signori* and *condottieri*, the merchants and bankers, were not only ruthless and rapacious but also intent on surrounding themselves with artists and poets and scholars, so that between wars and business they might discuss with them the latest trends in art and learning, have palaces and churches built in the latest style, cover the walls with murals and pictures and fill their halls and gardens with sculptures. Today, when such private enthusiasts have vanished and the public treasury is plagued with hundreds of more practical and more important demands, it all sounds like a fairy-tale. But it created an atmosphere which reached into even the humblest dwellings.

On the other hand the genius for music was awakened in the conditions which are traditionally held responsible for the decline of the visual arts in Italy: the loss of national independence, the Spanish occupation, the counter-reformation. Everything which is said to have killed the one brought the other to life. This alone must point to a fundamental difference between music and the other arts. Whatever this difference may be, music is more self-sufficient and less demanding than the visual arts. But there must have been something that encouraged it—something that fired musical ingenuity. For the first time it achieved equality with the other arts.

This did not happen overnight, just as the Renaissance in Italy did not develop in one single generation. Both rose from a hesitant beginning to become a veritable flood of enthusiasm and achievement. In the visual arts there were at first a few masters tilling virgin soil. From generation to generation their numbers grew until they became an army, dozens of men of genius and hundreds of men of great talent, scattering the immeasurable treasure of their works all over the Western world. So deep into the constitution of men does this unexpected gift spread that, in the visual arts, it passed from fathers to sons, brothers, nephews, to whole families such as the Vivarinis, Bellinis, Robbias, Lombardis, Pollaiuolos, Ghirlandaios and Lippis and many others. Musical talent does not seem to have been so hereditary, and cases are rarer. The Bach family are the outstanding example, but it also happened with the Couperins and Scarlattis and with the Johann Strauss family.

In the seventeenth century it is music which, like the visual arts in the fifteenth, attracted the men of genius and talent. At the end of that century Italy was overflowing with music and musical enterprise—overflowing in the true sense, because music now captured the imagination of all Europe. Musicians from the North came to Italy in large numbers to learn this new music, Heinrich Schütz and later Handel among them. Italian musicians were to be found at European courts from Paris to St Petersburg. In the eighteenth century there were as many great composers as there were painters in the sixteenth. Was this new outburst of talent in one particular art not some kind of miracle? What brought it about? What created the public enthusiasm which accompanied it? Again, there is nothing in the environment to explain it. This was not an exceptionally prosperous or contented time. One can search in vain for any special conditions of life in those days which could be said to have promoted the musical gift. There was no material inducement such as, two hundred years before, had led even minor talents to painting or sculpture. The composer in those days never rose to the importance and opulence of his Renaissance colleagues, and a genius like Vivaldi could lie in an unknown grave while Michelangelo's remains were treated like those of a saint or a king.

Since then life and art have changed beyond description, but the excitement of these two great movements can still be felt and their light glows on the horizon of our existence. Every year thousands of people make the pilgrimage to those places where the revelation of the arts took place. A large industry has developed out of this latter-day reverence. A whole vocabulary of unforgettable gestures, postures, faces and expressions has engraved itself upon the European mind and has withstood all the changes of time and taste. And likewise the music of that glorious time fills the concert-halls and opera-houses of the world. It lives with us and is as familiar to us as if it expressed our own feelings no less than those of its first listeners and performers. It still seems natural to us although, as in the visual arts at their greatest period, the precious moment of first achievement is lost for ever.

We know, by comparing Renaissance art with the art of preceding and following periods, which qualities the arts had to acquire in order to become as great as they were at their best in the first quarter of the sixteenth century and which qualities they had to lose in order to decline again.

Which then are the qualities that music had to assume in order to achieve equality with the other arts, in order to rise from small beginnings and become a 'great' art, creating works destined not only for the moment but for the future of mankind?

The first step, no doubt, was the abandonment of an over-complicated technique and a concentration on the contents—a simplification of 'how' and intensification of 'what'. Although there is only an ephemeral similarity between music and language the simplification of musical expression seems to correspond to a process philologists believe they can observe with languages. Modern philology says that simplicity of grammar is a sign of perfection. The language of the Eskimos is called primitive because it is complicated, using, for instance, different forms of a verb to indicate whether a man is alone or in the company of others; whether he is standing on a hill or on a plain, while the English language, with an almost rudimentary grammar, is capable of expressing the most difficult thoughts or observations in the shortest and most precise manner. Similarly, music escaped from an involved grammar and so could become simple and beautiful. This is the problem Italian music set itself in the seventeenth century, when it shed its contrapuntal complications and increasingly surrendered to the sheer beauty of sound. It entered the eighteenth century in full possession of a new and original power: from the *melos* of former times it had distilled 'melody'.

This new-found melody is, I believe, the greatest invention of musical genius. It is a purely musical creation, in the real meaning of the word—that is to say, something which does not exist unless and until it is created. Melody is the purest thing in all music. Rhythm depends on the experience of the surrounding world. It is an exaggeration or regularization or, if you will, a sublimation of noise-patterns, or instinctive or observed movements, of language itself. The web of juxtaposed or imitating parts is an intellectual game, as Leibniz described it. Harmony is governed by the natural phenomenon of proportionate oscillations. But melody has no model, no example in the external world, not even in bird-song. It is the free creation of the human mind and does not need the crutches of a text or the erudition of a difficult technique. For the first time in its history melody introduced free and unfettered imagination into music, an imagination akin to that which created Dante's *Paradise* or Botticelli's 'Primavera'.

Nothing in Western music fills me with greater admiration than this. Its discovery did not merely affect music as the discovery of such technical aids as perspective or oil painting or the study of anatomy affected painting and sculpture; it was the discovery of a new world. In the light of the music of the last fifty years, this may sound almost childish. But the significance of melody in European music was immeasurable: it introduced the individual into music. And in all European art it has always been the individual, not the type, which is capable of greatness. This is one of the great dividing-lines between the European and the non-European minds which, if carefully followed through the history of public and private life, may explain the cultural, ethical, and political supremacy of European man. Longer than any other art music seemed to have been held down by the 'type', but melody eventually made the art grow in stature and importance and filled it with a new creative impulse and a new joy in itself.

In the north people watched with misgiving as all the learning disappeared from music. To many it seemed that it was losing its seriousness, that it was about to be debased by free and easy living. Even with Richard Wagner one can hear the echo of these old objections. But while Handel came back from Italy a different man, the works of the greatest composer of that crucial period, J. S. Bach, who never knew Italy and the Italian masters of his time, display the struggle between old and new music in a dramatic manner. There are his well-known exercises in pure beauty, where part-writing recedes into the background (though without being

forsaken altogether), and other pieces—and they are the majority—
where the old craftsmanship is developed to perfection, reducing
inspiration to invention. Between those two extreme types there
are many pieces, such as the organ fugue in G minor, where a fugal
theme becomes a 'fugal melody'. Like many old musicians in our
own time Bach, at the end of his life, turned away from all the
new music. I have said before that his 'Art of Fugue' was the
legacy of 'old' music. New music rejected it.

Hindemith once expressed his regret that there was no textbook
on melody similar to those on harmony or counterpoint. But
melodies are born and not made, there is no rule or recipe, they
spring from that much maligned inspiration which can neither be
taught nor learned. But listen to the unaccompanied cor anglais
in the third act of *Tristan*, the 'sad tune'. It is so eloquent that it
makes all explanation superfluous.

The listeners to that new Italian music soon felt the change.
Greater and lesser princes and noblemen dispensed with their
court poets and reduced their court painters to portraitists, for
practical rather than artistic purposes, but they engaged court
musicians. A steadily rising passion for music, fed by an ever-
increasing stream of new works, spread all over Europe. As the
visual arts had in the sixteenth century, so music in all its forms
became the favourite art in the eighteenth.

This must have been a great encouragement for the further
development of new music. Up to and including J. S. Bach and his
Italian contemporaries every piece of music was monothematic
and avoided all contrast. The rule was to elaborate the one subject,
and when this was done the piece came to its natural conclusion.
This kept the individual piece rather short and concise. But even
the conservative Bach tried his hand at the combination of several,
though not sharply contrasting, subjects in the same piece and his
works grew more extensive, as for example the 188 bars of the
organ prelude in E flat. Only when the subject or theme became a
real melody did contrast find its proper place and justification.
Italian composers then turned almost exclusively to opera, discovering and exploiting the capacity of new music to be 'characteristic'. They added many new shades and facets to melody proper,
while in the North 'absolute' instrumental music grew and
developed. In the last quarter of the eighteenth century a new
balance between inspiration and craftsmanship was found—the
right balance as we, with our knowledge of its results, are entitled
to say. It was a precious, irretrievable moment.

Then, just as Michelangelo had come to the visual arts three centuries before, came Beethoven, the man of destiny. In his hands music acquired yet another unexpected quality which confirmed it as a 'great' art, capable of expressing great emotions and great ideas, however vague. This latest acquisition was monumentality: of thought, conception and size. Beethoven's music is amazingly expansive. The dimension of his works is no longer achieved by the uniform pattern of sequences which, in Baroque music, remain on the same level of expression. With Beethoven the length of a work is determined by an increase in expression, feeling or temperature. His 'Eroica' of 1804 is, compared with all preceding music, a real monstrosity, reminiscent of Michelangelo's athletic supermen. Such increase and intensification become the essential elements of Wagner's gigantic music dramas, of Mahler's gigantic symphonies, introducing the gigantic into music, a striking departure from its old 'miniature' world', small in scope and size. Even in Beethoven's Opus 7 of 1797 a phrase of ominous import raises a warning finger. This E flat minor phrase recurs in the music of the following century in innumerable variants, just as the gesture of the Eternal Judge in Michelangelo's 'Last Judgement' is repeated in painting and sculpture over and over again. With it, something dangerous crept into music, something which Haydn had already foreseen. Nothing shows the spirit of this new music more clearly than Beethoven's enormous fugues, where no breath of the old masters is felt.

It is a matter of taste rather than objective judgement where one believes that the summit of an epoch in the arts is to be found, in Raphael or Michelangelo, in Mozart or Beethoven. For me it is in the *Magic Flute*, where inspiration and the 'science of composition' enter into an ideal communion, where melody is of the purest beauty and greatness not yet monumentality.

With Mozart and Beethoven music reached a state of perfection comparable to that of the visual arts in Raphael's Vatican frescoes and Michelangelo's Sistine ceiling. The contemporaries of either may not have been as aware of it as we are, and may have expected that the arts would for ever remain on that exalted level. But they did not and could not.

Jacob Burckhardt says, perhaps too severely, that after Raphael's death in 1520 no other perfect work of art emerged. There were still great works to come, the *terribilità* of Michelangelo's 'Last Judgement' and others. But it is certain that by the middle of the sixteenth century the flower began to wither, that the former revelation became mere mannerism. All the groupings, gestures and postures, all the effects of light and shade, the facial expressions and the drapery, were exhausted. It is as if Michelangelo (and Beethoven after him) had led art into a cul-de-sac. Around him the once mighty flood began to slacken and general interest grew weary, as if in secret understanding with the spirit of decline. The once clear lines of the design began to be twisted out of shape, greatness became grandiloquence, inner feeling became outward decoration. Again, like a natural phenomenon, within fifty years of Michelangelo's death, the rich abundance of the previous hundred years had disappeared. There are still a few great names, but would one seriously place Guido Reni on the same level as Raphael or compare Bernini with Michelangelo? Italian genius vanished as mysteriously as it had come. The curtain falls, the great spectacle is over. The day is not far distant when the impoverished descendants of the patrons of the art will sell their treasures abroad to fill other palaces and future art galleries.

One would have thought that the talent so widely spread over the whole of Italy, from Como to Messina, and proved by thousands of major and minor works by hundreds of major and minor masters, was inherent, a phenomenon of biology that could never again be lost entirely. But, as Professor Collingwood so rightly observed, art is not inherent, but conditioned by all those facts and their inscrutable, cumulative effect which are understood under the collective name of 'history'. And never again have the arts risen in Italy to any comparable level. Respectable artists were to come, great virtuosos such as Tiepolo, but none of them had the attraction, the panache of their greater predecessors. It was to be the turn of the Dutch and the Flemish. More precisely than the Italian Renaissance this much shorter artistic upsurge coincided with political and economic prosperity and produced a bourgeois art of landscapes, *genre* pieces, still lifes and portraits of municipal dignitaries centred around the Italian-trained virtuosity of Rubens and disturbed only by Rembrandt's daemonic personality. Concentrated as it was in a small strip of land, among a small number of people, it is not surprising that it vanished without trace.

All this is not without precedent. In their own time the Chinese, Indians and Arabs lost their intellectual and artistic powers. So the question remains unanswered: is genius always dormant, ready to emerge, or are there times when it does not exist at all? The present day is not the time for great artistic ventures, and no genius could force them upon us. We need roads and schools, factories and hospitals, machines and yet more machines. And even the *avant-garde* artist finds himself in the *arrière-garde* of modern life.

But most of the shoes the world is wearing, many of the cars the world is driving, new fashions in pullovers and cardigans, are all designed by Italians. Perhaps, in these materialistic times, one should look for minor manifestations to discover the faint glow of some imperishable gift awaiting another chance?

I have dwelt at some length on the visual arts at a crucial time in history, because here was a rise and decline which is most fully recorded and known to us in every detail. In the field of the arts the events were as momentous as the fall of the Roman, Spanish or, more recently, British Empires were in the political field. Even Vasari, when he published the second edition of his *Vite* in 1568, could not have believed that it was possible.

How does it all compare with events in music?

With his late works, with the Ninth, the *Missa Solemnis*, and the last string quartets, Beethoven passed the crest of the musical art. There is a certain snobbery which rates the works of his last years higher than those of his 'middle period', the 'Eroica', the Rasoumovsky quartets, the Violin Concerto. I certainly have no wish to decry the last works. There are movements in almost any of them which belong to the greatest achievements of music. But spiritual and technical difficulty are not necessarily signs of accomplishment. These works brought a new spirit into music, just as Michelangelo's Library in Florence introduced a new and destructive spirit into the arts. And indeed, what happened to music during and after Beethoven's life was exaggeration, exaggeration of melody, expression and dimension which disturbed the classical balance. In Italy, with Rossini, Bellini, and Donizetti, musical 'science' is reduced to a mere shadow, and unbridled melody becomes almost immorally beautiful in its best moments and trivial in its worst. North of the Alps, romanticism drove expression to extremes, depriving literature of subjects and inspiration which it could no longer satisfy in itself. With Wagner music became an inflated monster feeling itself to be and presenting itself as the crowning of all the arts, the *Gesamtkunstwerk*. All this is no longer the language of the Golden Age but, as Burckhardt said of Baroque art, a barbarous dialect. Brahms may have tried to stem the tide, but it was too late. The century after Mozart could do no more than squander its rich heritage.

But music led a high life. It outpaced all the other arts. The whole of Europe revelled in it and found its greatest sensations in it and in its colourful artists. Opera in particular became a major entertainment, better and bigger than anything literature or the visual arts had to offer. There was a general clamour for new and yet more new music which, in retrospect, far exceeded the supply of good works. Those were the days when the great virtuosos, the great singers and performers and eventually the great conductors achieved almost greater honours and commanded more respect than the composers themselves.

In the end it seemed to be too much. People grew tired of gross pleasure, of beauty and monumentality and uninhibited expression. What had made music a great art ended up, as Paul Dukas said, in Ravel's refinement and Stravinsky's boldness which, he thought, could not be surpassed. Wagner had dreamed of a 'music of the future'. At the end of the century there were wicked thoughts about a 'rejuvenation' of music. It was inevitable: music was no longer satisfied with itself. After *Tristan* it could not continue in its old ways.

And it did not. Almost before our eyes music has foresworn everything that raised it from the old insignificance to the greatness of the late eighteenth and early nineteenth centuries, when it was capable of great works and great designs. It first lost its equilibrium by breaking all the rules, then it swung back and barricaded itself behind a wall of still harder rules which restricted scope and size as they had done five centuries earlier. Melody was lost in the process, although Schoenberg insisted that his music was melodious and Alban Berg wrote that twelve-note music, 'like any other music', was based on melody, on the leading voice, on the theme. But leading voice and theme belong to another category than melody, which is as unmistakable as it is indefinable. With melody went contrast, and the new works contracted in size, as Webern most convincingly demonstrated.

The works of new music are once again short, like those of 'old' music. When a composer of the *avant-garde* tries to write a long piece, such as Stockhausen's 'Gruppen', it is only long for no obvious reason. It does not have the continuity which requires length; it could stop at any moment without seeming abrupt or could continue for much longer without necessity. But the desire for long works is rare in new music and new composers resolutely face the consequences of new techniques and a new spirit. This new spirit is, however, new only by comparison with the spirit of music as it has developed in the last two hundred years. And quite consistently this old new spirit brought with it the old objectivity. With Beethoven music had become a highly personal means of expression, with *Tristan* an obtrusive self-confession. But new music gives away nothing of its creator save his cleverness and his intellectual powers, just as it did before the Golden Age. 'Music should express nothing but itself,' said Stravinsky, and the 'old' masters would heartily agree with him. This does not prevent an innovator such as Boulez from explaining how, in his 'Improvisation No. 2 sur Mallarmé', a lace curtain is represented by the coloraturas of the soprano and its reflexion in the window by the 'glassy' sound of celesta, vibraphone and harp, which is no more than a sophistication of Haydn's often ridiculed musical descriptions of rain and snow, of proud eagles in the sky and great whales in the sea.

One might feel some disappointment at this development. When Debussy showed how music could be written after and in spite of Wagner the world was justified in believing that a new era of great music, perhaps a new Golden Age, was about to begin. The obvious kinship between Debussy's music and the great upsurge of French painting and poetry seemed to disclose new rich sources for all the arts. Now, fifty years after Debussy's death, we have to admit that what we took for a promising dawn was a glorious sunset. Stravinsky, on the other hand, never promised more than a complete and ruthless change. So the historic mission devolved on Anton Webern, who, in the critical years, might have been overlooked altogether. But, as I have said before, the destinies of an art do not depend on one single genius. The whole edifice of music had to be brought down so that new music could build its own home. To this destruction all the composers since Beethoven in his last period have contributed, Richard Strauss as well as Stravinsky, Debussy as well as Schoenberg. It was the sustained effort of a century.

This, then, is the point at which new music has arrived: it is again a small art, an art of complicated structures for their own sake. The lofty purpose of the Golden Age has been lost. To calculate intervals or to have the probabilities of a given tone-row calculated by a computer or to improvise noises are not the subjects of a great art. And with almost mathematical exactitude the vast public turns away from its new music and assumes an attitude of complete indifference. It is frightening to see how very few works written in the last fifty years have become as familiar with music-lovers as the hundreds of works of the Golden Age from J. S. Bach to Beethoven.

How well the average music-lover of the nineteenth century knew 'his' music and how little he knows about 'his' music now! Even the greatest names of our time seem pale compared with the great names of a hundred or a hundred and fifty years ago. 'The time of great masterpieces is over,' wrote the often-quoted Boulez, meaning both old and new masterworks which everybody who claims to have any knowledge of music should know intimately.

It is a striking—and strikingly contradictory—coincidence that in the midst of all the new and easy methods of listening a kind of music is being created which tells the listener so little about itself. It must be realized that music has never before found more favourable conditions: it enjoys a highly refined and effective system of protection which is widely held to be an encouragement of the art; it is preservable and transportable and, therefore, more easily accessible than ever before; and, last but not least, the Western world is very prosperous and music is an important item in the budgets of the individual and of the community. There is nothing in the visible circumstances of life that could justify a decline of the art. But music has declined, however harsh, however unbelievable it may sound.

If external conditions tend to make the composer comfortable, there must be internal causes which make him uncomfortable. Our age is commonly and perhaps somewhat summarily called the 'technological age', which hints at materialism too. There were in the known history of man certain periods which produced certain popular tendencies or propensities. At times people were given to religious meditation or fascinated by the arts, there were mass passions for charity or nationalism and all of them were more than the mere quirks of a leader. Now it is 'technology', the impact of the most adventurous discoveries and inventions man has ever made within the short space of less than two generations. Technology, which embraces every aspect of scientific research and application, is an irresistible attraction. It opens a new world with the expectation of large monetary rewards, it has every quality of attracting the best brains, the most fertile minds. But the whole demonology of the human race, religion, and the arts, has been left behind by this world of bold but closely calculated projects.

Narrative or descriptive literature flourishes to some extent, perhaps because the problem of existence in the midst of all this 'technology' is an inexhaustible topic for discussion, though discussion may not have advanced far enough to bring about such final results as are required to produce a lasting masterpiece. But poetry in the narrower sense has become very scarce. There seems to be as little inclination for writing it as there is for reading it. It may be too personal, too individual for an age which has robbed individuality of much of its former relevance. Everywhere (and nowhere more than in the arts) individuality seems to be withdrawing behind a shield of uniformity.

It is equally hard for the visual arts to make proper contact with the times. Enormous demands are being made on architecture. Whole towns are being built or rebuilt, with all the old requisites of private dwellings and public buildings, theatres, concert-halls and sports arenas. But the artistic use which architecture is making of these unique opportunities is astonishingly small. New architecture is striving to make buildings and designs 'functional', and this accounts for the uniformity, for the narrow orbit within which imagination can move. Where the function of a building is not practical, with churches for example, or theatres, this new architecture is, as I have said before, embarrassed, as embarrassed as painting and sculpture are today. It is not incompetence which throws a few blobs of colour onto a canvas or transforms a shapeless block of stone into a different but equally shapeless block, but perplexity. There is much to think about in this brave world of ours but little that is worth seeing. There is a fatal consistency in the endeavour of the visual arts to free themselves from the visible. But they are and remain chained to the world of shapes and colours, real or imaginary. This is their great problem, which prevents them from creating works of lasting merit, and explains their difficulty in communicating with a larger public.

And, other things being equal, this is the problem of new music, which cares so little for sound and so much for intellectual effort; for music is and remains an acoustic phenomenon. There are frequent congresses of composers and experts of new music which discuss the burning question of musical creation and communication in our time. Such a congress recently dealt with the theme: 'Does the composer need the public? Does the public need the composer?' More correctly formulated the question should have read: 'Do we need new music?' Then the answer could have been an unequivocal 'Yes', instead of the time-honoured hope that later generations may appreciate the present struggle and its achievement. If after half a century new music is still outside the main stream of musical life, the inescapable conclusion is that it has not created masterpieces which could compare with those of the Golden Age. There is no reason to believe, there is indeed no indication, that the new music of our time in its most outstanding manifestations is not masterly within the limitations imposed upon it by all the known and unknown conditions of our spiritual existence. But ours is a post-Periclean, post-Augustan age and while the best works of new music are undoubtedly the best that can be written today they are not the best ever.

It seems that at least some of the theorists are beginning to realize this inherent imperfection. They speak of the 'chaos of the material' confronting the composer today, meaning the chaos of sounds or noises, the raw material of music. They speak of an experimental stage, which every unbiased listener or student of new music will readily confirm. But experiment alone will not solve the problems which are now facing music. Something must have thrown into chaos what at the beginning of our century seemed a reliable order. Something must have rendered the experience of our fathers invalid and inapplicable and must have sent a new generation forward on its road to the unknown. This something, this malaise, must be overcome before chaos reverts to order and experiments become successful. This does not and cannot mean that we shall ever return to the old order. Mankind has never returned to the abandoned dwellings of the past. But we must accept that, with all the present-day experiments groping in the dark, the new order is nowhere in sight.

The public, as a supreme and incorruptible judge, senses this experiment with unerring instinct and will have no part of it. It cannot be expected to follow, to encourage or to like it. Nothing less than achievement will kindle its enthusiasm and secure its approval. Until it is presented with positive achievements, it will remain as indifferent as it is today.

It may be said that I am dismissing my readers with cold comfort. But when I said before that our new music is neither the salvation nor the destruction of music I expressed my belief that one day mankind will regain its inner balance, which is the precondition of any self-assured art. It may be hard to be patient, so far as the arts are concerned, in an impatient, militant age. But patient we have to be. It would be disastrously wrong to discourage the experiment, the desire to come to terms with the times and with ourselves. If the urge to create were lost, however adverse the conditions, all art, old and new, would be lost with it. The true merit of experimental new music is not to be found in its results, which may be no more than documents of the struggle, but in its endeavour. For all hope for the future lies in the quest of today.

3

Date Due